THE POLITICS OF LOVE

By the same author:

Bursting the Wineskins
Chasing the Wind
The Passing Summer

THE POLITICS OF LOVE

Choosing the Christian Way in a Changing South Africa

Michael Cassidy

HODDER AND STOUGHTON
LONDON   SYDNEY   AUCKLAND   TORONTO

British Library Cataloguing in Publication Data

Cassidy, Michael
   The politics of love.
   1. South Africa. Apartheid – Christian viewpoints
   I. Title
   261.7

   ISBN 0-340-54609-3

Love never fails
1 Corinthians 13:8

The world languishes because love is being tried so little. It is imperative that it should be admitted into the field of political thought
Edgar Brookes

Whatever makes [people] good Christians makes them good citizens
Daniel Webster

For Nellis du Preez
Assistant Extraordinary
Wise Counsellor
And Valued Friend

and

With
Special
Gratitude
To Derryn Hurry
For Monumental Help,
Prayers and Encouragement

Contents

Foreword

by Archbishop Desmond Tutu

We really do have an extraordinary country. Only in September 1989 did we have a racist election in which people protesting peacefully against it were being shot and killed; when it was impossible to walk on segregated beaches without running the gauntlet of security forces armed to the teeth; when the ANC was being demonised by the government in its electioneering scare tactics; and when it was illegal to wear insignia bearing the ANC colours or those of other then-banned organisations. And then to come to the point we have reached, quite unbelievably, when the ANC logo and those of other political organisations are being carried on our TV screens and when Mr de Klerk can hold joint press conferences with Dr Nelson Mandela. It is surely breathtaking – that apartheid could soon be a thing of the past and that we could actually have the kind of dispensation for which so many have worked and prayed, and for which so many others have been detained, banned, imprisoned, exiled and even killed. This new South Africa, non-racial, democratic, just and non-sexist is now no longer just a remote possibility but something within our grasp despite the possibility still that the negotiation process could be derailed by the upsurge of violence and unrest and subverted by others intent on sabotaging Mr de Klerk's courageous initiatives.

To be sure, we do have a crazy country which has not only such land and natural resources that we are the envy of the world, but also remarkable human resources – all of which have been wantonly wasted in the all-consuming business of either defending or opposing apartheid. We have wonderful people of all races if only we could get our act together. If only we could realise that we can survive only together, black and white together; we can be human only together, black and white together; and we can prosper and be free only together, black and white together.

Yes, we have everything, but we have lacked justice which is love working itself out on the macro-political level. However, let me recall an instructive incident when I was still General Secretary of the South African Council of Churches. We had a multiracial group of women travelling to West Germany. One of them, a black woman, on the plane ate a dessert which contained peaches, to which she was allergic. She became seriously ill and had to be removed to hospital in Nairobi. One of her companions, however, a white and an Afrikaner to boot, decided she should stay on with her in that land of Kenya where South Africans are not welcomed too enthusiastically, especially white South Africans. This sort of almost fairytale happening struck me as the kind of thing that can only be birthed out of South Africa. And it illustrated for me the remarkable degree of goodwill and love still around, in spite of the way it has disgracefully been dissipated by some politicians through their reckless policies. However, it at last appears that we just might avoid Armageddon if we can get our act together.

In *The Politics of Love* Michael Cassidy attempts to show just how we could accomplish the daunting task of translating neighbour love, so frighteningly demanding and bracingly realistic (since it is not a wishy-washy sentimental pretending that things are fine) into transforming by Christian choices the structural and other injustices of apartheid.

He also speaks of repentance and restitution. I attended the celebrations in Windhoek when Namibia so miraculously became independent. Mr de Klerk, a little surprisingly, but deservedly, received a very warm ovation. He gave a splendid speech. But it would have set the world alight and thunderously applauding had he in terms of *The Politics of Love* also seriously asked for forgiveness for the pain and suffering inflicted on Namibia and then followed through with a commitment to return Walvis Bay as an act of restitution.

The point is that love has to do with repentance, forgiveness, contrition, reparation and with knowing that it is people you are dealing with. Sadly, I have not yet heard anyone in the white establishment formally and officially say 'Sorry, forgive us and *we are willing to make amends*'. Without this, our reconciliation and starting afresh may flounder because the foundation is not true.

God grant that we may try out Michael Cassidy's suggestions in *The Politics of Love*. We have little time left.

Author's Preface

In 1980 I spent a number of months overseas with my family for some rest, reading, reflection and prayer. South Africa's drama was starting to intensify and my spirit was in great anguish over the situation. On my last morning in Oxford I was walking along the banks of the Isis River and praying fervently about my country. Almost immediately I had the sense of a word from the Spirit of God edging into my heart: 'I have a way through for South Africa, but it will take a listening people.'

I never forgot that experience and have it etched upon my soul that God does indeed have an answer for South Africa if we will seek it. I have accordingly tried to the best of my ability over these years to do some listening and to encourage others in South Africa to do the same. The first fruits of that effort I brought forth in my last book, *The Passing Summer*. Now here in *The Politics of Love* I expand on Part Six of *The Passing Summer* which bore that title.

My purposes in doing so are fourfold. First I wanted to update some of this thinking into the De Klerk–Mandela era.

Second, in producing a shorter and more popular-style paperback I wanted to press out to many more people, both in the pew and beyond it, the vital and practical importance, especially in South Africa, of being led and guided by the Light of God's Love and by Christian principle in these difficult and dangerous times. My great fear, especially for South Africans, whether black or white, is that we may imagine we can work out this political conundrum simply by human wisdom and in the perilous pragmatics of secular politics. My conviction is that the darker or more difficult a historical situation, the more vital it is not only to hold on to Christian principle but to choose the right and loving thing and leave the consequences to God.

Third, I unashamedly want by this volume to give further life and impetus to *The Passing Summer* where I feel there is still much material of relevance for both Church and State in this unfolding drama, surely one of the more important of our whole century.

Fourth, I want again to call people across the world to prayer, both for South Africa generally and for the key players particularly in this 'workshop of the world'. I am fully convinced that it is by prayer alone that we will win through to the place where this unlikely land will not only find its own healing but become a blessing to the nations of Africa and the world.

As in *The Passing Summer* I have here and there changed people's names to protect their identity.

I must also record several special words of appreciation. First and foremost to Derryn Hurry for constant and prayerful counsel and for truly massive and often exhausting labours of cheerful and glad assistance with editing, rewriting and research. More than anyone else she has patiently steered both author and project from start to finish and I cannot adequately express the debt of gratitude I owe her. Her husband, Lynn, an educationist and ecologist, was also extremely helpful, particularly with my chapter on Facing the Giants (Ch. 13). Encouragement also came from Archbishop Desmond Tutu, who has most kindly written the Foreword, and from Rev Mvume Dandala, head of the Department of Mission of the Methodist Church, and Bishop Matthew Makhaye, Suffragan Bishop of Natal, both of whom in different ways helped me feel I was on the right track.

For much of the statistical data I am greatly indebted to researcher supremo, Teddy Langschmidt, director of Integrated Market Research in Johannesburg, which works in association with Market Research Africa. In Chapter 13 most of those incredible statistics come from Teddy and from his epic work *The Third Alternative*, published in August 1990. Thank you also to David Wavre, Carolyn Armitage, Karen Harris and others at Hodder's for all the work at their end.

From my Africa Enterprise colleagues, especially Malcolm Graham and Nellis du Preez and from our Board and Chairman, Dr Mmutlanyane Mogoba, came constant encouragement. Karen Buckenham from Canada gave the project many hours of much appreciated labour. Then also there is Colleen Smith, my secretary, a star if ever there was one, who pulled off her usual and huge efforts of typing with incredible speed, diligence and cheerfulness. Thank you, too, to my colleague Marylee James for all that fine work on Action Options (see Appendix A). Nor must I forget Dave and Penny Brady who let me use a cabin in their garden for several weeks of quiet and uninterrupted work. I should add here that I alone must be held accountable for the views set forth in this volume.

Finally, I owe perennial gratitude to my beloved Carol, and my children Cathy, Debbie and Marty, who are all so wonderfully patient and supportive of this funny man in their house who keeps vanishing to his study or elsewhere to grapple with that anonymous monster called 'the book'!

So here it is now, *The Politics of Love*. May it work for the blessing of many, especially in the Beloved Country, and in the power of the Spirit of God may it encourage all people everywhere deliberately and decisively to choose Love's ways in the world.

Michael Cassidy
Pietermaritzburg, October 1990

Part One

A NEW DAY DAWNS

Forget the former things; do not dwell on the past. See, I am doing a new thing! Now it springs up; do you not perceive it?

Isaiah 43:18–19

1   Rounding the Corner

A wise man changes his mind, a fool never.
                                    Spanish proverb

History unfolds itself by strange and unpredictable paths
                                    Winston Churchill

. . . As 1989 drew to a close . . . De Klerk was facing the
crucial, the awful, the soul searching decision from which
earlier Afrikaner leaders had shrunk – that of placing the
interests of the nation as a whole before that of his own
people.

                                    Journalist Peter Younghusband

Turn from evil and do good; then you will dwell in the
land for ever.

                                    Psalm 37:27

As far as I am concerned, you can have overnight flights. In
fact one of my modest theological conclusions is that they
are a major manifestation of the Fall of Man! At least if their
consequences in the human spirit are anything to go by. You
know – disorientation, exhaustion, that lost look and a general
inability to think straight.

My feelings at Heathrow Airport early on February 2nd,
1990, after British Airways overnight flight 94 from Philadelphia via Montreal to London were no exception to this. I
was 'bombed', as the saying goes, and was busy entertaining
serious doubts as to whether I still belonged to the human race.
And when it is 2.30 a.m. body time, it's somewhat maddening to

meet a world of breezy airport officials, all expecting one to have ready answers to demanding questions such as one's name, address, where one will be staying in the UK and how much one spent abroad!

Having negotiated these intellectual hurdles at customs, I flopped down on a bed in a nearby airport hotel, thankful BA were picking up the tab for my transit costs before the flight that night to Johannesburg. I had a few hours to sleep. And needed them.

BBC 1

By the bed was a TV remote control monitor. On impulse I picked it up, pressed 'on', plus BBC 1 for a few moments of the world's most civilised TV channel.

To my surprise I saw at once the shining dome of F W de Klerk's head and that pleasant face, slightly creased by its omnipresent but ever-so-enigmatic smile.

'Oh yes,' I grunted to myself. 'That's right. Parliament opens today. Well, so what? More of the usual. Bunches of banalities. Clusters of clichés. All about how great we really are as a country if only we weren't so badly misunderstood by that naughty outside world.'

I reflected on the previous day in Philadelphia when black US Civil Rights' leader, John Perkins, and I had been hooked up to a New York radio station for a one-and-a-half-hour talk show with a question and answer 'phone-in'.

'What will happen tomorrow when your parliament opens? Will Mandela be released tomorrow?' asked one caller.

'Well,' I mused like the wise old owl in danger of growing pessimistic. 'We've been told not to expect too much tomorrow. And we've had lots of rhetoric in the past about government intentions. So I'm not too excited. And to be sure, Mandela won't be released tomorrow because he will not allow himself to be released into a vacuum. The ANC, PAC, SA Communist Party and other liberation movements will have to be unbanned before he'll agree to come out. And it will, you know, take more than a miracle for the government to do that.'

My caller grunted in disappointed acceptance, as if some
Olympian oracle had spoken.

Yes, that was yesterday, February 1st, 1990. But now, it is
February 2nd and what is this I hear today? It can't be. But it
is. I know I'm beat up and all that. And *non compos mentis*. So
my mind is getting it wrong. But no, the President is saying it:
'The focus now has to fall on negotiation . . . There is no time
left for advancing all manner of new conditions that will delay
the negotiating process. The steps that have been decided are
the following:

> The prohibition of the African National Congress, the Pan
> Africanist Congress, the South African Communist Party
> and a number of subsidiary organisations is being rescinded.

My benumbed mind refuses to register. ANC, PAC and even
SACP unbanned? By a Nationalist Government? Am I
dreaming?

The President goes on:

> The media emergency regulations as well as the education
> emergency regulations are being abolished in their
> entirety . . .
>   The restrictions in terms of the emergency regulations on
> thirty-three organisations are being rescinded.

'Great thundering doodle-bugs!' I expostulate within.
'South African politics and life *normalising* – rounding the
corner. Can it be?'

Then the President goes ahead and spells it out:

> These decisions by the cabinet are in accordance with the
> government's declared intention to normalise the political
> process in South Africa without jeopardising the main-
> tenance of good order. They were preceded by thorough
> and unanimous advice by a group of officials which included
> members of the security community.

MANDELA

Now what about Mandela, I say to myself, as if echoing the question on the radio programme. I continue to listen trans-fixed to the BBC news bites as they come in:

Our country and all its people have been embroiled in conflict, tension and violent struggle for decades. It is time for us to break out of the cycle of violence and break through to peace and reconciliation. The silent majority is yearning for this. The youth deserve it.

With the steps the government has taken it has proved its good faith and the table is laid for sensible leaders to begin talking about a new dispensation, to reach an understanding by way of dialogue and discussion.

The agenda is open and the overall aims to which we are aspiring should be acceptable to all reasonable South Africans. Among other things, those aims include:

A new, democratic constitution;
universal franchise;
no domination;
equality before an independent judiciary;
the protection of minorities as well as of individual rights;
freedom of religion;
a sound economy based on proven economic principles and private enterprise;
dynamic programmes directed at better education, health services, housing and social conditions for all.

At last the sensational utterance:

In this connection Dr Nelson Mandela could play an import-ant part. The government has noted that he has declared himself willing to make a constructive contribution to the peaceful political process in South Africa.

I wish to put it plainly that the government has taken a firm decision to release Dr Mandela unconditionally. I am serious about bringing this matter to finality without delay.

The government will take a decision soon on the date of his release.

The Mandela moment. It has come. After twenty-seven years. My mind skips back to an afternoon on the veranda of Alan Paton's home in Botha's Hill near Durban. 'When Mandela is released you will have the biggest political meetings in South Africa's history', the old political patriarch had prophesied. Yes, indeed. I see them coming. And what then?

My mind also skipped back some two years to the day in 1987 when I sat in a rondavel on the edge of the Umgeni Valley near my home and penned in my book, *The Passing Summer*, my thoughts on the unbanning of the liberation movements and the release of Dr Mandela.

I was commenting on the needed negotiation process, and wrote:

> Another precondition, if negotiation is to work, is that all sides stop demonising their political adversaries. If the liberation movements are all demonised into being just a bunch of violent Moscow-controlled terrorists, and if the South African Government is cast as an irretrievably illegitimate bunch of lost-cause, racist brigands who can somehow be wished away, we won't get very far. Indeed, for as long as all the different South African groupings decline to accept the true legitimacy of the other groups, true negotiation is forestalled (pp. 401–2).

Now here was De Klerk hopefully putting an end to the demonising process.

As I had gone on to write in *The Passing Summer* (pp. 402–4)

> The Christian belief in the equality of all before God must commit us, professing Christian country as we are, to the inclusion of *everyone* in negotiations.
>
> This surely means that the Government cannot exclude the ANC or PAC, nor can the liberation movements exclude major Afrikaner political groupings. This is not to pronounce on whether the liberation movements or the

Afrikaner groupings are 'goodies' or 'baddies', but only to recognise that they are major parties to this dispute, all of whom profess strong claims to the land . . .

The inclusion of the South African liberation movements in negotiations would in my judgement not only make political sense, but would also be a means of demythologising ordinary groups of intelligent black politicians, who are neither gods nor demons but are key figures who cannot be ignored. Moreover, in open debate and interface in the country their fallibilities and humanness would be as evident as their positive contributions and undoubted abilities, which are currently being wasted on frustrated acts of protest and destabilisation.

It is my strong conviction that the same applies to Nelson Mandela, who also needs demythologising. At the time of writing he is still in prison after twenty-five years. And with each passing day the myth becomes greater than the man, to the point where one trembles at the consequences of what would happen were he to die in jail. Languishing there, his influence is restricted. But let him die there and the real reign of the martyr will begin. . . .

Many feel that, if released, Mandela could be the man to save this situation. Clearly he would need to come out as a real statesman, somewhat in the way Jomo Kenyatta emerged from prison and acted to calm irate blacks and nervous whites.

Mandela would need to come out activating the Christian faith he apparently professes. The EPG people said they found in him 'no trace of bitterness', and this suggests he could be a real force for reconciliation.

He would, moreover, need to come out as a true patriot rather than as the communist some have portrayed him to be. If he was such twenty-five years ago, he apparently no longer embraces that philosophy.

A great service to the situation would also be rendered if as a key leader he would constrain some of his constituency to hold out the olive branch to Chief Mangosuthu Buthelezi of KwaZulu, who is also a significant figure in the situation, as President Kaunda said to me back in 1986. (This is also held to be self-evident by many thousands of blacks and

whites, the detractors of Chief Buthelezi notwithstanding.)
Chief Buthelezi himself has repeatedly called for the release
of Nelson Mandela, and I have personally heard him say
that he would be prepared to serve under a democratically
elected Mandela.

Of course in such things as the release of Mandela and the
unbanning of liberation movements there is a risk. But there
is no course open to us in this land without risk, and nothing is riskier than the course on which we are presently
embarked.

Real negotiation between *all* the actors in this drama
remains the safest way.

Thus my thoughts nearly two-and-a-half years previously.
Nothing at that moment had happened to make me alter my
thoughts. And now it all seemed to be happening or going to
happen.

CAPE TOWN

Down in Cape Town, President de Klerk is wrapping up his
speech.

Therefore I repeat my invitation with greater conviction
than ever: Walk through the open door, take your place at
the negotiating table together with the government and
other leaders who have important power bases inside and
outside of parliament.

Henceforth, everybody's political points of view will be
tested against their realism, their workability and their
fairness. The time for negotiation has arrived.

. . . I pray that the Almighty Lord will guide and sustain
us on our course through uncharted waters and will bless
your labours and deliberations.

Oh yes, I say to myself, we'll need the Almighty Lord. That's
for sure. Otherwise the wheels will come off and all will be
wrecked.

The TV off, the room now silent, my mind continues to reel. It seems inconceivable, but it is true. At the very edge of the abyss, South Africa has at one minute to midnight screamed round the corner of history on two wheels, somehow without turning over, and has headed itself on to a new road. It is as if the vehicle of our body politic now has us trundling awkwardly not straight into the chasm, but with breathless hope, after a dramatic left turn, along the very edge of it. A still-precarious place to be, in all conscience, but no longer a hopeless place. Pray God, I thought, that forces on the far right or far left do not continue to push us over.

TIME AND OPPORTUNITY

But God is good, I thought. In wrath He has remembered mercy. And I had surely been right with the title of my previous book *The Passing Summer*, though I know some black readers had said, 'Michael should have called it *The Passing Winter* – because the South Africa we've known has been no summertime for blacks. It has all been bleak midwinter – cold and dark, menacing and agonising.'

But my title was misunderstood because the reality is that when the people of Judah in the sixth century BC made their poignant lament, 'The harvest is past, the summer has ended, and we are not saved' (Jer. 8:20), they were talking about the summertime, not of a great and happy situation, but of opportunity to change, turn and repent from a dreadful situation. For them the summertime of opportunity to save the day had tragically passed. Nor is anything in life ever so lost as the lost opportunity. And truly they lost it. For the judgements both of history and of God had accordingly overtaken them with the Babylonian destruction of Jerusalem and then a seventy-year captivity of the people.

Perhaps these utterances now from an Afrikaner president, of all people, were turning us away from our Babylonian captivity, especially if this marked the beginnings of true repentance as a nation and not just some political pragmatics because there was no option. I prayed it was the former and not the latter.

MESSAGES

By now Flight 94 was getting the better of me. I turned over and tried to sleep, but sleep eluded me.

'This is no time for slumber,' said jaded brain to jet-lagged body. 'This is a time to rejoice and congratulate and praise and pray!'

Seizing the phone I called our African Enterprise London office. The call was answered by the indefatigable Pat Strange, never surprised by when or whence AE team members phone in. 'Pat,' I gulped out, 'I guess you've heard it's all happening.'

'Yes, indeed,' she exulted. 'Fabulous!'

'Pleeez, Pat, get two messages off for me. A fax to President de Klerk and a telex to Thabo Mbeki and the ANC in Lusaka.'

The deed was done. To both belonged words of congratulations and most especially the assurances of prayer for God's extra-special wisdom in the days ahead.

I did not know President de Klerk personally – though opportunity would come some weeks later – but here certainly was political courage of the first order. He seemed to have faced the fact that white political hegemony was coming to an end and that in politics nothing is 'for ever'. I put in the fax: 'All this has required supreme political courage and great faith in our Lord.' I could add sincerely: 'You have already won a place in history but you will need the support and prayers of all, especially Christian believers.'

With the ANC, as I listed the salutation to Thabo Mbeki and seven or eight others, the message was not to strangers. Successive ministry visits to Lusaka over many years had afforded me many opportunities to get to know most of the main ANC players there to one degree or another. After every such encounter I felt soul-sick because of all that had landed black patriots longing to be home in the agonised displacement of exile. To be sure this had driven some to methodologies or even ideologies which were not mine. But who was more to blame? They or that miserable system which had driven them, after fifty-two years of fruitless commitment to non-violence, to that place of desperation. Even so, I had no brief for ANC or any other violence. That is not Christ's way. But I understood it.

During these Lusaka visits I had always been struck by the sheer waste of such able people. And so gracious and patient too, as if knowing their hour must come. An hour, as I said, when among other things they would be demythologised: they were neither gods nor demons but only fellow South Africans. As the President had just said, all reasonable South Africans were now concerned for a new day of justice and equity for all.

BACK IN SOUTH AFRICA

Back in South Africa it was all happening. Exuberant marchers and throngs did the toyi-toyi dance past the hallowed gates of parliament while the state president's guard, soon to be disbanded, stood rigidly in the sun.

Police on Cape Town's Green Market Square watched quietly from the shade of trees as ecstatic crowds danced the day away. One policeman even smiled.

The MDM (Mass Democratic Movement) protest march against the Tricameral Parliament suddenly underwent a magic metamorphosis and became a victory dance of jubilation.

Archbishop Desmond Tutu, a champion of champions for the oppressed, exulted: 'All this has taken my breath away.' For Frank Chikane, of the South African Council of Churches, there was at last 'A sign of hope.' Andries Treurnicht, leader of the right-wing Conservative Party muttered: 'It was a most revolutionary speech. Mr de Klerk has no mandate for the sweeping plans announced.'

In Johannesburg, shouts of 'Viva ANC' and 'Viva Mandela' rang from a group in Marshall Street. Then, as if to celebrate the incongruities of an incongruous country, they cried: 'Viva Comrade F W de Klerk. Viva!' At which point, as if to keep up the incongruities, some police teargassed them!

In Soweto, joy reigned supreme for Thema Phiri – 'The beginning of a new era', he exulted. But some tempered such thoughts with important realism. Said cautious Mr Kgaye: 'It is a bold step, worthy of a standing ovation. But looking at what still has to be done one wonders if disappointment is staring at us!'

Sandy Jackson in the white suburb of Rosebank expressed what many felt: 'Watching black and white reaction to F W's announcement was the most joyous thing I've ever experienced and heard.'

In Sandton, Mrs Alice Byron felt very differently: 'Seeing this government has handed us to a certain ANC and Marxist government, perhaps they would be kind enough to lift the restrictions on our money going out so that we can take whatever funds we have accumulated out of the country and start another life elsewhere.'

Another Johannesburg housewife moaned: 'He's gone too far, too quickly and God should help us all.'

Frank Drumberg in Northcliff felt apprehension as well: 'If these changes lead to black majority government then this country is doomed.'

In Pietersberg, Northern Transvaal, heartland of Afrikaner conservatism, Anglican Bishop Philip le Feuvre, of the Diocese of St Mark the Evangelist, heard the news over the phone: 'When I put down the phone I was close to tears. I went into town smiling like a Cheshire cat, looking for someone to tell. We had been told to look out for a right-wing reaction, but when I announced the news in a shop a very large Afrikaner just shrugged and said, "It had to come, didn't it".'

In another Northern Transvaal town some whites pulled up at a petrol station: 'Kom, kom; maak gou jou verdomste kaffir' (Come, come, hurry up you damn kaffir), they shouted at Motlatsi Lebona, the petrol attendant. Continuing to take his time, Motlatsi beamed back at them: 'Don't you know? Don't you know? Haven't you heard? There are no more kaffirs in this country. The ANC is unbanned! Mandela is coming out. It's a new day.'

And so, the few laments apart, the land applauded and rejoiced. So did the world. And so did I on a foggy day in London town.

For the Rubicon had, it seemed, at last been crossed.

2 Mandela: the Myth and the Man

Many feel that, if released, Mandela could be the man to save this situation.

The Passing Summer p. 404 – Jan 1988

An old man emerges from prison. He went in an activist. He comes out a myth.

Breyten Breytenbach

I have cherished the ideal of a democratic and free society in which all persons live together in harmony and with equal opportunities.

Dr Nelson Mandela

Set me free from my prison, that I may praise your name.

Psalm 142:7

Sunday, February 11th, 1990, was no ordinary day for the indefatigable Desmond Tutu, eleventh Archbishop of Cape Town. For this was the day when Nelson Rolihlala Mandela, the world's most celebrated prisoner, and at that moment undoubtedly the hope of South Africa's majority, would walk free from the Victor Verster Prison, near Paarl, after nearly twenty-seven years of incarceration.

The charge had been treason and attempting to overthrow the State by violence. The sentence? A little notice on one of his previous prison cells provided the cryptic answer – 'life plus five years'.

Sitting recently in the shade of a bush outside a church in the

Cape Peninsular where we were both ministering in a conference on evangelism, Archbishop Tutu fixed me with excited eyes as he relived the extraordinary emotions of those days.

'On that Saturday we were having a christening party in the garden of my home in Soweto when some journalists came and told me there was to be a press conference at 3 p.m. that day when it was believed the State President would announce the release of Nelson Mandela. We listened to the conference direct from Cape Town. And then the announcement came that Nelson would be released the next day. All heaven was let loose. The women raised the roof and all went dancing up the road. Our house is only about a hundred yards from the old Mandela house, so Leah and her friends went dancing up the street. I started dancing as well. I cannot describe my emotions.

'I mean, when you think of what happened only last September [1989], when we couldn't even walk on the beaches and the police were threatening to shoot us and using tear gas, and we had about twenty people killed for protesting! To have that as a backdrop for this, for which we had all been working and praying! We felt someone had to pinch us because it had all the qualities of a dream.'

'Did you anticipate all this happening?' I asked the Archbishop.

'Well, I'll tell you something. In January this year I was asked by one of the TV crews what was my New Year's resolution. I had answered somewhat gleefully, "I want to improve my dance routine because I think we will be doing quite a lot of celebrating this year." That was in January. Perhaps it was wishful thinking, a little bit of whistling in the dark. But, you know, I also knew God was around, what with the Berlin Wall coming down and freedom breaking out all over.'

INCREDIBLE NEWS

'You know, Mike,' he went on, 'words are totally inadequate to describe what it meant for us, for the world, and in the sense of bringing us an affirmation of a God who hears, who cares, who does come down and deliver His people. It was just incredible.'

Anyway, on Saturday, February 10th, after a midnight TV interview in Soweto with the International Television Network, Desmond went to sleep, excited beyond telling.

Next morning the baptism proceeded at Holy Cross Church in Soweto. To the three Xhosa names the little child was to be given, a fourth was added – 'Nkululeko', meaning 'freedom' or 'liberation'. Desmond preached on the 'God of surprises' to symbolise all that was taking place.

'I also spoke on new life', said Desmond, 'and new beginnings, God's promises being fulfilled, and freedom. So there we were having a kind of miniature enactment of what was taking place on another level in our country with its new hope and vistas all opening, which we had not expected, certainly not at that time.'

At which point the 'God of surprises' seemed to pull off another one. Midway through the service, media officer John Allen handed Desmond a note: 'There are two seats on a BBC plane flying to Cape Town just now.'

Desmond's heart leaped. The day before, he had been unable to get a flight since they were all full. Yes, the God of surprises. At which point the service picked up a little extra speed! They could make it and be there for the monumental moment.

As the BBC's plane with Desmond raced towards Cape Town the man of the moment must have been experiencing an extraordinary and bewildering set of emotions.

'But he also seemed quite calm', Archie Gumede, Mandela's life-long friend told me later. 'We were with Nelson at the prison and our emotions too could not be put into words. But he seemed amazingly calm.'

How could this be, I wondered, as Archie told me about the build-up to this moment.

LONG ROAD

It had been a long road. Mandela was convicted and sentenced for planning revolution and sabotage, imprisoned for twenty-seven years, forgotten by whites, never forgotten by blacks, eulogised by the outside world, mythologised by his own world, unknown, yet famous beyond the telling.

'He always had a sense of destiny', Archie Gumede told me. 'He never doubted his time and moment would come.'

In the days leading up to his freedom, Mandela thought back to his childhood and his tribal heritage as the son of a royal family in the Thembu tribe of the Xhosa people. He remembered how, when he was a boy in Transkei, his tribal elders had gathered in huts night after night to discuss the injustices of land-grabbing by avaricious whites. Even as a youngster – he was born on July 18th, 1918 – he took exception to the tribal system and began to rebel against the South African emphasis on tribe.

By the time he reached the University of Fort Hare, where he read for a BA degree, his political instincts were deepening. At university he formed a friendship with a fellow student called Oliver Tambo. The young hotheads soon got themselves suspended for organising a boycott of an election for the Students' Representative Council.

Opting out of an arranged tribal marriage, Mandela headed for the University of the Witwatersrand in Johannesburg where he gained a law degree. Thereafter, with classmate Oliver Tambo, he set up the first black law practice in South Africa in 1952.

Not to be intimidated by laws stipulating 'whites only' neighbourhoods, Mandela and Tambo set up their practice in just such a neighbourhood. They specialised in representing blacks who were in any kind of legal trouble, particularly relating to Pass Law offences when blacks were caught in white areas without the dreaded and hated Pass Book in their possession.

TURBULENT YEARS

These were, of course, turbulent and deeply depressing years
for blacks as the National Party began to put in place its
massive superstructure of racist laws (see *The Passing
Summer*, ch. 8).

The ANC, founded in 1912 after the racist Union Constitution of 1910 had been put in place, was now planning
various campaigns against the Pass Laws. Mandela, as one of
the key leaders in the Youth Wing, was inevitably in the thick
of it. Along with more than eight thousand other people
convicted or jailed for Pass Law offences in 1952, Mandela
received a nine-month suspended sentence.

But all who came under the charisma of this extraordinary
young man recognised that here was a political presence and
power of no mean proportions. The young Mandela quickly
became president of the Transvaal branch of the ANC.

Together with Tambo, Mandela was particularly keen to
encourage the ANC Youth League which the two young men
had formed in 1944, encouraging a programme of action calling for strikes, boycotts and other acts of civil disobedience
in protest against South Africa's racist way of life.

South Africa's way of dealing with such people took its
course and soon Mandela found himself issued with the inevitable banning order: he was confined to a limited area, turned
into a sort of non-person, and forbidden to speak or write for a
public audience.

The ANC then put into operation what was known as
the Mandela Plan (or M Plan) to develop a mass-based
membership built around the cell system.

Not long after, in 1955, came the famous congress at Klip-
town, which produced the celebrated Freedom Charter which
to this day forms the basis of much ANC thinking. The
following year came the famous treason trial when Mandela
and some 150 others, including the then ANC President, Chief
Albert Luthuli, were charged with high treason. At the time I
had stood with fellow Cambridge students outside South
Africa House in London in protest.

An absurd five-year delay in the sentence ended with
Mandela and his fellow accused being acquitted.

His first marriage having failed, Mandela found solace in the love of a young social worker by the name of Winifred Madikizela, familiarly known as Winnie, whom he married in June 1958 when he was almost 40. Their life together was fast-paced.

Nelson, by then nicknamed the 'Black Pimpernel', flitted in and out of meetings with the security police always hot on his trail.

With Mandela still very much in the thick of black protest politics, events began to move swiftly in the run-up to the Sharpeville tragedy in 1960 when police killed sixty-nine black protesters and sent shock waves not only throughout South Africa, but around the world. The ANC itself was now banned as an organisation, along with the breakaway Pan Africanist Congress.

Sharpeville did something to the soul of Nelson Mandela. It seemed to him whites would not listen to reason or accept the black way of peaceful protest. Mandela and others now formed Umkhonto we Siswe (The Spear of the Nation) as the military wing of the ANC. A fifty-two-year commitment to non-violence had come to an end: black patience had run out.

Mandela was now permanently involved in cat-and-mouse chases with the security police as he slipped in and out of South Africa to address meetings abroad, and gave secret interviews to the press from secret telephone booths. He had had some eighteen months on the run when, disguised as a chauffeur, he was trapped at a roadblock in Howick, Natal, very near my own home.

Mandela was jailed for five years for incitement and for going out of the country without being in possession of a valid passport.

With Mandela safely incarcerated, Minister of Justice John Vorster decided to crack down on the banned organisation. The police in July 1963 swooped on an ANC hideout at Lilliesleaf Farm in Rivonia, one of the northern suburbs of Johannesburg.

Walter Sisulu and Ahmed Kathrada were among those held in what was considered at the time a security coup of the first order. This came in the train of months of security police investigation into the activities of Umkhonto we Siswe.

Not surprisingly, Mandela was seen as the mastermind behind the ANC battle-plan (Operation Mayibue) for the revolutionary overthrow of the South African State. This was the document being studied when the police burst into the Lilliesleaf Farm.

Mandela, of course, was already in prison at this time, but was brought into the dock in Pretoria to face the devastating charge of high treason.

Rivonia Trial

Nelson Mandela was in the dock with nine others. Many consider it probably the most significant political trial in South Africa's legal history. It was also sensational. For it not only produced evidence of a huge underground conspiracy but it resulted in the life imprisonment of Mandela, who now became the ultimate symbol of black resistance to apartheid in South Africa.

Mandela's defence was basically an exposition of the ANC's view of apartheid, its reasons and motives for resisting it, along with its long-term hopes and goals for the future.

In the language of a trained lawyer, Mandela's statement became a manifesto for the whole black cause against apartheid and all its works.

Mandela admitted being the founder of Umkhonto we Siswe and also a member of the ANC executive who had received military training, arranged for recruits to receive similar training and solicited financial help from abroad.

Rightly or wrongly, Mandela felt they had not been involved in recklessness in their planning for sabotage. Nor had this been out of any desire for violence, but because he felt the political situation had driven him and his people to desperation over any other way to secure freedom for themselves. 'We believe,' he said, 'that as a result of government policy, violence by the African people has become inevitable.'

He also admitted that the ANC had refused to dissolve themselves when banned by the government. 'We believed it was our duty to preserve this organisation which had been built up with almost fifty years of unremitting toil. I have no doubt

that no self-respecting white political organisation would dis-
band itself if declared illegal by a government in which it had
no say.'

As to the charge that the ANC had gone Communist,
Mandela indicated that there had often been close co-
operation between the two organisations, the ANC and the
SACP, but that this was brought about by their having a
common goal, namely the removal of white supremacy, rather
than because they had an identical ideology. He indicated that
he was not a Communist, and had never been a member of the
party. Mandela said that while communists regarded the
system in the West as undemocratic and reactionary, he
personally admired such a system.

'I regard the British Parliament as the most democratic
institution in the world and the independence and impartiality
of its judiciary never fail to arouse my admiration,' said the
accused.

Elaborating on what had driven them to violence, Mandela
said: 'Always we have been conscious of our obligations as
citizens to avoid breaches of the law where such breaches can
be avoided, to prevent clashes between the authorities and our
people where such clashes can be prevented, but nevertheless
we have been driven to speak up for what we believe is right
and work for it and try to bring changes which will satisfy our
human conscience . . .

'Government violence can do only one thing and that is to
breed counter-violence. We have warned repeatedly that
ultimately, if there is no dawning of sanity on the part of the
government, the dispute between the government and my
people will finish up being settled in violence and by force.'

Then came the famous conclusion to the famous speech: 'I
have cherished the ideal of a democratic and free society in
which all persons live together in harmony and with equal
opportunities. It is an ideal which I hope to live for and to
achieve. But if need be, it is an ideal for which I am prepared to
die.'

While the black world and the wider world marvelled, the
South African judiciary passed its sentence, later attached to
the prison cell 'Life plus five years'.

Comment

In its editorial on the sentencing, *The Times* of London
presented its conclusion: 'The picture which emerges is of men
goaded beyond endurance . . . And the verdict of history will
be that the ultimate guilty party is the government in power.'
The *New York Times* put its conclusion in American categories: 'To most of the world, the Rivonia eight are heroes and
freedom fighters, the George Washingtons and Ben Franklins
of South Africa.'

PRISON YEARS

Then came the interminable years of prison. Mandela spent
most of them breaking rocks in a quarry, campaigning for
better prison conditions and then studying by correspondence
for a law degree.

When he and others arrived there, they were told by the
warders: 'The world has now forgotten you.' And so no doubt
it must have seemed. Their Robben Island prison was bleak,
forbidding and bereft of any means of escape. Home became a
stone cell 2 by 2 metres for the first few years, and they were
kept on a wretchedly tedious diet of porridge and vegetables.
For the first few years the prisoners were allowed a half-hour
visit and one letter every six months.

From January 1965, Mandela and the other prisoners were
frog-marched off to a limestone quarry, presented with picks
and shovels and told to break rocks. This was their daily
routine for an unbelievable ten years. At the quarry, Mandela
suffered regular persecution and verbal abuse from a white
warder who endlessly harassed him for supposedly not
working hard enough.

Later the prisoners were removed from the quarry and
taken to a prison yard where they were given old clothing
which they had to sew. Repair work on roads was also required, but in between there was time for study. Mandela took
courses in Afrikaans, economics, history and law.

Former inmate and companion to Mandela, Mac Maharaj,
once said: 'He often guided us in our campaigns for better

prison conditions and he showed tremendous persistence. We have waged hunger strikes. We have waged go-slows. We have petitioned, filed written and verbal complaints.'

And no doubt it must for ever have seemed as if the world had forgotten them. 'Sometimes I feel like one who is on the sidelines, who has missed life itself', Mandela wrote in 1979.

Letters

A very great trauma, of course, was the experience of being removed from his wife. And when he did see her, it was to hear of her own continual brushes with the authorities, or her own experience of banning for two years, or her various experiences of detention and, finally, being banished to the Free State dorp of Brandfort under house arrest. Mandela's official biographer, Professor Fatima Meer, in her book *Higher than Hope*, tells of his moving and prolific letter-writing to his wife and family. Thus, on April 15th, 1976, Nelson wrote to Winnie saying: 'Your beautiful photo still stands about two feet above my left shoulder as I write this note . . . I dust it carefully every morning, for to do so gives me the pleasant feeling that I am caressing you as in the old days . . . I even touch your nose with mine to recapture the electric current that used to flush through my blood whenever I did so . . .'

On October 26th, 1976, he wrote: 'I have been fairly successful in putting on a mask behind which I have pined for the family, alone, never rushing for the post when it comes until somebody calls out my name . . . Letters from you and the family are like the arrival of summer rains in spring that liven my life and make it enjoyable.'

Several years later, on May 6th, 1979, he penned these words to his wife: 'Had it not been for your visits, wonderful letters and your love, I would have fallen apart many years ago.'

And then, after eighteen years in prison, he could still write: 'I love you all the time, in the miserable and cold winter days and when all the beauty, sunshine and warmth of summer returns. My joy when you are bursting with laughter is beyond measure.'[1]

In all this Nelson felt heartrending anguish at the plight in which he had left his wife. 'I have often wondered whether any kind of commitment can ever be sufficient excuse for abandoning a young and inexperienced woman in a pitiless desert.'

As Mandela had made Robben Island famous, he also made Polsmoor Prison famous when he was moved there in 1982.

Towards the very end of the interminable sentence came the incongruity of his being imprisoned in a luxury home in the Victor Verster prison outside Cape Town. Beautiful bedrooms, lounge, kitchen and swimming pool were all laid on as South Africa dithered about what to do with him. He was able to receive fax messages in the prison and in the evening listen to the early television news and all radio broadcasts. He would go to bed about 10 p.m. and then be up early for two hours of exercises with an exercise bicycle, weights, push-ups, running on the spot and skipping. Daily newspapers were then delivered to him as well as *Time Magazine* and *Newsweek*.

Spiritual Food

Over the years in the different places and conditions, Mandela received spiritual sustenance from various chaplains, some Anglican, some Assemblies of God, and some Methodist. Seemingly he was a regular receiver of the sacraments and a regular reader of the Scriptures. I have met several of the men who chaplained him at different times, and all spoke movingly of their impressions and experiences.

My own boss, Dr Mmutlanyane Mogoba, President of the Methodist Church and Chairman of African Enterprise, told me once of visiting Mandela in Polsmoor Prison. Mogoba and Dr Jack Scholtz, a Methodist colleague, gathered with Mandela in a little threesome for communion. 'The prison chaplain standing in for the prison authorities was by the door,' said Mogoba. 'Please join us', the group urged. At which the Dutch Reformed chaplain drew to the outer edge of the little circle. 'No, come closer,' they said, at which he joined the circle and completed it. I remember how moved I was when I heard this story. Imagine if we all asked each other to 'come close', as Joseph had urged his brothers in Genesis 45:4.

More recently I met the Rev Harry Wiggett, an Anglican chaplain who pastored Mandela over two periods of five and seven years respectively. Harry cast his mind back and reflected: 'I remember the day I saw him after a break of about twelve years: he embraced me and I just felt totally loved by him. That must have been about ten years ago, though I first met him over twenty years ago.

'My impression of him was of a real, vital, dynamic and Christian presence. He had no reason to come to any of my services, but he did so because he wanted to worship and share the Scriptures, and be with the Christian body. That was thrilling in itself for me as a young deacon in 1965.'

Wiggett then recounted an experience similar to Mogoba's. 'One incident I remember as specially significant happened when we were celebrating the Eucharist. It was probably the second time I saw Mandela at Polsmoor. Suddenly he turned to the warder and said, "Are you a Christian?" The man said, "Yes." "Well, you ought to be joining with us," he said, at which the warder received communion with us. It was Nelson's doing. On that occasion there were seven of us together. Being confronted by someone of his stature, as a young clergyman, I was particularly struck by the utter simplicity of his approach to the Christian faith, and his utter simplicity in receiving what the Lord was giving through just a channel like myself. It took me by surprise, this humility with which he accepted the Word of God.

'As he works out his destiny now,' added Harry, 'I cannot imagine that his Christian faith would not be part of the process because of his participation in the Eucharist and Bible study and his sharing through the ministry in the prison over twenty years. I think his faith must play a relevant part in his attitude towards those with whom he is dealing. I hope and believe this is so also with the State President, who likewise has a strong and prayerful Christian basis to his life.'

On March 3rd, 1985, after Philip Russell had become Archbishop of Cape Town, Mandela wrote him a remarkable letter of congratulations.

The letter opens:

Dear Father,

I hope you received my message from Robben Island in which I sought to congratulate you on your elevation to the Archbishopric of Cape Town.

I consider it an honour and a heavy responsibility indeed for one to become the head of the Church of the Province, whose high profile goes far beyond the scope of purely religious affairs. It is an institution which has produced literally a constellation of eminent and committed clergymen whose concerns and efforts help to focus attention sharply on diverse aspects of our society which require to be rebuilt.

If today the churches take the view that they cannot ignore issues of human rights involving members of their congregations, the Anglicans will have made a substantial contribution to the acceptance of that view.

To be entrusted with the spiritual direction of an institution which espouses such a cause is a great challenge to the incumbent. When, therefore, I heard the good news that you had moved to Bishopscourt, I thought you would need all our support and encouragement, and that you would not be offended by a message of goodwill from one who has been so impressed by members of your church . . .

In the 'fifties I was privileged to meet Father Trevor Huddlestone, and I watched him in action as he put his Christian principles into practice during the painful days of Sophiatown. As you may be aware, there has always been a hard core of whites who had since the early 'twenties worked with blacks in an organised effort to improve the quality of life of all South Africans. But the realisation that there existed white priests in this country, who were totally blind to colour questions, who could preach the gospel from resplendent pulpits and then venture out to the streets and slums to identify meaningfully with the poor and downtrodden, made an indelible impression on all those who knew Father Huddlestone. He initiated several welfare schemes, one of which was the building of a swimming pool in Orlando which was widely patronised, especially by children.

Current circumstances do not allow me to expand on this theme. It is sufficient to know that friendships formed under difficult prison conditions can endure for a lifetime. Apart from our families, who could only see us once every six months, the only other people we could meet were priests. The interest they took in prisoners, especially during the turbulent days of the 'sixties, was a source of considerable strength and, in such an environment, each sermon made us feel that we had a million friends, a feeling which made us forget the wretchedness which surrounded us.

And so, midst anguish and hope, midst the human and the inhuman, midst being totally forgotten and being ever remembered, Nelson Mandela served out his epic sentence till finally his lost and broken nation concluded that national healing and political salvation were impossible without him.

P W Botha fumbled around with this conclusion. F W de Klerk reached it. And acted.

3 The Mandela Moment

Nelson Mandela is free. The news reverberates around
the world.

Breyten Breytenbach

Here stood a single symbol of long overdue freedom and
the hope of negotiation.

Debbie Cassidy, age 15

Hell, man, what have we let loose now?

Afrikaner Conservative

The Lord sets prisoners free.

Psalm 146:7

The excitement in the aircraft was almost unbearable as
Desmond Tutu's BBC plane raced to Cape Town's airport.
Desmond himself felt like parachuting down as he beheld the
vast throngs lining the road from the Victor Verster prison
towards town.

'I had never seen anything like it,' bubbled the Archbishop.
'The effect one man can have, a man who has been incarcerated for decades and who has not spoken for all that time to his
people. There *has* to be something called spirit, or how else
does one explain the impact of that one man? But I suppose
there was this solidarity with a person who summed up a
people in himself and in his own stand.'

Down below it was 'wall-to-wall' people from Paarl to Cape
Town.

The BBC plane touched down. The film crew raced to the
prison. Desmond and John Allen sped to town. The afternoon

advanced. The magic hour of 3 p.m. came and went, and there
was no sign of the man of the moment. Back at home I watched
the poor TV commentator, lost for words, dangling at the end
of a verbal rope and dying a thousand deaths with the disappointment of each passing minute.

By the time Tutu reached the City Hall and saw the tension
there in the frustrated, waiting throng, he was worried indeed.
What was going on? Why was Mandela not there? Some said
Winnie was late. Others said ANC colleagues were reworking
parts of his first speech in freedom! Who knows?

RELEASE

Finally came the magic moment. It was 4.16 p.m. South African
time. The date was Sunday, February 11th, 1990. After
twenty-seven years, six months and six days since he was
captured in the little town of Howick, Nelson Mandela walked
out of the front gates of the prison, hand-in-hand with his wife,
Winnie, and stepped towards the waiting car and the awaiting
destiny. With South Africa and the world glued to its TV sets,
the old man raised what looked like an anxious, almost
nervous salute with his clenched fist. Beginning in the road
near the prison and all the way into town, pandemonium broke
out in the vast throngs.

Back at the Cape Town City Hall Desmond Tutu and a
crowd estimated at somewhere between fifty and a hundred
thousand people waited anxiously. A few shop windows were
broken. Some looting began. Liquor was lifted out of a
restaurant and some members of the crowd began to drink
while others pelted nearby police with bottles, bricks and
stones. Some of the police responded with birdshot. As the
gunshots rang out, Allan Boesak, an indefatigable labourer
for liberation, appealed to the crowd to sit down and remain
calm. Two hours went by.

Meanwhile, at the Victor Verster prison, Mandela's car was
seeking to crawl through the clutching throng. Journalists who
had been there at 8 a.m. began to roll their cameras as if they
would never shoot another film.

Some hundred uniformed police stood round the prison

gates, and others loitered in the pine trees on an adjoining
rugby field. Two other truckloads of police looked down on
the scene from a nearby mountainside. Plain-clothes police-
men scuttled through the bushes and nearby vineyards. Four
TV helicopters, tipped off by radio, now hurtled in over the
hills and zigzagged back and forth as they sought to follow the
laborious progress of Mandela's car down the road. Shouts
and cheers were almost hysterical. Photographers here, there
and everywhere stampeded over each other and everyone
else, perhaps believing that fame and fortune lay in getting
a magnificent shot of Nelson Mandela at this moment of
unfolding history.

MUSES MOVE

Back in Paris, exiled South African poet, Breyten Breytenbach, watches it all on TV, a lump constricting his throat. His
poetic muse lays hold upon his soul and he begins to write:

Nelson Mandela has been released! Old women lift their
skirts to step up to the memory of a youth of rhythm and
stomp. The reeds bend with the light. Old men marvel at the
trembling of history and drown in thick beer this day, and
the hump of accumulated days scarred with the pain of
poverty.

On Robben Island, in Polsmoor and Victor Verster and
Zonderwater and Brandvlei and Barberton and Diepkloof
and all the other hell-holes of humiliation, prisoners bang
their tin plates and chant: 'Man-de-la! Man-de-la!' And in
the quieter quarters of dehumanisation, the politicals stand
taller to look the warders in the eye . . .

Nelson Mandela is free! The news reverberates around
the globe . . .

In Warsaw and Berlin and Accra and London the lost and
scattered children of SA and some from Azania, the broken
warriors expelled from the movements, are getting drunk
and obnoxious.

In India a fat wrestler changes his name to that of Mandela so as to draw larger crowds to the fairgrounds. In New

York a trembling hand writes: 'Dear Mister Mandela, my husband is lamed, we don't need much. I have no one else to turn to.'

. The powerful of the world issue bloated statements, and confidentially ask their ambassadors: 'How long will he last?' . . .

An old man emerges from prison. He went in an activist, he comes out a myth. A horizon lights up, he brings hope, and he never knew the world, nor the soft caress of empty days under drifting clouds. If he ever did, he no longer remembers. Perhaps there is now a little more sense to our dark passage on earth. He has kept body and soul together with pride and the impossibility of love. He will succeed. He will fail. He lives. He will die. Nelson Mandela is opening a door.

In my own home my then fifteen-year-old daughter, Debbie, is likewise moved and takes her pen. She calls her lines 'Turn-about', for despite her youth she knows that it is indeed a 'turn-about' which is striving to be birthed in the South African soul.

TURN-ABOUT

The lonely bird held hostage in a barred cage flies free at last,
As the sun beams through both shadows and stripes
Now covering the aged feathers,
Finally showing the mysterious greyness of twenty-seven captive years,
Wasted, haunted and cut off from the reality of ebony and ivory.
Meanwhile outside the blackness of the den is further darkness, violence, hatred, greed,
And the multicoloured land slowly starts to disintegrate into small pieces of grey ash.
Until the word was given, the cage door opened
And the bewildered bird is welcomed by flashes of black, green and yellow
As jubilant songs and cries fill the crowded air.

Here stands a single symbol of long overdue freedom and
    the hope of negotiation
For many a dark skin, a leader released, and a road to
    freedom from the trappings of discrimination.

Afrikaner

Back in Pietermaritzburg, ex-Free Stater and Afrikaner,
Marie van Nieuwenhuizen, was beset by conflicting emotions.
On the one hand her Afrikaner history almost forbade the
happening under way before her eyes. On the other hand her
Christian commitment called her to greater generosity.

So there she was in front of her TV struggling. And praying.
And watching all those blacks, delirious with delight.

'Suddenly,' she said, 'I found something amazing happening
deep within me. I found in my heart no hatred, resentment,
anger, or criticism, but instead a deep love and compassion for
all those people. I started weeping and, being all alone, could
let my tears flow freely. I found myself praying and interceding
for all those people. Before, I would have been filled with
anger, bitterness, resentment and rage. But now a new Spirit
within me cried out "Love them and pray for them! Don't
judge and condemn." And then as Dr and Mrs Mandela came
walking down that pathway, I found that as soon as I set my
eyes on them, I was absolutely overcome with love, compassion and sympathy. I sensed a softness on Dr Mandela's
face and in his eyes. And the Spirit within me so worked that I
just began to weep and weep. I lifted up my hands to the
television screen and prayed, "Father let your love enfold
them, let your peace surround them and let your light touch
them. And, Lord, may there be in them no spirit of vengeance,
hatred or bitterness, but fill their hearts with love and
forgiveness."'

Marie then spent an anguished period of time confessing to
God the sins of our nation, with all its hatred, prejudices and
racial discrimination.

'The most precious thing,' Marie later told me, 'was that
when I prayed for Dr Mandela I found myself calling him

Brother Mandela. What a release this has brought within my spirit.'

Marie sat down right away and wrote Mandela a long letter. 'Now,' she says, 'I feel I must write a second one, make a personal confession for myself and my people and ask for forgiveness for all the pain which we have caused to Nelson Mandela and his family.'

Amazing

As Mandela's car edged its tortuous way through a sea of humanity and headed towards Cape Town, he turned to his wife and said: 'Winnie, this is amazing. This is a new South Africa. Look at all these whites out there waving to me and celebrating. This really takes me aback. Truly amazing.'

Chaos

'This situation is becoming chaotic and dangerous,' said Desmond Tutu to John Allen, 'and now we hear that Nelson is lost somewhere and you've no idea when he's going to arrive. We're going to have heavy trouble, especially with all these young people if we don't do something. Some of them are getting very angry.'

The young, like everyone else, wanted to see their hero, come what may. Many were in no mood to cope with the buzzing rumour that he was not now going to make it. And darkness was not far away.

By the sad stroke of some mysterious muse, or else a chauffeur's momentary lapse, Mandela's car landed in a blocked-off sidestreet. Leaping from the vehicle into the yard and then into the home of a startled and overwhelmed white housewife, Mandela reached for the phone and finally made it through to Desmond Tutu at the City Hall.

'I don't know how I'm going to be able to make it, Father,' he groaned.

'You've got to,' said Desmond, 'or there'll be a riot. Press

on hard. We'll wait. But you must get here. The people must
see you and hear from you.'

The Archbishop raced back to the City Hall balcony to try
and calm the crowd with assurances that Mandela was coming.

'You see, Mike,' Desmond told me later, 'we were now
facing a very severe problem of crowd control. A lot of people
were being pushed against the wall, there were no barriers to
hold folk in check, and we were even getting reports that some
people might get crushed to death. Others had clambered over
the balustrades on to the balcony and were coming into the
City Hall itself, and even into the Mayor's Parlour. We were
facing a chaotic situation. So I went out on to the balcony and
asked everyone to be calm and assured them Nelson was
coming. But nobody, just no one paid any attention to the
Archbishop of Cape Town! I remembered that in September
last year after the big march, I asked 30,000 people to keep
quiet, and they listened. But today, no. That was when I
realised that the chief actor for whom the seat had been kept
warm had now arrived and lesser lights like myself could shift
off centre stage. But I felt a tremendous sense of achievement
in a way, and relief that what so many had been working and
praying for was now going to happen. Our leaders were going
to come. Now we could become more clearly the church than
ever before. I mean, we had spoken at so many rallies which
should properly have been addressed by our political leaders.
All that was most unfortunate.'

Political Arena

'Desmond,' I interjected, 'you say that at that moment when
Mandela was moving to centre stage, you felt a sort of relief.
Please elaborate.'

'Well, it's like this.'

'You see, although many people view me as so political, I
was in fact reluctant to be thrust into the political arena. First
of all there is all the abrasiveness that comes when you have to
say things that are unpleasant. And that is something totally
contrary to my nature. The experience of a Jeremiah was very
much my own experience. You know, one of my chief weak-

nesses is that I love to be loved. I can't bear being an ogre. And being seen as one by many whites has been one of my greatest burdens to bear. Of course there is a proper place for the church in political affairs. But in this last period of South African history we in the church all had to do too many things which were almost "party-political". But the people who should have been doing them were not around or did not have the space to do them.'

I was interested to hear Desmond say this himself as I had often, especially overseas, offered this explanation to various questioners who asked whether Tutu wasn't 'a bit too political'.

The Archbishop went on: 'You know, I have always hoped I was being prophetic to both black and white. But I suppose the situation has been so horrendous that I was almost always speaking to one side only. Of course now in the matter of violence, as you know, one has to speak strongly also to blacks. But one hopes people will realise clearly that the church does not have a party political role. The church has constantly to keep what the Latin Americans call a "critical distance".'

District Six

As the afternoon of Sunday, February 11th, advanced towards evening, marshalls began to panic. One begged the Archbishop, 'Please come and speak to a crowd of young people who have forced their way into the City Hall foyer.' John Allen recalls, 'On the spur of the moment, the Archbishop put into effect an earlier plan to relieve the crush. He led the youngsters out of City Hall, up to our church in District Six and than arranged for Nelson to make a stop there on his way to town.'

The plan worked. In part at least. 'It was quite a sight to see the Archbishop leading about two hundred kids away, like a sort of Pied Piper,' John Allen told me later. 'In due time some three thousand or so were up in District Six.'

But then up near the church the youngsters got ugly when, after a long wait, Mandela did not arrive.

'You've tricked us. You and the Boers have tricked us,' yelled some of the youngsters at Desmond. 'We trusted you before, but now we see you are a stooge and part of the system. And the system is using you to deceive us.'

Desmond stood there stunned. And pleading for reason.

'Let's deal with him now,' shouted one crazed youth.

John Allen's blood ran cold. 'These kids are going to attack,' he said to himself. 'This is touch and go.'

Several were held back forcibly.

'All right,' said Desmond, 'I'll take you back to the City Hall. I promise you'll see Dr Mandela there just now.'

The youngsters bulldozed their way back to the greater throng.

'Desmond was almost in a state of shock,' John Allen told me later. 'A very nasty experience.'

At Last

Mandela arrived at last at 7.45 p.m. amid mob hysteria in the City Square below the balcony. And both nation and world heard the voice which had been silent, yet speaking, for nearly thirty years.

'I don't think it mattered much to anybody what he was saying,' Desmond reflected later. 'He could have said anything and they would have cheered. It was incredible. Really remarkable.'

After being introduced to the excited crowd by former ANC General Secretary Walter Sisulu, Mandela launched into his speech: 'Friends, comrades and fellow South Africans, I greet you all in the name of peace and democracy for all.'

The place erupted with a roar like the sound of Krakatoa erupting.

Mandela went on: 'I stand here before you not as a prophet, but as a humble servant to you. Your tireless and heroic sacrifice made it possible for me to be here. I therefore place the remaining years of my life at your disposal.'

He said he had not personally conducted any negotiations on the future of South Africa as yet, apart from insisting on a meeting between the government and the ANC. He then

Church Umbrella

When Mandela and the ANC delegation finally went to bed it
was in borrowed pyjamas and nightdresses because the original plan had been for them to head straight back to Soweto as
Mandela had wanted to have his first night in a black township.

But, according to Archbishop Tutu, others had said 'No!
You must go to Bishopscourt.'

Added Tutu: 'We didn't speak about the symbolism of him
spending his first night almost under the umbrella of the
Church. But I think it was seen as such more by the people
outside. Many people in the States said to me that the impact
for them was powerful. In any event, the message it carried
was that the Church had played a very important role to get us
to where we were at that point.'

A New Day

Early next morning, Archbishop Tutu and his household
celebrated an early Eucharist service, as is their daily custom.
Mandela slept in after the exhausting previous day so as to be
rested for the huge international press conference set for 10 a.m.
in the shady and colourful grounds of Bishopscourt. No doubt
the shades of a few past archbishops were approvingly present
and appropriately relieved that at last South Africa had
rounded the corner of history and turned away from Apoca-
lypse into a new day.

As a professional in the media, John Allen was amazed how
Mandela coped with surely the most excited and perhaps
largest press conference in South Africa's history.

He turned to Tutu later and observed: 'You know, Father,
all the business about his being a myth has been exploded
today in the way he handled that press conference. They were
asking him questions that would have tripped anyone up. Yet
someone who had been in jail for twenty-seven years seemed
to know instinctively where all the pitfalls were. Remarkable.'

The press conference happily negotiated, the ANC party
now began to gear up to leave for Johannesburg.

Cyril Ramaposa, Chairman of the National Union of Mineworkers, excitedly phoned his colleagues in Soweto. 'We are on our way. Prepare to be hit by a one-hundred-ton express train!'

Outside Bishopscourt, a coloured traffic cop asked Mandela for his autograph.

Mandela signed. And then added a message of good wishes. In Afrikaans.

4 Kroonstad Prison

Remember those in prison as if you were their fellow-prisoners.

Hebrews 13:3

On Monday, February 12th, while Nelson Mandela took Soweto by storm, Billy and Basil, two young men from a black township near Kroonstad, basked in the euphoric joys of their hero's coming out the previous day and his name occupying every available headline in every available newspaper.

South Africans felt new that day. Their hearts were rejoicing. Feeling that joy should be not only unconfined but shared, they hit on a thought: 'Let's go up to the prison and see if we can see Charlie Bester and celebrate together with him.'

'Great idea!' And off they went, blissfully unaware that Sunday, not Monday, is prison-visiting time. Charlie, who is my nephew, had in fact been visited the previous day by my sister, Judy, and brother-in-law, Tony. They had been doing the two-hour drive from Johannesburg most weekends ever since December 1988 when Charlie had been sent to prison as a conscientious objector who refused to have any part or lot with the South African Defence Force (SADF). At the time of his trial he had said that he saw the SADF underpinning the policies of division of that particular nationalist administration. 'Evil is manifesting itself in a political system,' he had gone on to say, 'and the government of the day is using the army and people of my age to uphold and defend that system.'

Not being, at that stage at least, 'a universal pacifist on religious grounds' (for which the sentence would then have been six years doing alternative service at the government's behest), but rather a 'political' objector to service in this particular army, Charlie had earned himself a six-year prison sentence. It was his religious convictions which produced his political protest, but this made no difference.

Following Christ

'My basic motivation,' he had written, 'for refusing to serve in the South African Defence Force is that I am a Christian, and as a Christian I must follow Christ. Christ's way is the way of love, and so in every situation I must try my best to follow a path of love. At the outset, I acknowledge that I am as fallible as anyone else and do not hold myself up as a better Christian than others, but I do believe that God sent His Son to die for us and so redeem us and set us free, so that, in our weakness and in His strength, we can be witnesses to Him.'

In his pre-trial statement he had written: 'I want to break down the barriers which divide us and I reject violence as a means to do so. If I were to serve in an institution such as the SADF which I see as perpetuating these divisions and defending an unjust system, it would be contrary to all I believe. I see it as incredible arrogance that eighteen-year-old boys, most of whom have never previously been to a township, let alone been involved in its life, are ordered to enter, armed, on the back of a military vehicle to impose "law and order" on a community they neither know, nor identify with.'

'In South Africa,' Charlie added, 'we have lived and are living under a political system which belies the fundamental tenets of Christianity, in that it has failed to meet the challenge of loving one's neighbour. The ideology of apartheid has been responsible for untold human suffering and humiliation in the pursuit of racial purity and the maintenance of power by a minority group. I would want to praise the government for its reform programme, but the principal bastions of apartheid remain in place . . .'

He concluded: 'The only way which I see that we, as white South Africans, can liberate ourselves from our spiritual oppression is humbly to seek reconciliation. Central to this is repentance before both God and man for the wrongs we have done. Only then can we begin to build a society on the firm foundations of justice, freedom and love.

'I am fully aware that I am breaking the law of the land, and have no guilt in doing so. After studying Christ's commandments and seeking God's calling in prayer, I personally cannot be obedient to this law and to God's calling. I shall submit to the authority of the State and stand trial. I believe that in order for me to follow a path that will best demonstrate my love for God, my country and my fellow South Africans, I must pursue the way of reconciliation and non-violence. I will therefore refuse to serve in the SADF, and take the consequences.'[1]

Sentence

I remember the moment of the sentencing so well. It came after Charlie, Robin Briggs – Anglican Dean of Pretoria – and I had testified, and lawyer Kathy Satchwell had put in her plea in mitigation of sentence.

As I have elsewhere[2] written:

The court was recessed for four minutes while the magistrate deliberated on the day. During this recess Ivan Thoms, another Christian conscientious objector, stood and asked me to say a prayer right there in the court-room. First Robin Briggs and then I prayed. We prayed for the judge, the prosecutor, the state, the government, Charles, the situation and for the healing of South Africa. This was a moving moment that touched us all. Even some police and soldiers present wept. My sister Judy looked up and saw tears streaming from beneath the cap of one bowed young white policeman.

On his return the magistrate took about forty-five seconds to pass the merciless sentence and close the case. He said, 'Six years is your sentence.' It was the only moment in the trial when he appeared to have the initiative.

Cries and shouts now came from the gallery. Some blacks led the singing 'Nkosi Sikelel 'i Afrika'. A police sergeant now barked out that the whole court was under arrest for contempt of court! All of us were duly shepherded down into the cells. Robin Briggs slipped out a back door to the colonel to ask him what on earth he was doing. The colonel replied 'They sang a freedom song.' Robin Briggs pointed out that 'Nkosi Sikelela' is a prayer. Moreover, how could people be in contempt of court when the sentence had been passed and the magistrate had left the courtroom?

Anyway, some hundred and fifty of us were now down in the cells. Charles was over in a corner, behind bars already. The little bag he had taken down with him with clothes, Bible and toilet bag had been confiscated. Charles pointed out that a friend of his in the Cape in similar circumstances had been allowed to keep his toilet bag. The policeman replied, 'This is the Transvaal. You can't have the bag.'

Eventually we prevailed upon the colonel to let Charles at least keep his Bible. This we handed to him through a little window in the wall of wire. The last picture I had of him that day was behind those bars clutching his Bible to his chest with a big grin on his face. He was quite undaunted to the last.[3]

And so it was that Kroonstad prison was the venue from which Charlie began to watch on TV the release of Mandela on Sunday, February 11th. He was rudely interrupted at 3.30 p.m. by warders who told him he had to get back to his cell. As he reluctantly left, Charles thought: 'Come on Nelson, after all these years, this is your moment and here I am waiting! Where are you?'

His joyful emotion at the whole thing quickly overcame the temporary frustration. All this followed the tremendous personal news just before President F W de Klerk's February 2nd speech that Charles's sentence was to be reduced to three years.

EMIGRATION

However, as I had written to the President eight weeks previously, Charlie should have been out altogether. I concluded:

Not only for the sake of Charles and his few other young friends who are currently in prison, but also for the sake of the country as a whole, I want to make a plea to you that first of all Charles and his friends should either be released from prison and given alternative service or have their sentences drastically reduced. Moreover, the law which has sent them there should be speedily amended.[4]

Most marvellously, the Appellate Division of the South African Supreme Court sitting in Bloemfontein a few weeks later would rule in a majority decision that Section 126 A(1) (a) of the Defence Act does not prescribe a mandatory sentence (ie of six years) for persons who refuse to render the service in the SA Defence Force for which they are liable. The Appeals of Charles's two friends, Dr Ivan Thoms and David Bruce, now released, were accordingly upheld and the way paved for Charles's sentence to be reviewed further.

In any event Charles's stand and his lonely lot in Kroonstad prison up to that point had made him quite a hero to many like Billy and Basil, though they were unknown to him. Charlie was and is in fact a powerful symbol of youthful white protest and the country boasts a surprising number of young South African whites marked by this kind of conviction and, of course, thousands of such blacks.

An Unorthodox Visit

'We want to see Charlie Bester,' said Billy and Basil to the startled warder.

'But it's Monday. Sunday is visiting time.'

'No, but we want to see him anyway.'

The warder, recognising determination when he saw it, and perhaps infected with a touch of their Mandela euphoria, vanished into the prison hinterland.

To Billy and Basil's amazement the warder returned with positive permission from the lieutenant colonel.

'Bester!' Charlie looked up, startled. 'There are some chaps here to see you. Go to B Section visiting area.'

'But I'm an A category prisoner,' said Charlie, still perplexed at the visitors coming at this unorthodox time and wondering about their identity. 'I have "contact" visits. I don't want to talk through that glass.' (I knew what he meant, having battled traumatically through such a barriered visit some months previously.)

'I know, man, but these are blacks. It's not prison policy for whites to have contact visits with blacks!'

'Come on!' expostulated Charlie. 'You know that's all wrong! I insist on seeing them in Section A.'

The warder, finding himself between the devil of Charlie's resolution and the deep blue sea of Billy's and Basil's enthusiasm, relented. Perhaps he knew that someone, who had had some 1,000 letters in the last couple of months was someone to be reckoned with.

'Oh, OK! Come on!'

And a contact visit it was! The young strangers, two blacks and a white, clutched each other in embraces of greeting and celebration.

'Charlie, we've just come to rejoice with you over what's happening and especially Mr Mandela coming out.'

Hearts melted, tears flowed. Black clutched white and vice versa. Hope soared. The land could be saved. A new day could come.

Watching white warders and guards clicked their tongues. And surely wondered.

It seemed the Rubicon's waters had even reached the inner recesses of Kroonstad prison.

They reached even farther on Monday, August 14th, 1990, when, after nearly two years in prison, Charles won a Supreme Court appeal against his six-year sentence. Just four months previously, the Appeal Court in Bloemfontein had declared the law by which Charles had been sentenced 'draconian and repugnant'.

And so Charles walked free in the De Klerk–Mandela era more than 600 days after his initial sentencing. As he posed ecstatically with his mum and dad for a bevy of photographers, he remarked: 'I would do it all again if I had to. I'm still convinced I made the right decision.'

But now there was this daunting challenge. Could South Africa really come through to a new day of harmony and equity? Charles believed it could but only if the nation would draw on the power of God and His love.

Part Two

GOD, MAN AND LOVE

I will show you the most excellent way
1 Corinthians 12:31

5   There and Not Silent

True liberation is not the right to do what I want, it is the *power* to do what is *right*.

Carl Ellis

Democracy is not a heresy, but democracy *divorced from God*, freedom and immortality, and from every moral imperative, is certainly a heresy and a dangerous one.

Edgar Brookes

'Woe to the obstinate children,' declares the Lord, 'to those who carry out plans that are not mine'.

Isaiah 30:1

Jesus answered, 'I am the way'.

John 14:6

God's Will

A little child, who had been learning the Twenty-third Psalm for Sunday School, was asked by the teacher to recite it. 'The Lord is my Shepherd,' she started out promisingly, 'I can do what I want.' Not so promising.

The fact is that we cannot do as we want. If God is there, as He is, and if He is not silent, as He is not, then He has a will, a plan and a way which He would convey to us. And woe betide us if we miss it. Not in the sense of a vindictive and capricious God pronouncing doom on us, but in the sense of our missing the best and perhaps only way to get a personal or national course of action right.

And I guess this is what I fear most for South Africa, that we

will try to leave it all to the politicians, and will disregard the
Lord, forgetting that He is there and has a will. Then each of
us, like Frank Sinatra in his song, will try to do it 'My way'!

For a nation professing to be a godly one, that will be
catastrophic.

This leads us to affirm several basic truths.

I   JESUS IS LORD AND KNOWS THE WAY

South Africa professes to be a Christian country, with 78 per
cent of its people owning allegiance in some way, however
nominal at times, to Jesus Christ.

What if we were really to take Jesus seriously, believe in His
deity, go His way, and draw on His power? Would it not be
marvellous indeed? And why shouldn't we? For He is there,
risen and alive and ready to come alongside us. And this in
spite of the fact that so often we whites have presented a
travesty of Him and of the Christian faith to so many blacks.
But He is there. And alive. And available to guide us.

Yet many wonder – is it really so? Is He really there? Really
alive? Really the Way? Really ready to help?

I believe so – with all my heart. And lest any would lose their
nerve on this, let's think about Him a moment. To do so is to
renew our faith in Him as utterly worthy of our trust and love.

In any event, no other influence has so mightily blessed and
affected our planet as that brought by the simple life of Jesus of
Nazareth. But the New Testament goes farther, as did He. For
this One is God in the flesh stepping on to planet Earth.

I remember once chatting with a student at Wits University
in Johannesburg.

'Oh! I think this whole Christianity thing is so boring and
tedious,' he said.

'Now listen to this,' I replied. 'You've heard the words
before – but just listen to them again. They come from the
opening chapter of John's Gospel. "In the beginning was the
Word, and the Word was with God *and the Word was God . . .
and the Word became flesh and dwelt among us*" (RSV)

'Now get this,' I went on to my student friend, 'don't let the
familiarity of the words blunt or dull their force to your heart

and mine – *the Word was God* – got it? *God*. The Word was *God – and the Word became flesh* and dwelt among us.

'It's breathtaking,' I said. 'Quite breathtaking. The Word was God and *the Word became flesh, became a human and actually dwelt among other humans on this earth*. They saw Him, experienced Him, touched Him, talked to Him and then put down their experiences of Him on paper so we could get the picture too.'

'When you put it that way I can see it is pretty amazing,' said the student.[1]

Quite so. For Jesus's life, claims and character are indeed inexplicable unless He is the logos, the Living God made flesh, the One in whose hands is vested 'all authority in heaven and on earth' (Matt. 28:18).

And having such power, it is not surprising that death could not hold him. And so on the third day He burst the bonds of death and of the worst that humans could grub up, and came forth risen and alive and gloriously relevant for us and for every situation.

Not friend or foe, not politician or citizen, not Judas or Pilate, not sceptical theologians or doubting disciples could conquer the unconquerable Christ.

St Paul puts the person and power of Jesus as eloquently as any have ever done:

> Christ is the exact likeness of the unseen God. He existed before God made anything at all, and, in fact, *Christ himself is the Creator who made everything in heaven and earth*, the things we can see and things we can't; the spirit would with its kings and kingdoms, its rulers and authorities; all were made by Christ for his own use and glory. He was before all else began and it is his power that holds everything together (Col. 1:15–17 LB).

Relevant

For me, the truth that Jesus is not just a prophet but the cosmic Creator has huge relevance to South Africa, not just in telling me that in Him there is a power available beyond all our feeble and fallible fumblings, but in alerting me to the fact that His stamp and way are written into the very fabric of the universe which He created.

I would like here to refer the reader to *The Passing Summer* and the pivotal chapter on Understanding (Ch. 12, pp. 199–223) where I spell out the implications of Jesus being the cosmic Christ. Suffice it here to note just a portion of what I elaborated there, because I believe this is crucial and fundamental *if* South Africa as a professedly Christian nation is to come through.

Jesus and Morality

Christians believe that what Jesus was, as seen in His earthly life and ministry, God is always. Jesus's nature is God's nature. Not only that, but in His humanity He was the natural, normal man *par excellence*, whose life was in absolute accord with the natural order and the cosmos.

Because he is the agent in creation, and seeing that 'without him was not anything made that was made' (John 1:3 RSV), all reality, and all the cosmos, has His stamp upon it.

What Christians believe, therefore, is not that Jesus imposed a morality on mankind, but rather that He exposed more fully and completely an intrinsic morality in the universe itself. A good and moral action will therefore have not only Jesus and Scripture behind it but the universe and the cosmos as well. Conversely, a bad or evil action will therefore stand not only under the judgement of God and Scripture, but also under the judgement of life and the cosmos.

Consequently, in each action we commit cosmos or commit chaos, according to whether the action is good or bad. A good action is integrative and constructive; a bad action is disintegrative and destructive.

Christian ethics are therefore always on the side of fullness, happiness, true fun, completeness, peace, health, political stability, justice, social harmony, and so on.

Laws cannot, therefore, be 'broken', but one can be broken by them. No one breaks a law: he can only illustrate it in operation. To jump off the Empire State Building is not to break the law of gravity – only to illustrate it!

Morality and reality

To be moral, therefore, for the Christian, whether in personal, family or political ethics, is not to be narrow, prudish or politically obtuse, but simply to co-operate with the moral and spiritual structure of reality. Moral obedience is not obedience to an arbitrary decree, but to the way things are.

The moral law, then, is seen to be part of the way the world is made. That which is 'good' is that which enhances life by obedience in its inherent constitution; that which is 'bad' is what is out of relation to the structure of the world and life as it has been designed by God.

The moral law is the law of nature, and the law of nature is the law of life. In other words the laws of God's world all interlock. When human beings are called to be sexually or financially or politically moral, they are simply being called to play the game of life according to the rules of the game established by the author of the game for our happiness and well-being (*The Passing Summer*, pp. 218–19).

Morality and contemporary politics

When governments segregate or discriminate or pervert justice, they violate the moral law of the universe, and the hugely negative and reactionary consequences serve only to demonstrate this violation. The law, in effect, has not been 'broken' – it has been illustrated!

The Lord can speak to ancient Judah, just before He judges them with Babylonian conquest, and explain that in their many sins of injustice, greed and violence they are 'sinning against themselves'. The moral law of the universe is catching them out.

God's word is simple and clear: 'Woe to him who increases what is not his . . . You have devised a shameful thing for your house by cutting off many peoples: *so you are sinning against yourself*' (Hab. 2:6, 10, NASB).

St Paul can say of the immoral person that he sins against his own body. (1 Cor. 6:18, RSV): he hurts himself. He does not break the law; the law breaks him.

In other words, whether in political, personal or social morality, to go against the Lord's ways, which are the rules of the universe, is to hurt oneself.

Apartheid and all its works dramatically illustrate this in that they constitute one gigantic national project of self-inflicted wounds. The discriminating way is the way of shooting ourselves in the foot. If pursued long enough, it must become the way of national suicide. The same is true of the politics of hate, violence, vendetta, or 'let's grab it all'. That way will also violate the Jesus fabric of the universe and be self-defeating.

We are free to choose in politics as in life, but we are not free to choose the consequences. A law which operates regardless will always have the last word.

The Jesus way is not just for those who accept or buy into the Christian Scriptures: it is for all. That's why it operates as much for those who would oppose apartheid and the manner in which they do it, as for those who propagate it.

The Jesus way and the South African way

The implications of this first seized my imagination back in 1969 as I began to see why and how Jesus could say 'I am the *way*' (John 14:6). It also explained why Christianity was described in the first century as 'the Way' (Acts 9:2; 19:9; 24:14; 24:22).

The point is that the disciples had found in Jesus not only the way for salvation (Acts 4:12) but for living life and making it work – in any and every sphere, whether personal, marital, social or political.

'The Way' is the way to do everything – the way to think, to feel, to act and to be, in every conceivable circumstance and in every relationship. It is the Way that is written into the nature of everyone and everything. This makes the moral universe all of a piece, with its laws inherent in reality itself.

The way we are made to work is also the way God wants us to work. Creation thus works His way or else works its own ruin. And the history of humanity is nothing but a long confirmation of this truth.

All this raises acutely the issue of how we do things, not only in our personal lives but also in our nations. The relevance for South Africa and its so-called 'way of life' is crucial.

It means there is a 'Way' and a 'Not-the-way' for South Africa to order its society. And the choices will confront us at every turn in our national life. Will it be the Jesus way of love and justice, or will it be the non-Jesus way, with all its dire consequences? (See *The Passing Summer*, pp. 220–1.)

What struck me most forcibly in President de Klerk's February 2nd speech was not just the courageous content of it, but the genuine prayer of divine dependence with which it ended. 'I pray that the Almighty Lord will guide and sustain us on our course through uncharted waters.'

And as Nelson Mandela emerged into that gentle Sunday afternoon light to change for ever the face and dynamics of South African life, I felt afresh our nation's need of the Living God if we would come through. I do not know it for sure, but I would imagine that Dr Mandela must also have been sensing deeply his need for God's wisdom and power and what Martin Luther King called 'strength to love'.

Deeply as one could imagine the sense of spiritual need in each of the hearts of these two leaders, however, I also knew that the spirit of faith and trust in the Living God might well prove as difficult for President de Klerk and Dr Mandela to sustain as for other major players in the unfolding drama, such as Chief Buthelezi or Dr Andries Treurnicht, and indeed for the whole nation, or other people of faith and goodwill in the wider world. This is because all humans, whether white or black, high or low, powerful or powerless, are creatures of frailty and prone to sin and failure.

This is the second major truth we have to grasp.

II HUMANS ARE FRAIL AND PRONE TO FAIL

In South Africa, as elsewhere probably, this frailty has several dimensions.

We are inadequate to cope with the pace of change

This inadequacy I see particularly in terms not just of coping with the pace of change generally, but with the rapidity of revolutionary change specifically.

It is true that in 1990 and early 1991 the changes in South Africa have birthed new hope, but they have also left us breathless and tense, anxious and fearful. In a brilliant essay in *Time Magazine* (March 1990), the writer comments on events across the world and in South Africa and says, 'Epochs these days are lasting only moments; epics are being squeezed into précis. If current history were on video, it would be stuck on fast forward and we'd all be out of breath.'

He adds: 'In the twinkling of human eyes, the world changes . . . how can anyone study history when it charges so recklessly ahead . . . history may be going places, but it is travelling too fast for anyone to check for directions.'

This was dramatically illustrated in the suddenness with which the Gulf Crisis blew up. The pace of it left the world gasping.

And it has been true in South Africa. We are bewildered by the speed of change, and desperately anxious about the violence and the future. The endless trauma is exhausting and confusing. For so long, the media has been tamely controlled in the extent of its quotation. But now the plethora of speeches and ideas befuddles and bewilders almost every South African mind, leaving us disappointed, even disillusioned.

And all this is set in context of the 'future shock' which characterises the wider world. Alvin Toffler coined that phrase to describe the shattering stress and disorientation which is induced in individuals who are subjected to too much change in too short a time.

In terms fittingly apt for South Africa he writes:

Can one live in a society that is out of control? That is the question posed for us by the concept of future shock. For that is the situation we find ourselves in. If it were technology alone that had broken loose, our problems would be serious enough. The deadly fact is, however, that many other social processes have also begun to run free, oscillating wildly, resisting our best efforts to guide them.

Urbanisation, ethnic conflict, migration, population, crime – a thousand examples spring to mind of fields in which our efforts to shape change seem increasingly inept and futile.

'With chilling clarity, Sir Geoffrey Vickers, the eminent British social scientist, has identified the issues: "The rate of change increases at an accelerating speed, without a corresponding acceleration in the rate at which further responses can be made; and this brings us nearer the threshold beyond which control is lost." '[2]

Most South Africans, black and white, know this feeling only too well. We feel close to a threshold where we are unable to control the march of events or their outcome. This is both exhausting and frightening.

A South African student probably spoke for many recently when he said: 'Pleeez – I don't want to read a paper, turn on the TV or listen to the radio. It's just too much.'

In such circumstances it is good that we have in the God and Father of our Lord Jesus Christ a power greater than our own, one to whose controlling guidance we can yield ourselves.

Human frailty and proneness to fail has a second manifestation.

We all have fears of the future

I think both whites and blacks here have deep fears about possible collision and conflict in the future. But love, and indeed the politics of love, can cast out fear in a society.

I must say I too have fears. They relate mainly to whites, but not exclusively.

In a gathering of some forty-three thousand Christians, the majority white, at the Ellis Park Stadium in March 1990, I felt constrained to spell out two of these fears.

My first fear is that like Judah our repentance on the white side may be too shallow. Jeremiah 6:14 says 'They dress the wound of my people as though it were not serious.' We are seeking as a nation in these times to repent, but let's not think the wound can be lightly healed. We have a million miles to go to true national healing, harmony, and a binding up of the wounds of the past. Our road of repentance, especially for those of us who are white, will not only mean constitutional change but massive economic and land reform, massive movements towards educational equality, the end of all group areas and residential separation, and the total restructuring of our society. Are we ready for that?

And in the Church – which is so very guilty for its many silences and its past participation in the system – the road of repentance means deep sorrow for our sin and the removal of all racism in our congregational, denominational and personal lives. And though in the face of accusation and unforgiveness this is hard, let's not fall prey, like Judah, to shallow repentance and superficial healing of our national wounds.

My second fear is that of starting to repent and then changing our minds as we see the full implications of it. In Jeremiah 34:15–17 we read about Judah where the Lord says:

> Recently you repented and did what is right in my sight: Each of you proclaimed freedom to his countrymen . . . But now you have turned around and profaned my name; each of you has taken back the male and female slaves you had set free to go where they wished. You have forced them to become your slaves again. Therefore, this is what the Lord says: You have not obeyed me; you have not proclaimed freedom for your fellow countrymen . . . I will make you abhorrent to all the kingdoms of the earth.

And of course that is exactly what happened as Judah finally went into Babylonian captivity for seventy years. They had started to repent and then changed their minds with cataclysmic consequences for them as a nation. Let's not do that in

South Africa. The consequences would be a South African Babylonian captivity, which, as one prime minister once put it, would be 'Too ghastly to contemplate.'

As to blacks, my fear is that in the understandable passions, sometimes euphoric, sometimes blind, sometimes unthinking, they will forget the perils of their own sinfulness and fallenness and repeat all the mistakes of the white man. That's why we have to register deeply that we are *all* sinful.

We are ALL sinful

This is the third reason why the Lord and His ways are so needed in this land at this time.

I am not one of those with optimistic views of human nature or utopian understandings of human history, or any settled convictions that the oppressed can never become oppressors. And in this I feel I have the Bible with me. Its Word is very simple and clear: 'The heart is deceitful above all things and beyond cure' (Jer. 17:9). The white heart, the black heart, the brown heart. Your heart. My heart. All alike are deceitful and corrupt. To trust euphorically and naïvely in untainted goodness and settled benevolence in the human heart is to trust a broken reed. This means, among other things, that as the last government was made up of fallen sinners, so will be the next one. Both oppressor and oppressed suffer from the same disease.

And let it also be noted that human proclivity to evil tends to intensify as people are put under greater pressure.

Of course, the sin of whites in South Africa is all too painfully evident. But it is perhaps less obvious that without constant prayer and care, human sinfulness will just as readily corrode the black freedom movements. We have seen something of this in black violence in the Natal townships in the last few years, and more recently on the Reef. A close national walking with the Lord is therefore needed, and a deep seeking of His righteousness and His ways all along the line.

Carl Ellis is a black American from the Southern States and deeply committed to the Black Civil Rights Movement of both past and present. His concern always has been to see God's power and righteousness dominating the sinful impulses

present in all of us and which he often saw imperilling the
Civil Rights Movement.

He put it this way:

> Righteousness will never liberate ungodliness to do its
> thing. Righteousness, both collective and individual, will lift
> a people above the frustrating effects of ungodliness and
> give them the will and power to realise their loftiest aspir-
> ations (Matt. 5:6). The quest for righteousness in every area
> of life must be on the top of the black agenda if we are to
> become the people God created us to be (Matt. 6:33).

This thesis leads Ellis to affirm that

> The less an oppressed people seek to construct their resist-
> ance to oppression around the Word of God, (1) the weaker
> will be the cultural power generated by their struggle, (2)
> the smaller will be the likelihood that the oppression will be
> broken, (3) the greater will be the likelihood that the
> resistance movement will be destroyed by the ungodliness of
> those involved in it, and (4) the greater will be the likelihood
> that they will lose their cultural cohesion and compassion for
> their fellow human beings.

Ellis concludes with a warning and a challenge:

> I believe that the secular black movement splintered into
> many fragments because it sought to do away with God and
> his revelation. This explains also why, when some of our
> people began to 'make it', they became wrapped up in the
> new me-ism. Because their own ungodliness was never
> challenged when it resurfaced, they lost their compassion
> for those who remained in the under class.
>
> True liberation 'is not the right to do what I want, it is the
> *power* to do what is *right*.' If we are going to achieve
> liberation in our historical quest, then we must go *beyond
> liberation* to righteousness – God's righteousness. Not the
> 'holier than thou' brand of self-righteousness, nor religi-
> osity, but an applied righteousness lived out in all aspects of
> culture.[3]

In South Africa the quest for a new day and a liberated, democratic society must be accompanied by the quest for God and His righteousness.

If it is not, we will in our sinfulness fall prey to a deadly set of false dependencies. This is fourth in our catalogue of evidences for our frailty and proclivity to failure.

We are powerfully prey to false dependencies

The experience of Judah in the sixth century BC is perhaps as instructive as any. Their false dependencies were at least threefold – false dependency on bad laws – false dependency on their own human wisdom – false dependency on armed might. Each of these earned a pronouncement of woe from God.

Bad Laws

'Woe to those who make unjust laws [or 'unrighteous decrees' as the Authorised Version puts it] . . . to deprive the poor of their rights and rob my oppressed people of justice . . . What will you do on the day of reckoning, when disaster comes from afar?' (Isa. 10:1–3).

In South Africa, we have with the monolith of apartheid laws 'decreed iniquitous decrees' and 'framed mischief by statute' (Ps. 94:20 RSV).

If we do not repeal all these laws, or if those who would repeal them are defeated by arch-conservatives or right-wingers who would reinstate them, then the God who is there and not silent about unjust laws pronounces woe upon us. Because unjust laws are not the Way. Likewise if those who will rewrite the statute books for South Africa ignore God's ways of justice and forgiveness, the same will be true.

The Lord through the prophet Jeremiah is equally plain:

This is what the Lord Almighty, the God of Israel, says: Reform your ways and your actions, and I will let you live in this place . . . If you really change your ways and your actions and deal with each other justly, if you do not oppress the alien, the fatherless or the widow and do not shed innocent blood in this place, and if you do not follow other gods to your own harm, then I will let you live in this place, in the land I gave to your forefathers for ever' (Jer. 7:3, 5–7).

Farther on, the exhortation is repeated with a record of Judah's stubborn response:

but I gave them this command: Obey me, and I will be your God, and you will be my people. Walk in all the ways I command you, that it may go well with you. But they did not listen or pay attention; instead, they followed the stubborn inclinations of their evil hearts. They went backward and not forward (Jer. 7:23–4).

If South Africa, or any section of it whether white or black, does not obey God then woe awaits us. We will go backward not forward. Mark these words.

Human Wisdom

The second woe relates to trying to do it all in our own strength and our own wisdom. And this relates as much to whites trying to work their way through to a new day as to blacks seeking to implement their political plans for the future.

In Isaiah's time, the nation of Judah, supposedly a godly people, refused to listen to God or seek His counsel or Way. They could do it all on their own. Result? Woe.

Read it: '"Woe to the obstinate children," declares the Lord, "to those who carry out plans that are not mine, forming an alliance but not by my Spirit, heaping sin upon sin; who go down to Egypt without consulting me; who look for help to Pharaoh's protection"' (Isa. 30:1–2).

Beyond that there comes stern denunciation on a 'rebellious people' who urge the prophets to speak words to tickle the national fancy while ignoring God. 'Give us no more visions of what is right! Tell us pleasant things, prophesy illusions. Leave this way, get off this path, and stop confronting us with the Holy One of Israel!' (Isa. 30:10–11).

Such smooth talk can come in South Africa from various church leaders, whether they are talking to whites trying to preserve and perpetuate the status quo or to blacks who are trying to overthrow it. The false word is 'God is with you while you do your thing, regardless of whether you plug in to Him or not.'

Oh, no! He ain't! That's why He speaks to both, calling all back to Himself and warning against improper self-reliance, a habit to which we are all prone, and all the more so when the pace of events speeds up and we begin to race along helter-skelter with them, thereby becoming too busy and pre-occupied or even proud to pause and seek the Lord's mind.

And so His Word reaches us afresh: 'In repentance and rest is your salvation, in quietness and trust is your strength, but you would have none of it. You said, "No, we will flee on horses." Therefore you will flee!' (Isa. 30:15).

And flee we do, so sure we can manage on our own. Meanwhile, says Isaiah, 'Yet the Lord longs to be gracious to you; he rises to show you compassion. For the Lord is a God of justice. Blessed are all who *wait* for him!' (30:18). In other words, He waits for us until we wait for Him. Then there is blessing.

The glorious Good News is that when we do finally get round to calling on Him, often once we've made a muck of things in our own wisdom, He responds to us with gracious and tender guidance as the prophet promises:

How gracious he will be when you cry for help! As soon as he hears, he will answer you. Although the Lord gives you the bread of adversity and the water of affliction, your teachers will be hidden no more; with your own eyes you will see them. Whether you turn to the right or to the left, your ears will hear a voice behind you, saying, 'This is the way; walk in it.' (Isa. 30:19–21).

And surely, surely to goodness, this is what lost, bewildered and bamboozled South Africa wants and needs most desperately to hear – a word from the Most High Omnipotent and Omniscient God saying: 'This is the way. Walk in it.'

And we can hear it. But only on condition that we surrender and repent of all proud self-sufficiency and self-reliance.

Armed Might

A third woe awaits us for another type of false dependency – on our own or someone else's armed might. This is probably the most attractive yet in fact the most broken of all broken reeds.

In penetrating and eloquent terms the prophetic word comes again:

> Woe to those who go down to Egypt for help, who rely on horses, who trust in the multitude of their chariots and in the great strength of their horsemen, but do not look to the Holy One of Israel, or seek help from the Lord . . . the Egyptians are men and not God; their horses are flesh and not spirit. When the Lord stretches out his hand, he who helps will stumble, he who is helped will fall; both will perish together (Isa. 31:1, 3).

Military might and armed struggle have a certain worldly wisdom and sometimes achieve certain goals. But more often than not, the achievements are dangerous ones, for in seemingly conquering some dread monster, they spawn a thousand others.

I remember some years ago seeing this well illustrated in the Luweru Triangle in Uganda. For that was where Milton Obote's people, the liberators from Amin's oppression, massacred some 200,000 Baganda, whom six months previously they had liberated! In many places I saw Ezekiel's 'valley of dry bones', with shattered skulls, macheted shin bones, and the remains of ten or more people piled live upon one another in huge latrine pits. At the time I saw this, I prayed to grasp why the experience was coming my way. The sense of divine response to my heart was this: 'I want you to see and register the full horrors of what happens when tribal violence runs riot.'

Perhaps that is why three years ago in *The Passing Summer* I wrote that 'a major fear among whites is of ongoing and escalating factional black violence in a post-apartheid society under black majority rule. The spectre, whether valid or not, of an ANC-Inkatha-PAC-UDF or even tribal slug-out has certainly intensified white despair that black majority rule would not bring an even remotely peaceful dispensation' (p. 392).

That fear will have its validity rendered null and void only if blacks as well as whites remain conscious of their sinfulness and deal with it.

The Luweru Triangle experience in Uganda was also an illustration of the monsters spawned when violence is used in the pursuit of liberation or gaining power or ascendency over another group. More on this anon when we think in detail of the problems of violence.

For the white right to call for 'a million guns' or for some blacks to depend on armed struggle partakes of equal folly. It is not God's Way. It is a false dependence.

Rather let all look to Him, for He is there and He is not silent and we will hear Him say: 'This is the Way. Walk in it.'

6 The No Failure Factor

He alone loves the Creator perfectly who manifests a pure love for His neighbour.

The Venerable Bede (673–735)

There is no way you can be born white and think differently unless by grace, and there is no way in which you could be born black and think differently except by grace.

Frank Chikane

Love never fails.

St Paul (1 Cor. 13:8).

I have often thought that 1 Corinthians 13, Paul's great hymn of love, is probably the most political chapter in the Bible. Political, but not party political as Archbishop Tutu would say. After all, no one who loved and lived like that could fail to be carried into the public or political arena in some degree or other. More remarkable still, for life and even for politics, is the chapter's promise that its message relates to a phenomenon which ultimately never fails. And in a land, such as South Africa, where failure is constantly evident, dangerously capable of overtaking us, and totally unaffordable, this should seize our attention.

It is well to see first in more general terms what it is we are speaking about. For no loving works or ways of ours will reach the public or political arena unless they are first being worked on in the personal and inter-personal arena.

If this Lord of Love calls us to love ('This is my commandment that you love one another'), then to what is He calling us?

A Threefold Commandment

The marvellous and matchless reality is that, with the experience and discovery of Christ in our lives, we enter in new ways upon a threefold love – love of God, love of self and love of neighbour. Jesus expressed these three loves in His famous summary of the commandments: 'Love the Lord your God with all your heart and with all your soul and with all your mind. This is the first and greatest commandment. And the second is like it: Love your *neighbour as yourself*' (Matt. 22:37–9).

Clearly here, the matter of primary importance is our relationship with God. Everything else flows from that, most particularly a right relationship with ourselves and then with others. Once we have been received, accepted and forgiven by God, we know we can receive, accept and forgive ourselves. Knowing we are loved by Him, we can love ourselves. Says St John: 'We love because he first loved us' (1 John 4:19). Knowing He has put away and forgotten our past, we too can put away and forget our past. Knowing His forgiveness covers us, we can forgive ourselves.

Suddenly an amazing thing begins to happen as we recognise that our own personal lives are of intrinsic value. Grasping this helps both a proper pride, a proper self-respect and a proper self-love. We begin to accord to ourselves the importance God accords to us. As a spin-off from the value He attaches to us we attach new value to ourselves. We will stop downing ourselves and hating ourselves.

Here then is a key for our relationship with our neighbour. The value, love, forgiveness, acceptance and respect which we accord ourselves, we now find we can accord in new ways to the neighbour. For we are to love our neighbour 'as ourselves'.

So when Jesus says 'Love your neighbour' (Matt. 22:39), what exactly does He mean?

This leads us from the threefold commandment to love God, oneself and one's neighbour into a discovery of what love is. Four kinds of love are talked about in Scripture, the fourth being God's great self-giving, unconditional and 'in spite of' love which He manifests to us and calls us to manifest to others.

The other three loves lead to this in a sort of ascending staircase.

Four Loves

1 Affection (Gk – 'storge')

The first of these is love *as affection*. While it includes family love, the kind of love of a parent for a child or a child for a parent, it goes much farther and speaks of all relationships in warm comfortableness with other people. It could be the butcher, the baker or the candlestick maker, or your dear old aunt or even some likeable and familiar public figure. C S Lewis used to say that *storge* or affection accounted for nine-tenths of whatever durable happiness we have in our natural lives.

He also writes:

> Affection is the least noticeable and least discriminating of our loves. No matter how attractive, almost anyone can be the object of affection. Affection ignores the barriers of age, sex, class and education. It is based on familiarity, not merit. By the time one becomes aware of affection, it has usually been going on for some time. It seeps through our lives.

> And affection broadens our minds. It unites people who find themselves thrown together in the same household, neighbourhood, school, or job – people who might never have chosen each other for companions. We choose our friends and lovers because of traits that attract us. But affection, when it occurs, teaches us to appreciate traits that wouldn't attract us.[1]

2 Friendship (Gk – 'philia')

Then there is friendship love. *Philia* is the warmest Greek word for love. It refers to that kind of devotion which people have for their closest friends. It refers to that world of freely-chosen relationships which are open, luminous and satisfying.

Philia speaks about companionship between those who share a particular interest together, whether in a drama club, a political party, a rugby team or a medical clinic. People who have *philia* between them will in all likelihood share not only outward things, but inward things and will care about the same truths and values. While lovers stand face to face, true friends with *philia* between them stand side by side looking outwards together at some third factor of fun or interest or value. Another beautiful thing in *philia* is that it is not jealous or exclusive and will never resent the addition of others to its circle.

With my colleagues in African Enterprise, I experience this type of love. It is a thing to be treasured.

3 *Romantic Love* (Gk – 'eros')

As I have written elsewhere:

> *Eros* describes the love of a man for a maid. It includes the sexual dimension and physical passion. On the other hand, sexual experience can occur without *eros*. While sexual desire may want only a physical experience, *eros* wants the beloved. It is also to be noted that *eros* is not so good over the long haul. While seeming very eternal to new lovers, *eros* is nevertheless the most mortal of our loves. *Eros* describes that kind of romantic love which we feel when we are 'in love'. But people don't always feel 'in love'. This is why those who depend on love simply as a feeling can become quickly disillusioned or disappointed when they find that feeling beginning to wane. Their tendency is to blame the beloved and then search for a new conquest. However, what we have to realise is that it takes humility, charity and God's grace to continue what *eros* has begun. *Eros* needs help. He needs the assistance of a higher love. In a nut-shell, *eros* needs God. This is why C S Lewis used to like the story about William Morris's poem 'Love is Enough'. Someone apparently reviewed the poem by saying simply, 'It isn't!' Quite right, it isn't. In fact, *storge*, *philia* and *eros* all need the most vital addition of the New Testament's fourth type of love.[2]

4 *Gift-love* (Gk – 'agape')

Now we start getting to the heart of things. Here we see God's pattern of love that we are called upon to imitate. Lacking nothing, God gives everything, regardless of how deserving or undeserving we are, in spite of how attractive or unattractive we are. Even if we do not reciprocate, He loves us still. This is love which is unconquerable benevolence and invincible good-will. It operates, or should, regardless of what other people do to us. Whether they insult us or hurt us or sadden us, we will not take revenge or allow bitterness to invade our hearts. Rather will we seek to regard them with benevolence and goodwill, seeking only their higher good. This is a way of love which involves commitment, action, resolution and the will. This is love as loyalty. This is love which behaves positively, generously and graciously, regardless of inner feelings which might not be positive. The surprising thing, of course, is that as we seek to love that other person in this way, positive feelings and warmth often emerge and develop.

And so into Paul's mighty and majestic chapter of 1 Corinthians 13, where the ninefold anatomy of love is spelled out.

Ninefold Anatomy of 'Agape' Love

The apostle begins uncompromisingly: when we do noble things, but without love, we don't score 50 per cent or 33 per cent or 10 per cent before God. We get zero. Our grand egos reel. Our self-righteousness protests. Our political zeal rebels.

First, the apostle takes up human speech. Whether it be the mighty eloquence of political orators or the charismatic utterings of the Christian faithful, if not done in love, the score is zero. To God's ears it is all simply a noisy gong or a clanging cymbal.

Second, if we have great prophetic gifts and can challenge both Church and State, and if we have huge intellectual or spiritual prowess or indeed mighty religious faith, nevertheless if it operates without love, it scores zero.

Third, if we have social concern and generosity or passionate political love for justice so that we would give our bodies to be burned, if we do it without love, our score again is zero.

In South Africa, where there are causes on every corner and in every second cluster of people, this Pauline word speaks to us with terrifying directness. If we are doing these things without love, God's *agape* love, they score zero and count in his sight as 'wood, hay or straw' (1 Cor. 3:12).

As we fight for the cause of whites or blacks or of the PAC, UDF, ANC, Inkatha, Conservative, National or Democratic Parties, or even for the cause of South Africa as a whole, if it is done without at least a sincere aiming for God's *agape* love, as the controlling dynamic, it scores zero in His sight. If someone would therefore say that love does not belong in politics or that the politics of love is mere sentimental twiddle-twaddle, and if they would go another way, then the sad score according to my Bible will be zero.

What then is required of us if we would score differently? The Apostle spells it out in terms of nine ingredients.

Patience: Love is patient.

Kindness: Love is kind.

Contentment: Love is not jealous.

Humility: Love is not boastful or arrogant.

Courtesy: Love is not rude.

Unselfishness: Love does not insist on its own way.

Good Temper: Love is not irritable or resentful.

Guilelessness: Love does not rejoice at wrong but rejoices in the right.

Fortitude: Love bears, believes, hopes, endures all things.

(i) Patience

'Don't be so impatient, Daddy,' one of my children once said to me. And it is true that we can spoil many things by impatience. One of the great gifts of black people across Africa, and most especially in South Africa, is the one of patience, or 'long-suffering' as the King James Version calls it. Someone like Nelson Mandela certainly suffered long for his beliefs. Such long-suffering makes people heroes. On the other hand it is not surprising if black patience has in many ways run out as they have waited so long for a new day and a new order. Now that day and order are, we hope, coming. But further patience in God's strength will be needed as the old order gives way to the new and as whites fumble around with their fears and hesitate with political change. Whites, too, will need patience as they see things go wrong in the black political movements. The 'I-told-you-so' posture will get us nowhere and will aggravate black impatience all the more.'

St Augustine once said: 'Patience is the companion of wisdom.' Certainly we will all be wise in South Africa if we are patient with one another through these tumultuous times. Love is patient, so it will work at waiting.

(ii) Kindness

Jesus was incredibly kind to people. It never ceases to amaze me how unbelievably unkind people can be to each other. Barbed words, spiked tongues, bitter attitudes prevail all round until people everywhere cry out with the Psalmist: 'Hear me, O God, as I voice my complaint; . . . Hide me from the conspiracy of the wicked, from that noisy crowd of evil-doers, who sharpen their tongues like swords and aim their words like deadly arrows' (Ps. 64:1–3).

Such bitter and cruel words, the opposite of kindness, sadly run riot in office, factory, church and home. They pervade politics, frustrate reconciliation and hamper rapprochement.

Says the poet John Oxenham: 'I will pass through this world but once. Any good thing that I can do, or any kindess that I can show to any human being, let me do it now. Let me not defer it nor neglect it, for I shall not pass this way again.'

Says Paul in Ephesians: 'Get rid of *all* bitterness, rage and anger, brawling and slander, along with every form of malice. Be kind and compassionate to one another, forgiving each other, just as in Christ God forgave you' (4:31–2).

(iii) Contentment

The Apostle's reference here is not to a crude condoning of an immoral status quo, nor to a wimpish acceptance of injustice, nor to passive acceptance of wrong. He is speaking of a love that is not jealous. It does not fall prey to the tyranny of envy. It does not want what other people have. It does not manifest ill-will to those more gifted than ourselves, more capable than ourselves, more powerful than ourselves, or more comfortable than ourselves. This generous-spirited love will not want someone else's position or prominence. It will not clamber over precept and principle to reach power. It will not demean, detract, belittle or diminish. This love puts its ambitions under God's control. How far we all are from this!

This astonishing faculty was well manifested by the Apostle Paul when even in one of Nero's prisons, he could resist complaint and affirm: 'I have learned to be content whatever the circumstances . . . I have learned the secret of being content in any and every situation, whether well fed or hungry, whether living in plenty or in want' (Phil. 4:11, 12).

(iv) Humility

I sometimes tease my children, asking them if they would like my new book on *Humility and How I Attained It* with its ten life-size portraits, all autographed! I guess we could all do with books on humility and how to attain it, although few would dare to write them! But every now and then one does meet genuinely humble people whose humility is uncontrived, untutored, unself-conscious and unrealised by themselve. It is a beautiful thing. And what a cruel curse is its opposite, the strutting, self-satisfied pomposity of pride. Most of us know it in our lives and also know it as a killer. Yet we cling to it even as it clutches at us. In our South African nation we have pride of race, pride of tribe, pride of party, pride of opinion, pride of power, pride of wealth, pride of position and a thousand others. On every side in political, trade union, business, or personal matters it works as a wrecker. However, our God would not have it so. As He says in the Old Testament: 'If my people, who are called by my name, will *humble* themselves . . . I will forgive their sin and will heal their land' (2 Chr. 7:14). The New Testament says it equally simply: 'Humble yourselves . . .' (1 Pet. 5:6).

To swallow our pride and walk humbly with each other in South Africa would certainly oil a million wheels on which a happier future could run. So, Lord, humble each of us and grant each of us that wholesome feeling of being extra-ordinarily small and incredibly unimportant.

(v)   Courtesy

I was staggered the other day to reread and seek to grasp the implications of Paul's word to his young disciple Titus when he told him to 'show perfect courtesy toward all men' (Titus 3:2).

I thought of my own multiple failures in home, at work, in the ministry, or in my own little struggles to contribute to a new South Africa.

And as I looked around the country I could think of many people, both high and low, who have been wounded, alienated and made intransigent by the cruel pricks of discourtesy.

On the positive side I was much struck by a newspaper report describing the first formal encounter in Cape Town between the South African Government and the ANC. The reporter described how everything was carried out with impeccable courtesy. Out of such things do new days come. That same courtesy needs to go in all directions. The biblical challenge is 'perfect courtesy to all'.

In his great classic on 1 Corinthians 13 Henry Drummond wrote:

> Politeness has been defined as love in trifles. Courtesy is said to be love in little things. And the one secret of politeness is to love. Love *cannot* behave itself unseemly. You can put the most untutored person into the highest society, and if they have a reservoir of love in their heart, they will not behave themselves unseemly. They simply cannot do it.
>
> You know the meaning of the word 'gentleman'. It means a gentle man – a man who does things gently, with love.

Drummond observes the whole art and mystery of it, that the gentle person, man or woman, cannot in the nature of things do an ungentle thing. 'The ungentle soul, the inconsiderate, unsympathetic nature cannot do anything else. "Love doth not behave itself unseemly." '[3]

Indeed. Love is not rude or discourteous.

(vi)   Unselfishness

Agape love 'does not insist on its own way'. The King James

Version translated that as 'Love seeketh not her own'. This ties into two striking biblical words – one from the Old Testament and one from the New. Says the Old Testament: 'Should you then seek great things for yourself? Seek them not' (Jer. 45:5). Why not? Because such things sought selfishly for oneself, or in overweening ambition, are not worth anything. Only selfless service in love is ultimately worth anything. As to mounting to high, senior or powerful positions, we are to let it happen, if it would happen at all, only at God's discretion and not by our scrambling, for 'No one from the east or west . . . can exalt a man. But it is God who judges: He brings one down, he exalts another' (Ps. 75:6–7).

The New Testament word is similarly couched: 'Each of you should look not only to your own interests, but also to the interests of others' (Phil. 2:4).

In many ways the whole South African catastrophe has been born of whites thinking only of their own interests and insisting for over a century, and especially in the last half century, on 'our own way'. (*'Onse eie en ons identiteit'* – 'our own things and identity' – say nationalistic-minded Afrikaners. 'Our privileged way of life', say the economically-fixated English.) And with the heady promises of a new day for South Africa there is a real danger of blacks doing the same.

But Paul here calls for generosity of spirit and unselfish consideration of the *other* person or group beside us. Beyond that he is challenging inflexibility of opinion.

How massively we are all divided by our rightness about everything under the sun. No views are tentatively or flexibly held. 'I am right. And God knows it.'

Like the Anglican and the Baptist arguing about the respective merits of their denominations: when they almost came to blows, the Anglican pulled himself to his senses and casually remarked, 'Oh, I don't know what we're fighting about. After all, we're all doing the Lord's work, you in your way, and we in His!'

The late David Watson pressed the point home. Commenting on Jesus's amazing picture: 'Unless a grain of wheat falls to the ground and dies, it remains only a single seed. But if it dies, it produces many seeds' (John 12:24), Watson writes:

In practical terms, it means dying to our respectability, dying to our rights and privileges, dying to our prejudices, dying to our ambitions, dying to our comforts, dying to our independence and self-sufficiency, dying to our self-preservation. Unless we die to ourselves in these and other ways, there will be no fruit, no harvest, and no hope for this world.[4]

How hard for us wilful South Africans to hear this, let alone to put it into practice!

Says the Apostle simply, 'Love does not insist on its own way.'

(vii) Good Temper

Love is not irritable or resentful. It is not easily provoked. Unbridled anger is a killer in human affairs. Will Rogers, the American wit, observed that people who fly into a rage always make a bad landing!

In South Africa, thousands of people, both black and white, are living on exceedingly short fuses. Anger and temper hover just beneath the surface, like a volcano about to erupt. So much pain and frustration have been inflicted on blacks that this is not surprising. On the white side fear, anxiety, fatigue and uncertainty constantly spawn anger. Photos of political rallies, especially among the Far-right and Far-left, reveal faces full of it.

We are a nation of irritable, resentful and angry people. A recipe for escalating sadness if ever there was one.

The Bible's posture challenges this and says that if we would be angry without sinning, we must not be angry with anything but sin.

A tall order, we would each confess. Yet the grace of a good temper can be given by our Lord. As His Spirit is allowed to penetrate ours, it 'sweetens, purifies and transforms all'.[5]

(viii) Guilelessness

'Love does not rejoice at wrong, but rejoices in the right.'

It is a curious thing, especially in this land where so much is wrong, to discover the astonishing degree in which many rejoice in the wrong. In seeming to lament it, they in fact wallow in it and love to narrate the latest horror as if basking in its beastliness.

It is in most of us a pervasive habit of mind. Sometimes self-righteous to a degree, but birthed by an evil system, it can so lay hold upon us that no good or right thing can be rejoiced over. No credit for anything good or positive can be given to the enemy or the other side. Everyone is made to walk small and no one but I dare walk tall. It is the working of shrivelled spirits, void of largeness of heart and the luminous, positive guilelessness of which the Apostle here writes: 'God, give us the grace to be guileless, not rejoicing in the wrong, but in the right, and knowing also that right is right, even if everyone rejects it, and wrong is wrong even if everyone accepts it.'

(ix) Fortitude

'Love bears all things, believes all things, hopes all things, endures all things.'

The capacity to bear and endure is a distinctive mark of the African. Had it not been, South Africa would have been a warring battleground decades ago. Black fortitude has been and is an amazing grace.

Whites are not much good at this, having had little practice. Our turn may come.

But for all, whether white or black, love's call is to bear and endure and to be full of faith and hope.

Interestingly enough the Apostle throws some extra light on the gift of fortitude in another of his letters. He is talking to the Colossian believers about how he prays for them that they may be 'strengthened with all power according to his glorious might so that you may have great *endurance* and *patience*' (Col. 1:11).

The Greek word here for 'endurance' (*hupomone*) means fortitude to cope with all kinds of *circumstances*, while the word for patience (*makrothumia*) refers to fortitude to cope with all kinds of *people*! How we all need both!

A story has it that some of the angelic host gathered round God after creation and said: 'Lord, look at South Africa. You've given it most of the world's minerals, a spectacular climate, sensational scenery with its mountains, beaches, forests and rivers. On top of that, marvellous agricultural potential and the whole bit. It's not fair when you look at most of the other countries of the world.'

'Ah!' said the Lord. 'But just wait till you see the sort of people I'm going to put there!'

Well, I guess we who inhabit this tip of Africa are a pretty complex and tricky lot. Certainly the diversity here is astonishing – every shade of the rainbow, with a cultural mix of extraordinary range and complexity. Result? We get each other down. Not only those people who are different from us, but even our own sort.

But in love's way of bearing, believing, hoping and enduring all things, neither circumstances nor people will get us down.

Starting Point

In the face of the massive challenge of this ninefold love, one would feel lost indeed if one forgot the starting point – namely that this God of Love, who really has a way for the world and indeed a way for South Africa, calls us clearly and unequivocally to come in surrender of ourselves to Him. The way Jesus put it in the first recorded words of His public ministry is like this: 'The Kingdom of God is near. Repent and believe the good news!' (Mark 1:15).

Repentance means a change of mind leading to a change of direction. It is what the Prodigal Son did when he changed his mind about the way he was living in the far country, when he decided that this was producing only destructive consequences and he then changed his direction. Instead of moving farther away from the Father, he turned back to the Father's love and the Father's household. It meant leaving the old life and involved, as a friend of mine once put it 'Giving the pigs a permanent wave!' We wave goodbye to the style of living on the husks of life and we go back to the bountiful table and loving provision of the Father. We change our mind and we change our direction.

The second exhortation Jesus gave was to believe that in Him, as King and Lord of Heaven and earth, the Kingdom of

God had drawn near to mankind and we needed to lay down our weapons of rebellion and come in submission to the King. This submission is not a ploy whereby we become exploited by an alien power. No. It involves rather an intellectual assent and a commitment of our destiny to one who has nothing but our good in view. It is like getting on an aeroplane. We not only believe in the plane's existence, power and workability, but we commit ourselves to it and to the pilot who will take us to our destination. Belief is followed by commitment of the will. A little child believes that Daddy, who is good, is there in the pool or river, and that he is strong and reliable and caring. Then she jumps into his arms.

We also face the fact that submission to Christ will call us to carry His Cross. It will not all be a bed of roses. Knowing Him and the power of His resurrection will also entail the fellowship of His sufferings. But how wonderful to know also that after we have responded in repentance and faith, God does something very special on His side. He forgives us the past and indwells us by His own power in the person of the Holy Spirit. Changes, sometimes sudden, but generally very gradually begin to take place within us. What the Bible calls 'New Birth' begins. We begin to discover the experience of Temple Gairdner of Cairo, who said after his conversion: 'That sense of newness is simply delicious.' United States Senator Mark Hatfield put it this way:

Following Jesus Christ has been an experience of increasing challenge, adventure and happiness. He is totally worthwhile. How true are His words, 'I am come that they might have life, and that they may have it more abundantly.' No cause, noble as it may seem, can be truly satisfying or purposeful without the personal direction of Jesus Christ. I can say with all sincerity that being committed to Him is indeed truly satisfying.

A Hindu who found Christ wrote: 'Without Christ I had been without hope and full of fear about the future life. Now by His presence, he has turned fear into love, and hopelessness into realisation.' A Moslem who made the same discovery marvelled that he was no longer caught up in 'mere acceptance of certain beliefs and dogmas' but in the amazing experience of 'living in close fellowship with Christ'. Kipchoge Keino, the world record-breaking long-distance runner from Kenya exulted after he found Christ in this experience. 'I now know God is guiding me and has a purpose and plan for my life.' A prominent research physicist at Stanford University tells about what happened after he surrendered his life to Christ: 'The Bible is a supernatural book to me. Old problems and desires have faded away. For the first time I feel complete as a human being.'

Recently, at a conference I met Jim Ryun who for eight years held the world record for the mile, having also been the first high-schooler in the world to do the mile in under four minutes. 'The fastest man alive' they once called him. Running had however become his god. And it left him asking: 'Why am I so dissatisfied?' Finally, he learned of Christ and how to receive Him. 'As I prayed and received Christ into my heart, the emptiness running had never been able to fill vanished, and I felt a joy and peace that the old Jim Ryun had never, ever experienced.'

Meeting Jim and his wife, Anne, I was struck primarily by people who had learned what it was to love. And they had an inner power to do so.

Love Lasts

So, then, there are the ninefold ingredients of *Agape* love which we are told to work out in the power of Christ and His Spirit. Personally practical? Obviously. Socially helpful? Manifestly. Politically relevant? Of course. For politics is only people trying to get along together. And if love facilitates that, and especially if finally it never fails, it must become the goal of all. More than that, *Love Lasts*. Love survives and lasts to all eternity. Pope John Paul II once said: 'Only love lasts for ever. Alone it constructs the shape of eternity in the earthly and short-lived dimensions of the history of man on earth.'

Henry Drummond put it this way:

Can you tell me anything that is going to last? Many things Paul did not condescend to name. He did not mention money, fortune, fame; but he picked out the great things of his time, the things the best people thought had something in them, and brushed them peremptorily aside. Paul had no charge against these things in themselves. All he said about them was that they would not last. They were great things, but not supreme things. There were things beyond them. What we are stretches past what we do, beyond what we possess. Many things that people denounce as sins are not sins; but they are temporary. And that is a favourite argument of the New Testament. John says of the world, not that it is wrong, but simply that it 'passeth away'. There is a great deal in the world that is delightful and beautiful; there is a great deal in it that is great and engrossing; but it will not last. All that is in the world, the lust of the eye, the lust of the flesh, and the pride of life, are but for a little while. Love not the world therefore. Nothing that it contains is worth the life and consecration of an immortal soul. The immortal soul must give itself to something that is immortal. And the only immortal things are these: 'Now abideth faith, hope and love, but the greatest of these is love'.[6]

7   Love Real and Reachable

Don't curse the darkness. Light a candle.

Chinese proverb

I was asked by Idi Amin what I would do if he gave me his
revolver. I told him, 'Sir, I would hand it back to you,
because that is not my weapon. My weapon is love.'

Festo Kivengere of Uganda

God has poured out his love into our hearts by the Holy
Spirit, whom he has given us.

St Paul (Rom. 5:5)

Outside Pietermaritzburg is the township of Edendale. Its
dark clouds of alienation, making it in these last years com-
parable with Beirut, have plunged South Africa into gloom.
Many other townships round South Africa are or have been in
similar pain. Nonetheless there is hope, especially in the
person of the black pastor – hidden, humble, imperilled, yet
rarely fearful and almost always faithful. In many ways he
stands dramatically on the South African sky-line to remind us
that the ninefold ingredients of *agape* love are reachable
realities in the hearts of humankind. Many of us who know
black pastors know that here stand a multitude of working
models to say that love works, is real and reachable.

This love, whatever the odds, will work by lighting a candle
rather than simply cursing the darkness. It will do what it can.
And by such things across the land and in every corner, South
Africa can be saved. The pastor will in love do what he
can, while he can. I pay tribute to him therefore, for South

Africa has no final answer apart from him. And he stands as example and inspiration to all.

One such is Ben Nsimbi, Methodist pastor, devoted husband, father of three, friend to many and to me. Also one of our African Enterprise Board members. In appearance he resembles a black, pocket-size version of Abe Lincoln. Like many black pastors across the nation he battles bravely with the multiple pressures of crisis. Prayer, preaching, politics and a thousand practical things of love and care occupy him day and night.

Thus it was not really surprising to have him turn up at my office one day to tell me, 'Mike, one of the ANC leaders wonders if you could lend him a PA system for Dr Mandela's press conference and rallies in the area today.'

Having previously committed ourselves to helping Ben all we could, his wish was our command. And so away we went, several of us from AE, plus PA system. But now began a goose chase to catch up with the Mandela cavalcade. Ben became flummoxed as to where they were and when, but seemed relaxed. 'We'll catch them up in Mpophomeni township near Howick,' he said. 'I gather they are now in town after changing the venue of the press conference. Too much crush of people out here. Then they're heading to Mpophomeni. Let's go by the Thuthuka Centre.'

Displacees

And so we went down to his church and the neighbouring community centre. Hundreds of what Ben prefers to call 'displacees' were in the centre, mainly women, children and older men, all of whom had either had their homes burned down or had evacuated in terror at the prospect. Soup and bread were being dispensed. 'Toilets are a great need,' said Ben, 'but we are working on this.'

Numbers of young 'comrades', as they are called, saluted Ben with clenched fists as we drove by.

'This is a UDF area,' he said, 'so I have to minister here to all these young comrades and try and hold up the Lord to them and to all these people who have fled from Inkatha. But out there in the hills and areas where my assistant and I have another thirty-five churches to pastor and look after, we have many Inkatha people to whom we must minister as well.'

And then chuckling, Ben added, 'My wife says to me – you must be careful, Ben, or you will get yourself killed because you are ministering to both sides. But what can I do? I must run the risks. It is my duty. And the Lord loves them all.'

That's it. We model our love not on man's sectional ways, but on the all-embracing ways of a God who so loved the *world*, all of it, that He gave His Son.

'Thirty-five churches, Ben?' said an incredulous Neil Pagard. 'You mean you look after thirty-five churches with just one other person?'

'Of course,' said Ben, as if it was all part of the norm in the black pastor's world.

As Ben's car limped up the hill out of the Edendale Valley towards Taylor's Halt and the Inkatha area, he suddenly stopped. We all got out with him.

'Down there,' he pointed, 'there was a terrible battle last week. And see those gutted houses. I am called out all the time to look for and identify bodies and minister to the families. Like last night at 2 a.m. – which is why I am a bit tired today. I got to bed at four.'

There was no bravado here or complaining. Just all in a day's work. My colleagues and I sat silent. I knew each one was marvelling.

Back Road

'I'm taking you all by a back road,' said Ben, labouring the obvious as he quit the tarred road and headed into the hills by a track which had long been stranger to any grader.

In a gentle vale of haunting beauty and quietness Ben pointed out some youths gathered by a store.

'They are preparing to fight or defend the area. They meet here daily,' he said sadly.

'We must go in here,' and Ben suddenly turned his car off the road into a little drive-way flanked by mealie patches and a couple of humble dwellings. 'My circuit steward lives here. It's an area that seeks to be neutral between the two sides. Sometimes they fear getting it from both! It's dangerous.'

Neil Pagard looked anxiously at his watch. I read his thoughts. At this rate we'll completely miss Mandela in Mpophomeni as well. But Ben is an African – an identity which precludes slavery of any sort to Western man's terrible tyrant of time! Savour the moment. See the people. Enjoy the day. Relax. Programme and agenda are secondary. Besides, there are people here who need encouragement.

An ecstatic Mr Gilbert Zondi, the Methodist society steward, with his wife and friends, greeted us all with delight while several fowls clucked quizzically around us.

Ben explained. 'We are en route to the Mandela meeting in Mpophomeni and just dropped in.' Delight all round.

'But oh, Umfundisi [pastor], things are bad,' said Mr Zondi. 'None of the kids here are in school. They're boycotting and keeping ready to fight. We wonder what's going to happen.'

'Ah yes!' murmured Ben, with the pained expression of relative helplessness. Then some more cheerful chit-chat, with Ben refusing to be downed. At last – 'Well, we must be on our way.' Neil and John Tooke looked relieved.

But first a prayer. In the stillness. And the beauty. And the danger. Some love, I knew, was left behind.

My People

In the middle of nowhere and halfway up the next rock-riddled and semi-vertical incline, while Ben's car registered every protest known to the Japanese motor industry, he pointed to a house on the right and said, 'Some of my people lived there – the Nhlophane's, but they have fled. They dismantled their building and took all they could to another area. I preach out here once a month.'

Two hundred yards farther up, Ben pointed to another skeleton of a house. 'Also my people. And see that big fresh-water tank? The people who evacuated from here want me to get it to town for them. But I have no truck. I must work on this.'

Toilets. PAs. Food. Bread. Pràyer. Preaching. And now water tanks!

'Ah yes,' I remembered. 'The African makes no dichotomy between secular and sacred. A Hebrew really, and not a Greek.'

At last we were on top of the world. All of Natal seemed to be below us. Poor stricken place, but lovely with the lavish endowments of Nature's hand. And there was Mpophomeni, way down there, dormitory township for Howick over yonder, yet all isolated in the veld, strange, aberrated creation of apartheid's mania for separateness.

We trundled down the back-side of our hill, passing as we did so several parked army casspirs set up as a remote watch-point complete with walkie-talkie radios into which a group of white and black soldiers seemed to be speaking strange solil-oquies. They stared at us. Quizzically. Ben drove by, as if he owned the place, a wry smile betraying some inner thoughts.

Were we too late for Mandela? Ben seemed unconcerned. Then we saw the stadium: it was not emptying but filling up, as this little township which has suffered much, disgorged itself from every house to hear their hero.

Mandela

And then, with precision timing, Ben found himself filtering into the Mandela cavalcade just as it arrived! Not a second too soon, not a second too late. It was nearly two hours since we had left Edendale! I looked at my colleagues and indulged in wide-eyed astonishment.

'Stick by me,' said Ben getting out of his car, as we stopped by a church. Disciplined marshals, all arm-banded in the brilliant green, gold and black of the ANC's colours, ushered Dr Mandela, Archie Gumede, Walter Sisulu, Harry Gwala and – you guessed it – Ben Nsimbi and us towards the church! By no design or plan we had inadvertently become part of the Mandela party.

The church Mandela was to inspect had been desecrated and the altar damaged by persons unknown.

Archie Gumede, one of the two co-presidents of the UDF

(United Democratic Front) called me over. I had known him for some years.

'Mike, come and meet Mr Mandela.'

And so we all met the man of the moment on whom so much would seem to hang. Tall, erect, impressive and strong.

'I hope you got my book in prison, Mr Mandela,' I ventured as I shook his hand.

'Yes, indeed, and thank you very much.' Then to my colleagues, 'I have heard good things of AE's work.' Pause. A twinkle. 'But perhaps they only tell me the good things!' Perhaps.

I had spoken to Sisulu and his wife on the phone. Now face to face. Harry Gwala I was meeting for the first time. What had all these impressive men suffered to come to this place? Certainly all knew the anguish of prison. But what else? Loneliness? Despair? Deprivation? Crushing depression? Regret over lost and wasted years? Emotional agony in separation from family and loved ones? Anguished wonderings if they would ever see the outside of a prison and the fruit of dreams and sacrifice?

But now for Mandela here in Mpophomeni was adulation. Possession. Adoration. More, surely, than any man could manage. And longing, looks of hope from a people wearied beyond the telling with oppression and despair. Ben's people, too.

One also felt strangely part of some dual kingdom, with here in Mpophomeni one of the heads of state and his court in tow, while in Cape Town would be the other king, the other kingdom and the other court. The political schizophrenia felt weird. We were peering awkwardly at what poet Breyten Breytenbach calls 'the twilight land of two competing legitimacies'.

Rally

Then the rally. Ben again was the ticket to our trailing in reflected glory as his car was ushered by marshals to follow those of the big men. 'They must know you, Ben,' I said.

Wild shouts and cries of 'Viva this' and 'Viva that' greeted

Mandela and his party as they took their places. Women ululated. Efficient and disciplined marshals controlled it all. My colleague, Mike Odell, chuckled to see a PA of sorts already in place. Our sound system's big moment had been missed!

Mandela's speech was brief and to the point. Continue in the struggle till it's won. This was the music of political ecstasy to many ears.

And then the fanfare, fire and passion of it all.

As we left the stadium behind the big ones a radiant black lady, who must have seen us in our mission to the area the previous year called out, 'When are you coming back to Mpophomeni?' This touched my heart. What a land of Gospel openness and need!

Hazard

Now came the hazardous part. Knowing Mandela was headed to Edendale and among other places his own community hall, Ben could not be left behind as the cavalcade set off for town at breakneck speed. 'I know blacks are in a hurry,' I thought, 'but this is mad.' Ben, adrenalin pumping, was caught up in it all. His little car in a line of ten or more did things neither it, nor he, nor Toyota had ever quite envisaged. I held on to my seat, said my prayers and reminded myself that I believed in a sovereign God. Amazing how doctrines of theology can help you at such times!

Edendale

Edendale at last. Mandela went here, there and everywhere. In Imbali a bullet flew past his car. At Slangspruit where many had died in previous weeks he said, 'Stop this violence.' At the ecumenical centre: 'We are not fighting against Inkatha. We are fighting against apartheid and the policy of racial oppression. We are here to make peace.'

At one point it looked as though Mandela's straightened schedule might not allow a stop at Ben's church hall. He looked crestfallen. 'Some people here, Mike,' he said, 'have waited over twenty-four hours to see Mandela. We must not let them be discouraged. It will mean so much to them if they can hear him!'

Again I was seeing the heart of thoughtfulness for others. Here were people, many of them simple folk and not important to the world's eyes, but not to be denied the chance to hear the man of the moment.

The huge number of widows and children in the church were Ben's 'displacees'.

Ben finally flagged down the Mandela vehicle, told of the waiting folk and urged they not be left out.

Finally we were all at Ben's hall. Once again the latter's directing hand pushed us into the platform party. Mandela did his 'Vivas' again and urged hope, patience, and ongoing labours for peace and victory in the struggle. Hearts of despair took hope. Ben looked gratified.

The party moved off again. By this time weariness was setting in. Keeping up with Ben, just for one day, was ushering in for me some premature ageing.

But suddenly he was missing. Vanished. Where was he? I waited and waited. Mike Odell from our team took some photos of the 'displacees'. My other colleagues had gone straight back from Mpophomeni to AE. But Ben? Where was he?

Half an hour later I saw him walking wearily up the hill to join me at his car.

'Sorry, Ben, I lost you.'

He looked a bit sheepish. 'I'm sorry, too, but I just had to take Mandela to the toilet!'

Ah, yes, the toilet. Incongruous intrusion of the minor into the momentous. Yet not without its message. It reminded of humanity. Frailty. Fallibility. And the fragility of the whole South African thing.

Rest

'I'm tired now, Mike,' said Ben. 'Let me take you back to town.' I saw a man, bone weary, yet able to consider me and my needs for transport back to town.

'Ben, you're not just tired, you're exhausted,' I said. 'And you've still got to speak at this public meeting in town tonight for the whites to get the story on the crisis. I think you'd better come to my home for a bath, some sleep and some supper.'

He needed little cajoling. Within seconds of getting on to a bed in my home, he was asleep.

Briefing

By 7.30 p.m. we were back in Central Maritzburg, the big Methodist church packed for the most part with anxious whites. John Aitcheson from the University gave the history of it all. Then Ben on his feet yet again. The last briefing I had seen him give had been the day of IDASA's (Institute for a Democratic Alternative for South Africa) fact-finding tour for leaders the previous week. Ben was then briefing Frank Chikane and out-of-town leaders of the SA Council of Churches. Now it was mostly local whites, many of whom longed to know and do more, but felt paralysed by uncertainty or a sense of helplessness.

Exhausted and battling a sore throat, Ben soldiered through with gracious explanations and practical counsel to whites to do the works of love for people in need.

'Well, Ben, my brother, it's been quite a day. Thank you so much for it all. Really extraordinary. Rest well, now,' I said as it came time to leave.

'Actually, Mike, I can't turn in just yet. I have my daily 10 p.m. meeting with some of the young people who will be guarding different places tonight.'

No, surely, not still more to come. I felt spiritually limp and emotionally lame as my wife Carol and I stumped off into the darkness while Ben went back to Edendale to shine his light and share Christ's love for just a little longer.

Thus the black pastor in South Africa today. And thus by grace the reality and reachability of love.

Part Three

LOVE'S PRINCIPLES FOR PEOPLE AND POLITICS

Whoever does not love does not know God,
because God is love.

1 John 4:8

8   Love's Necessity in Nations

I have decided to stick with love. Hate is too great a
burden to bear.

>   Martin Luther King

Love is a political virtue . . . The world languishes because love is being tried so little. It is imperative that it
should be admitted into the field of political thought.

>   Edgar Brookes

We must also consult the foolishness of the dove if we are
to build the Beloved Country.

>   Prof Douglas Irvine

Hate evil, love good; maintain justice in the courts.

>   Amos 5:15

While love may penetrate and control the hearts of the Ben
Nsimbis of this world, the question is whether it can operate in
the political realm. And at such a time.

Frederick van Zyl Slabbert, former leader of the opposition
in Parliament, and currently founder and director of policy
and planning for IDASA sees these times in this land as both
'The best of times and the worst of times.'

On the negative side violence grips different parts of the
country. Then 'extravagant, irreconcilable demands are made
on the polar opposites of the political spectrum; those who
drive the centre towards "talks about talks about talks" get
bogged down in position bargaining and internal constituency
urgencies, and so on.'

But we have moved into a new era, no question of that.

Writing in the first part of 1990, van Zyl Slabbert voiced the view of many South Africans when he wrote:

> All the major factors that shape our future are geared towards a positive outcome: the international community wants negotiations to succeed; the region desperately needs it, and domestically, despite the distressing signs of conflict and tension, we find the major players still committed to avoiding catastrophe and finding a workable consensus for transition away from domination towards democracy.

However, as he and others readily grasp, we have no quick fix situation.

> The experience of oppression and struggle and the comforts and insulation of domination do not evaporate overnight. We are beginning to move from structural inequality and discrimination towards liberalisation and democratisation. Only beginning. It is going to be a painful learning process for all concerned – and we have no option but to go through it.[1]

By contrast in the *latter* part of 1990 optimism was draining from the hearts of many South Africans, both black and white, and giving way not only to the realism manifest in van Zyl Slabbert's utterance but often to pessimism, gloom and even outright despair and disillusionment.

The spectre of hate-filled right-wingers vowing to fight for every inch of the Fatherland, and of blacks killing each other, suddenly surfaced.

A combination of apartheid's alienations along with conservative white selfishness, black inter-necine power struggles plus perhaps some right wing *agents provocateurs* among the police, along with Third Force spoilers seemed, at least in the minds of many, to lie at the root of all the conflict. Whatever it was, whether among blacks or whites, it was the opposite of love whose rules and principles, if followed, would never allow this sort of degeneration into the ways of hate-filled violence.

In any event if our situation is not to slide into endemic civil strife, then it is along two routes, as Sowetan editor Aggrey Klaaste says, that our nation must travel. The first is the reconciliation route involving a deep commitment 'to thinking and behaving positively' (Christian Forum, October 1988). And the second is what he calls 'the spiritual route'.

In fact, says Klaaste, in the black community 'there is a thirst, however masked, for the spiritual route'. The need, as he views it, is for a 'spiritual resonance to underpin' whatever people are engaged in politically.

This speaks of God's way. But neither Klaaste nor any other black or white thinkers are under the illusion that the way into the future, even drawing on all spiritual resources, will be anything other than long and arduous.

Marathon

I agree. Some years ago I had a strange dream. In it I had the mysterious sense that God said to me: 'In the South African struggle you are not caught up in a short race. You are in a marathon. Be prepared for this.'

The very next Sunday in church a woman came up to me and said, 'Michael, I feel God wants me to pass a message to you.'

'Oh, yes,' I replied all eager and alert, 'and what is it?'

'He says you are to know you are in a marathon.' Life and the Lord have their mysteries, I thought. And their messages.

The next week I secured an enlarged photograph of two of South Africa's greatest runners, Bruce Fordyce and Hosea Tjale, as they raced side by side in the legendary Comrades Marathon from Durban to Pietermaritzburg. I had the photo mounted and framed and hung in my office with the caption beneath 'Run with Patience . . .'

It hangs there to this day, with a chunk of the Berlin Wall on top of the frame to remind me that all walls do finally come down, however permanent they may have seemed midway through the marathon.

Pain and Suffering

Speaking of the Comrades Marathon and the spirit in which it is run, there are perhaps here in parable form some special lessons for all caught up in the political marathon in South Africa. One commentator on the 1990 race spoke of the fact that the common denominator for all runners is the pain and suffering of the race. Obviously this is minimised in some measure according to the training and readiness of people for it. Nothing could be truer for all of us in social and political life in this land.

Thus there was the 'unconscious runner', collapsed at the entrance to the stadium, only minutes short of making it in the time which would earn him a medal. Yet there were some of his friends and compatriots, oblivious to the risk of losing their own medals, struggling to carry him home. Perhaps in the end what counts is that we run the race, not so much to obtain our own goals or fulfil our own agendas as to assist and encourage others to reach theirs.

Then the pain of the first runner who was to miss his bronze medal by being only one second outside the time. His brave response, despite the dulling and discouraging effects of pain and failure, was simply and eloquently stated: 'Next year I will try again.'

In this roller-coaster land of ups and downs and often more failures than successes, how much do we all need the spirit which says, 'I will resist disillusionment and despair. I will try again.'

It is this marathon, as an extended and politically painful process, whose full resolution will take a decade or more, which emboldens me to push out to South Africa this simple volume of Christian reflection and principles for meaningful application in our society. Why? Well, because I feel first that the darker, more difficult and more demanding a historical context is, the more the guiding light of principle, especially Christian principle, must be embraced and clutched to the heart.

Second, I stand convinced that it is most especially the love principle, sincerely embraced and earnestly applied, which will more than any other shorten the pain, relieve the difficulty and hasten the advent of a new day in this strategic and much-watched land.

Norway Conference

This conviction was deepened for me when in August 1990 a major international conference was convened in Oslo, Norway, on 'The Anatomy of Hate'. Senior national and international figures from all over were there, including our own Dr Nelson Mandela and Mr Leon Wessels, deputy Foreign Affairs Minister.

What intrigued me was the fact that here were distinguished figures from all over the world together isolating *Hate* and *the Politics of Hate* as the chief destroyer of social harmony and political justice. And they were asking, 'What is this killer called *Hate* that has us all so defeated and on the ropes all across the world?'

The conference was great, a landmark exercise, a Norwegian triumph, but it would have been even greater had it gone on to ask two more questions. First – 'What is love, as the opposite of hate, and what are the Politics of Love by which the Politics of Hate are put out of business?' Second – 'Whence comes the power to overcome hate and discover the ways and works of love?'

Maybe next time round the Elie Wiesel Foundation of Norway will mount an international conference on 'The Anatomy of Love and the Politics of Love'.

One might note here in passing that Leon Wessels's utterance at this Norway conference, coming thankfully from the heart of a deeply convinced Christian, came the nearest to being the kind of acknowledgement of white guilt for the past which the situation requires. He acknowledged that, 'Apartheid was a dreadful mistake which blighted our land and its people. It was also morally unfounded. It was moreover inhumane and indefensible.' Let such a word be fully and formally embraced and owned by white South Africa and we'll move a giant step closer to peace. We'll say more on this in Chapter Nine.

Constitution Not Enough

It still needs noting that even if we suddenly had a 'quick-fix' in South Africa so that by the time this book is out we have a new constitution, even then, and perhaps most especially then, would these principles of love need to come into play. Constitutional change alone is not a solution, it only points the way to one.

After all, a constitution is only a piece of paper prescribing the governmental shape of a country. Real reconciliation between people and groups of people still has to be worked out once the constitution is in place. Social harmony still has to be sought and found. A good constitution is not enough. It is only the very beginning. It's how people love and relate over the longer haul which really counts. A new South Africa is being born, but coping with extended labour pains is going to tax us. That's why we need more than human resources.

A few months ago I was in the office of Tex Harris, the larger-than-life six-foot-seven-inch United States Consul in Durban, now back in the USA on promotion.

Not only can you not miss Tex, but he makes points in a way you can't miss!

Suddenly, in the middle of our conversation, carried out in a high-rise with all Durban majestically displayed below us, right over to those townships gripped in mayhem and violence, he leaped to his feet and pulled from a cupboard a plastic packet with replicas of bullets from the American Civil War – a war on the race issue in which America lost more people than in all the other wars it has ever fought combined: First and Second World Wars, Korea, Vietnam and the rest.

With the bullets safely in my hand, he fixed me with a steely look: 'That war happened when we already had a truly great constitution in place. You see, Michael, it takes more than a constitution. In fact, through Christ and His Spirit we have to bring the broad mass of individual people to the concept of nation-building. This nation can only be built in human hearts, not at some negotiating table. It is frightening to me as an American and a Christian, in looking at this country, that so many people are afraid as individuals to make a commitment to work for a new day. Everyone sees this as someone else's work. The Church has the potential ability to move people in their hearts to bring about change. Through people's faith in Jesus Christ they can act on the basis of a set of principles which at the basic bottom line are nation-building in nature. It is in the hearts of people that the real answer lies. Not in some distant political achievement worked out at the top.'

Tex then told of an American social vision labelled 'A Thousand Points of Light'.

'There is a parable,' he said, 'of a guy walking down a beach where thousands of starfish had been washed up. As he went along he was throwing one fish at a time back into the ocean. Someone came up to him and said, "This beach goes on for a hundred miles. In an hour the sun will be out. It will kill all these millions of starfish washed up by this unusual tide. You can't possibly save enough to make it worth your while." But the fellow just carried on. As he picked one up and threw it back in the water, he said, "Well, my efforts sure meant a lot to that one!"'

Nation-building

'Somehow,' concluded Tex, 'that kind of spirit has got to become operational in South Africa. There is a sense of defeatism among so many – an inability for ordinary people in their individual and personal capacity to get going and do the loving, caring, relationship-building thing. It's as if they are witnesses to a drama instead of participants in it. This has got to be overcome. For Christians in this country, it is that kind of force that needs to be set in motion. It is essentially a *spiritual nation-building process* that has to get going.' This, I think, is also what Sowetan editor, Aggrey Klaaste, was writing about.

The bullets in my hand convinced me Tex was right. Perhaps they should hang clustered with my Marathon picture plus the Berlin Wall fragment – a threefold reminder of perseverance, hope and peril, all juxtaposed.

The principle and power needed for this hour can and should be provided by what we have already referred to as the Politics of Love. *I define the Politics of Love as those politics and policies which are controlled by Christian principle and the biblical love ethic.* Such politics begin their reasoning sacrificially and unselfishly from the Cross of Christ. From these they take Christian principles and the biblical love ethic of thinking of the other person and other group first, and build them into political, social and economic structures and policies in terms of justice, compassion, dignity and freedom.

Love's Law in the Ledger

At the end of 1989 the British journal, *The Economist*, assessed 1989's place in the sweep of world history:

> It was a wonderful year, 1989, a year your great-grandchildren's schoolbooks will spend a whole chapter on; but it does not quite rank with the great years of history. In the great years, something new is written into the human ledger – 1989 was an erasing year. It did a splendid job, clearing the page for whatever comes next; but that is not exactly the same thing.

The Economist then went on to observe:

> In 1989 one of history's bigger mistakes began to be rubbed out. The institutions of Leninist communism – one-party rule, a 'planned' economy – collapsed in much of Eastern Europe, looked pretty doomed in the Soviet Union, and were preserved in China only by the desperation of a communist party that had failed to learn that you cannot sit on a throne of bayonets, not for ever. Half-noticed in the excitement about all this, one of the last outposts of an older and murkier mistake may also have started to crumble, as South Africa's new president took a new look at his country's chances of preserving one-race rule.

De Klerk's decision turning away from that is now history.

The article then did a sweeping survey of history's high points leading up to the events of Eastern Europe and the beginning of the end of 'Lenin's 1917 revolution'.

It then noted:

> It may also be the end of the wider error that began exactly
> two centuries ago: the notion that politics is a science, that
> people can be governed out of a laboratory.
>
> And is the bright white space on the page, thus rubbed
> clean, to make way for something new? The puzzle of 1989 is
> that nobody seems to have any clear idea what the next entry
> in the ledger might be. For the first time in centuries, no
> novel political idea urgently offers itself.

That may be. What we do know, however, out of Oslo,
Norway, is that the *Politics of Hate* which have dominated in so
many places won't do. All the same, my biblically pessimistic
view of human nature, and my non-utopian view of history,
also make me hedge my bets on man's millennial moments,
such as Eastern Europe 1989 or South Africa in February
1990, because these moments are notoriously prone to go
wrong unless the Lord is allowed to have His way in the hearts
of men and women. That bright white space, that new entry for
which the political ledger waits, must be filled not only with the
Politics of Love and Christian principle, but with the supernatural power of God's Spirit to enable them to come forth and
be worked out.

In South Africa, it is true a new day dawns. But some new
idea or spirit has to be in place and at work on the one hand to
stop factional or even tribal violence from taking root in the
power struggle for a new government, and then on the other
hand to arrest that radical white right-wing spirit which refuses
to accept that the days of the old white supremacy are now
over.

A white policeman in Durban said to a black: 'I know black
majority rule is coming. But you are two hundred years too
early.'

The policeman knows what the future is bringing. But a
fight, perhaps a desperate one, looms among some whites,
perhaps more than we care to recognise, on timing. Deep
down they may know white supremacy's days are numbered,
but now is not the time, they feel, to call it a day on that
ill-fated philosophy.

So what can unlock that policeman's heart and a myriad of others? What can head us away, even if we get a new constitution, from the horror behind Tex's bullets?

The answer is the Politics of Love and the policies of Christian principle, because the Christian faith is one espoused, even if often in distorted forms, by nearly everyone in this country. Perhaps it remains only for all major groups plus all the rest of us to examine where we have distorted the true biblical understanding of what God in His Word requires of us, so that we can more accurately see our way into the future.

Politics of Love

My deepest conviction is that along this way lies the answer for South Africa. Fortunately South Africa is one of the best-equipped nations in the world to walk this way. And for four reasons.

First of all, in all our constitutions thus far we have identified ourselves as a Christian nation. This makes us honour-bound to work out the appropriate politics flowing from such a religious confession.

Second, there stands the astonishing fact that 78 per cent of South Africans profess to be Christians. This means that South Africa, more than any other nation, acknowledges and cannot escape a commitment to the politics of the Christian way. So 'Let the time that is past suffice' for being nationally content with the wretched expedient of professing one thing and doing another.

Inspirationally, the politics of love sets before us as a nation the epic challenge of living out our faith and confession. By doing this, the nation will be both saving itself and inspiring this tired old world with new visions of hope.

And practically, the politics of love make sense because every person, not to mention every Christian, from far right to extreme left, can unite and agree around the way of love. It provides a dynamic principle of unity and common resolution which has more intrinsic controlling power within it than plain patriotism and love of country, the latter being so much more prone to the corruption of selfish interpretation and sectional interest.

Love Breaks Logjams

More than that, love's concern for the other person, party or group can break the logjams of polarised conflicts and challenge the traditional human mechanisms of fight, flight or freeze.

Love says – Don't *fight* in order to ensure that you remain or become dominant. Don't *flee*, thereby allowing forces of domination or evil or violence to triumph. Don't *freeze* into helpless paralysis where bad and violent people triumph simply because good and peace-making people do nothing.

Love speaks positively and says, 'Be a positive part with your adversary of *fixing* the problematic situation to your mutual benefit.'

If opposing people sense in the other side a concern not just for themselves but for the other, along with a profound commitment to reach answers mutually beneficial and ultimately best for one and all, then a chemistry of mutual co-operation is beautifully released.

Outright violence may need a neutral peace-keeping force to bring things to a point where some of these principles may have a reasonable chance of becoming operative.

We will say more on this in due course.

Suffice it for the moment to register the necessity in this nation of attempting to fix things by love's resources and not any other. Indeed who knows what power might be unleashed if we could rise to walk this more excellent way!

Love as a Political Virtue

What we are really calling for is the acceptance of love as a political virtue. Once that happens we are A for Away.

The late, great Edgar Brookes, parliamentarian, historian and professor of political science said,

Love is a political virtue – shall we call it the unfound political virtue? And one to which we must strive to approximate. If justice is a political virtue, then so is love. Justice, too, can never be more than an approximation in states as we know them, but that does not mean that it must not be tried. The world languishes because love is being tried so little. It is imperative that it must be admitted into the field of political thought: only so will at least an attempt at an approximation be made.[2]

As far as the modern philosophy of politics goes, Brookes recognises that 'all this must seem to many foolishness – an intrusion of emotional sermonising into the philosophy of politics'. But, he asks, 'Has the exclusion of love been so wise? Have fear or suspicion and common sense brought us very far? Can we not [therefore] apply love in public life?' . . . and even when 'we cannot know whether we shall succeed in the ordinary human sense of the term.'[3]

And lest we consign Brookes to some sentimental past, not relevant for South Africa in the 1990s, let it be noted that Professor Douglas Irvine, professor of political science at Natal University in Pietermaritzburg, quoted him with approval in his inaugural lecture in April 1990. He observed that Brookes would have seen it as the worst kind of disloyalty to pretend that one's deepest convictions should be denied when it comes to political life.

Professor Irvine said he would never defend that sort of disloyalty. He then went on to quote the paragraphs from Brookes which I have used above but added this one:

'What is certain is that love will persist. I do not know if we have the right to ask more. Love cannot die if we are to be faithful . . . Since in this whole universe of life which we inhabit, love is the only thing that is fundamentally worth-while, let us be on the side of love.'[4]

Irvine concluded his lecture with these compelling words: 'We will surely need the wisdom of the serpent in making a constitution for the new South Africa to accommodate diversity and otherness and tame power, while meeting as far as possible the justified demands for a redistribution of land, wealth and resources. But we must also consult the foolishness of the dove, if we are to build the Beloved Country.'

Young Blacks

Of course there is a problem here when it comes to many of South Africa's young blacks. To mention Christianity, politics, love and constitutions all in one breath is to conjure up for them the vision of a myriad of traumatic experiences of apartheid, a policy which emerged from a seemingly Christian government professing to be doing this with concern for their highest interests.

Says young Manuel Ntuli, reflecting in an interview on Christian national education: 'The "love one another" line of you white people has ended up making us inferior. In fact various departments of education taught us not to love one another. Christian education, especially the DET (Department of Education and Training) taught us as blacks that we have to treat the white man as a superior. It hasn't taught us to love you as my sister and you treat me as a brother.'

This is indeed an embarrassing historical albatross around the necks of any and all Christians.

What can we say other than, 'We profoundly regret the desperate distortions of the so-called Christian way which apartheid inflicted on you. That was not, is not, nor ever will be what the true Jesus way or Politics of Love are all about. Please therefore give Christians another chance to show and work out more truly the way of their Master – and please be part of that.'

Two Historical Precedents

In closing this chapter let me note two great historical precedents to encourage the view that the true way of Christ's love is not only humanly possible but politically practical. Both come out of England where the political history of the eighteenth and nineteenth centuries was profoundly affected by two men who came to a love of Christ and thereby of their fellow men. Beyond that they moved heaven and earth to let love work in the political life of their day.

One was William Wilberforce (1759–1833); the other was Lord Anthony Ashley, better known as the seventh Earl of

Shaftesbury (1801–85). Both men demonstrated that love, far from being too sentimental to affect the tough political world, is the greatest political virtue of all.

For Wilberforce, his love of Christ and his love of people drove him to labour relentlessly for some fifty years in the British parliament to secure the abolition of slavery. Love of Christ and of people bred in him a profound sense of human dignity and value, and this was the primary motivation in his epic crusade.

Beyond that, says one of his biographers, 'Wilberforce believed that England's destiny lay safest in the hands of men of clear Christian principle and that submission to Christ was a man's most important *political* as well as religious decision.'[5]

For Wilberforce and others who were caught up in the eighteenth-century Wesleyan drive, Christian love led naturally into a sense of *responsibility* to care politically for the poor, the broken and defenceless. While not all were guilty of making others poor, all were responsible to do something about it. And so it was that Christian love in Wilberforce and his friends gave birth to a moral sentiment that permanently changed England's attitude to distant and defenceless peoples and to her own brutal and degraded masses at home. Love was no sloppy irrelevance: it was the engine of change.

In Shaftesbury's case the well-springs of his Christian love were moved by the plight of children (as young as six years old) who were forced to work more than ten hours a day, sometimes almost naked, down mines in awful conditions.

Shaftesbury said he took up the issue 'as a matter of *conscience*, and as such I am determined to carry it through . . . I cannot feel by halves . . . I take it I suffer very often much more than the people do themselves.'

The horrors of these and many other social abuses drove him to untiring efforts to change the political structures which produced these aberrations.

In consequence Shaftesbury got this whole situation not only before the British parliament, but before the conscience of the nation.

With an illustration of the consequences of the politics of love historically evident, we dare not deny that love is a relevant virtue for public and political life. Indeed it is the highest and noblest.[6]

Finally, let us examine the ringing and wistful words of the French philosopher and theologian Teilhard de Chardin (1881–1955): 'Some day, after mastering the winds, the waves, the tides and gravity, we shall harness for God the energies of love, and then, for the second time in the history of the world, man will have discovered fire.'

9   Love's Laws in Politics

The People, though we think of a great entity when we use the word, means nothing more than so many millions of individual men and women.

James Bryce

Do to us what you will and we will still love you.

Martin Luther King

Do not be overcome by evil, but overcome evil with good.

Romans 12:21

One Cockney trader said to another just after proposing a deal 'Now, them's my principles. But if you don't like them, I've got others!'

Clearly that sort of thing won't do! A principle is not a principle if it changes round every corner. So once again this is just where love's laws and ways come to our rescue.

In the social and political arena, I believe love has four laws and seven controlling principles. We look at these in our next two chapters. The laws are:

1 *Love sees politics as all about people.*
2 *Love deals with its own heart first.*
3 *Love loves, humanises and forgives its enemy.*
4 *Love hears and sees the other side.*

These laws basically deal with how, under God, we handle ourselves and our neighbours.

I LAW ONE: LOVE SEES POLITICS AS ALL ABOUT PEOPLE

Politics is all about people, ordinary people, and for the most part very ordinary people, and we do well not to forget it. Some have principles and some don't. We shouldn't forget that either!

I remember when I was a little boy when getting autographs was the rage. So I duly acquired an autograph book which I avidly filled with the first and second elevens of soccer, cricket, hockey and any category I could think of. One page was labelled 'Wall of Friendship' and was set aside for special friends. Then I had another page headlined 'Ordinary Friends'.

On the train with me once as I went back to school was a very dour Scot from the old Basutoland colonial service, a man with a wry sense of humour. He later reported to my parents with something of a pained expression that he had been requested by me to sign his autograph book under a page which was headlined 'More Ordinary Friends'!

The fact is that we are all, politicians included, ordinary people, and for the most part 'more ordinary people'.

The politician, like any other ordinary person, is subject to moods, ups and downs, personal family pressures, irritations and tensions. The way he is handled even privately affects how he responds publicly.

I remember going once in the mid-1970s on the first of several visits to Ian Smith and other leaders, black and white, in the old Rhodesia. When I went into Smith's office he appeared to be on the edge of apoplexy. I wondered what the matter was.

The moment our introductory formalities were behind us, he waved a letter at me which he said he had just received a few moments previously from the notorious Idi Amin. Amin's letter said that he was coming to liberate Rhodesia personally! Smith was so outraged that his equilibrium for the day was clearly upset. Maybe he made one or two wrong decisions that day. He was not God or superman but an ordinary human being, in a state of plain, ordinary human distress over a letter. This is the kind of thing which can happen to you and me even without Idi Amin writing to us.

The politician will also think, say or do things according to controlling factors of very ordinary humanity such as fatigue, domestic trauma or a critical word in the press.

The day before the historic first meeting in Cape Town between the South African government and the ANC, I not only felt a strong constraint to pray for Mr de Klerk and Mr Mandela, in terms of God's wisdom, but to cable Mr Mandela urging him to take care of his health. Although extraordinarily important, he is an ordinary person and vulnerable like any of us to excessive physical stress.

Likewise on numerous occasions I have said to Chief Mangosuthu Buthelezi, 'You must take more breaks.' The fact is that excessive exhaustion in any human being can imperil wise decision-making.

Not only are all our political leaders ordinary people, but other ordinary people put them in or out of power. Fears, antagonisms, loves, hates, insecurities and ambitions all play a major part in shaping the political process.

So it's people we are dealing with. The other person. But me too. So I'd better begin with me. Someone said, 'It takes all sorts to make a world and I'm glad I'm not one of them!' But you are. And so am I. This brings us to the second law.

II LAW TWO: LOVE DEALS WITH ITS OWN HEART FIRST

This is where it must all begin – with our own hearts. Leo Tolstoy once said, 'Everybody thinks of changing humanity and nobody thinks of changing himself.'

And that applies as much in one's social or political thinking and action as in any other. For this is where the primary battlefield lies.

As to South Africa, as I noted in *The Passing Summer*;

What is allowed to conquer each heart will conquer the country. If hatred conquers my heart, I must not be surprised if it conquers South Africa. If bigotry and prejudice conquer your heart, they will conquer in your country, wherever you are. If despair and defeatism rule in your heart and mine, they will rule in the citadels of the land and prevail in its policies, and we will reap the bitter fruit in full measure.

However, if love and forgiveness conquer in individual hearts, then love and forgiveness will conquer the country. If largeness of heart can vanquish shrunken narrowness of mind and spirit in you and me as individuals, if love can banish fear, if hope can overwhelm despair, if the positive can swamp the negative, then the nation can be born again.

But it has to start in the individual human heart. If enough people win there, the nation wins. And if enough lose there, not only does the nation lose, but the nation is lost.

This is not simply a matter of generating some warm feelings of benevolence towards broad groupings of people, such as 'the blacks', or 'Zulus' or 'Afrikaners' or 'the English', or even in narrower terms to the ANC, Inkatha, PAC, UDF, Cosatu, National Party or Conservative Party.

In South Africa the first test, the real one, is on the level of that one problematic black man or Englishman or Afrikaner who is either in your own circle or who, though a distant public figure, nevertheless straddles the emotional horizon of your own political soul like a colossus, obstructing your pathway to the politics of love. By God's grace conquer, there – there in the microcosm of one person – and you are home and dry.

How can that be? It is because if you conquer in the microcosm of your attitude to an individual, you are then freed to deal with the macrocosm of the group. If you come to Jesus in love (not necessarily in agreement) for that problem individual, be it F W de Klerk, Buthelezi, Mandela, Treurnicht, Terreblanche, Makwetu, Ramaphosa, de Beer or whoever, the highway then opens up to the politics of love. Deal not with your intellectual agreement or lack of it, but with your *heart-attitude* to your political problem person and a new world of political possibilities opens – because love has won.

To some friends of mine the late Bishop Alphaeus Zulu once said, 'You must never allow hatred in your heart ever for anyone.' To someone else he said, 'You may hate the sin, but never the sinner.'

When love has conquered in our relationship with our problem figure we can then move on. Not that this means arriving at a place of agreement or even affection, for we can love someone we do not like. Love simply means desiring the highest and the best for the other person, respecting his or her dignity and viewing him or her with compassion and forgiveness. I don't think it requires affection, but it will sometimes lead to it.[1]

One person who came to this powerfully and deeply in the political arena was the Jewish Christian, Paul Ostreicher, whose father had suffered much as a Jew in the First World War. In an interview Ostreicher described how he reached a self-critical attitude to his own heart.

Being a Jew by background, even though he'd become a Christian by the time Hitler came to power, my father knew that the moment would come when he would have to flee or die. But he constantly said, 'It's only good fortune that I have Jewish parents. If I didn't have Jewish parents and had grown up in a different context, I might be the persecuting Nazi. When I look inside myself I know that the persecutor could be me. And I can never face Hitler without seeing Hitler in myself as well.' This idea that your opponent – the person who thinks differently, the person who actually wants to destroy you – is less human than you are was something my father never allowed me to accept.[2]

This sort of thing is, I believe, part of the spiritual Great Trek upon which all South Africans must embark – the trek from intransigence to a change of heart. As the former Dutch Reformed Moderator, Johan Heyns, says, 'Unless a complete change of heart takes place in South Africa, there will be no political solution.' And if I don't let it start in my own heart, I cannot expect it to start at all.[3]

Confession

Once we have looked into our own hearts, we will quickly
know that there are attitudes there which are far from right.
We will then in humility bring these not only before God but
before those who have been hurt by our actions or policies.

In this regard, South African whites generally, and maybe
even the National Party of South Africa specifically, perhaps
in one of its congresses, need unequivocally to say first to God
and then formally to blacks: 'Apartheid and all its ways were
not just a tragic political error but *sinful and wrong*. We are
deeply sorry. We repent. Please forgive us. And help us to
mend the awful consequences of the past.' This needs to
happen even in the context of the present changes.

Individual utterances along this line have come from certain
nationalist leaders, such as Leon Wessels, referred to in the
last chapter. But somehow this needs to be formalised so that
every ear in the nation hears it. This is not to rub people's
noses in the past, but to acknowledge a spiritual principle that
the sins and mistakes of the past can never be truly left behind
until adequate confession and restitution are made.

In a perceptive article, journalist Alastair Sparks, once
editor of the deceased *Rand Daily Mail*, and now with the
Observer, writes of the awesome task facing President de
Klerk.

> To dismantle apartheid, to allay white fears of the black
> majority, to demythologise Afrikaner nationalism after
> generations of indoctrination in the notion that theirs is a
> special nation with a right to rule in their own God-given
> land, is an undertaking that may be even more daunting
> than Mr Gorbachev's.

But, adds Sparks, what the government have yet to do adequately is to explain *why* this 'remarkable U-turn' is taking
place. Sparks points to the need for a real 'acknowledging of
the guilt of the past. There has,' he notes, 'been no equivalent
of Mr Gorbachev's de-Stalinisation,' and at no time has the
country's present leadership 'renounced Hendrik Verwoerd,
the chief architect of apartheid who put most of its laws on the

statute book between 1948 and his assassination in 1966.'

Sparks stresses that if there is no serious formal acknowledgement of past wrongs then there is no acknowledgement that blacks have legitimate grievances, or that these now require redress.[4]

What blacks really need to know is that all this apparent change of direction is not just a matter of political pragmatics because we have no option, but due to a *change of heart* on the part of whites.

Of the Lord's forgiveness, if that is truly sought, we may be assured. Perhaps even more remarkable in human terms is, I believe, that we can be assured of black forgiveness. One of the black person's most amazing capacities is that of forgiving hurts. We whites do not deserve it. But if it is truly sought, it will I am sure be truly granted.

This was something Germany, but most especially German Christians, were faced with at the end of the last war.

A biographer tells how Niemoller moved beyond the idea of German error to plain sin, which had to embrace the plight and place of the 'sinned against'. In a sermon he said, 'Not only is Germany suffering because of her own sins, but *also* Holland, France, Finland and Poland . . . The churches too often were silent.' The great pastor then went on at an ecumenical gathering, says his biographer, to acknowledge that the Church, along with the German people, had taken a wrong way, and thus grievously afflicted the future of the whole world. 'We pray that God may forgive us,' he said. But he also hoped that this admission of guilt could bring a new start and give Germany a new and better role in the world.

In January 1946, Niemoller met a German Jew who had lost everything – parents, brothers and sisters, too. 'I could not help myself,' said Niemoller. 'I had to tell him, "Dear brother, fellow man, Jew, before you say anything. I say to you: I acknowledge my guilt and beg you to forgive me and my people for this sin."'

Much guilt lies heavily on all South African whites. Although many in both Afrikaans and English churches have faced this, and some conceivably in government too, but I'm not sure that all whites have truly faced our *moral guilt* before God for apartheid.

One very honest Afrikaner said to me, 'Many of us are changing because we must, because of political pragmatics, but not because of a deep heart change, with sorrow and repentance.'

Maybe that is changing. But I suspect many whites are still there. Yet if we truly deal, as love requires, with our own hearts, we will not only root out hatred and bitterness but face our personal and political sins, confess them and seek both divine and human forgiveness. Thankfully this spirit of confession pervaded the National Church Leaders' Conference at Rustenburg in November 1990. (See Appendix B for summary.) Which brings us to love's third law.

III LAW THREE: LOVE LOVES, HUMANISES AND FORGIVES ITS ENEMY

In South Africa we specialise in enemies. Everyone is someone else's enemy. Every group is hated by some other group.

Almost nowhere are people rising to the heights of Martin Luther King who once said to Southern whites: 'Do to us what you will, and we will still love you.'

1 Love Humanises

Part of the problem is that we have never adequately made the effort to humanise our enemy and see him or her as anything other than a member of this race or that, this political grouping or that, this party or that.

In April 1988 in Maputo, ANC lawyer, Albie Sachs, had his right arm reduced to a stump by a bomb going off in his car. *Business Day* editor, Ken Owen, ran a headline 'Live by the Sword, Die by the Sword'. But when Owen finally met Sachs face to face in Paris, the chemistry of the encounter deeply touched him as Sachs stood before him.

Sachs himself has said about the bomb incident which changed his life.

I'm curious to meet the people who planted the bomb and talk to them. I can't bear the idea of this cold assassination. I want to push a kind of humanity right in front of them so that I become transformed from just a target to be eliminated into a human being.

I feel a need to do that, and if the price for peace in South Africa is that those involved in these terrible murders go unpunished, it's worth it. What is the objective of punishment? It's not there to satisfy a desire for vengeance; it's to make a country better and make people behave better. If we can find other ways of doing this, then it will be a big plus.[5]

In life, and especially in South African life, we need to grasp that there are two ways of seeing. Either we can see the hatred, bitterness, selfishness and insecurity in the other person – and it is certainly there for us to behold – or we can take the eyes of Jesus and see other *humans* around us – all lost, struggling, imprisoned in their own histories, but valuable and precious. Often they are nursing wounds which make them hate or kill or simply slander and dishonour. And sometimes the latter, the slandering and dishonouring, is even more dreadful when people follow the dictum of the nineteenth-century Russian revolutionary Sergei Nechayev who said, 'It is not enough to kill an adversary. He must first be dishonoured.'

Ben Jele

In the Pietermaritzburg area where I live, massive enmity exists between Chief Buthelezi's Inkatha group and other political groupings. Ben Jele was an Inkatha councillor in the Imbali township. Those who have met him have found him gracious, warm and welcoming. But Ben is also a devastated human being for he has had one son badly injured by stabbing and the other murdered.

He says he wonders why it was done. Some would say it is in vengeance for what Inkatha has done. But is he now to wreak his own vengeance and kill an antagonist's son on the other side? Or does he try to love, humanise and forgive the enemy? And can his own enemy on the other side similarly love Ben and his group?

In the meantime, Ben battles with his family's shock and the memories. He remembers Mpho and the day he came home cheerfully for dinner. It was a joyful family meal. Mpho was in good form. Then he jumped up happily after the meal, wagged his finger accusingly at his dad as if to say, 'Now don't try to stop me trying to go and see my friends. I'll be back, Daddy, in just a few minutes.' That was the last they saw of Mpho. Fifteen minutes later a distraught mother came dashing down the street to tell Ben and his wife that Mpho was lying dead with a bullet through the back of his head.

Whatever the political or other rights and wrongs in the Maritzburg townships, here sits a grieving father and his stricken family.

Inkatha has done many similar things to people on the other side. And there, too, sit grieving and weeping people battling also with the options of forgiveness or vendetta.

2   Love Forgives

So in South Africa we search for the key with which to end conflict. And the key lies in enemy-love and forgiveness.

Of course we need God's grace and power to love and forgive (hence the message of this book), but if we manage it we will be amazed at how well the engine of change will start and run! Not that forgiveness requires us to condone sin and violence. Love, while condemning sin, and even absorbing its devastation and hurts, will forgive the sinner and the perpetrators of those hurts, whether individual or group.

It is instructive here to note that forward-moving countries have not wasted time 'getting even'. Said Abraham Lincoln, 'The only way to destroy your enemy is to make him your friend.' To get even with your enemy is to set his enmity in concrete and keep you for ever apart. Enemy-love, however, embraces the principle that you so resist your enemy in love that you not only change the situation, but you transform your enemy. So the goal of enemy-love includes not only transforming the bad situation but the enemy responsible for it. If we don't do it this way we actually don't change the situation at all.

In our land so many have become enemies that what the New Testament has to say about enemy love is marvellously relevant.

First is the astonishing example of Jesus Himself on the Cross: 'Father, forgive them; for they know not what they do.' This is love at its best. Martin Luther King wrote:

> We shall not fully understand the great meaning of Jesus's prayer unless we first notice that the text opens with the word 'then'. The verse immediately preceding reads thus: 'And when they were come to the place, which is called Calvary, there they crucified him, and the malefactors, one on the right hand, and the other on the left. "*Then*," said Jesus, "Father, forgive them."' *Then* – when he was being plunged into the abyss of nagging agony. *Then* – when man has stooped to his worst. *Then* – when he was dying a most ignominious death. *Then* – when the wicked hands of the creature had dared to crucify the only begotten Son of the Creator. *Then* said Jesus, 'Father, forgive them.' That 'then' might well have been otherwise. He could have said, 'Father, get even with them', or 'Father, let loose the mighty thunderbolts of righteous wrath and destroy them', or 'Father, open the flood gates of justice and permit the staggering avalanche of retribution to pour upon them'. But none of these was His response. Though subjected to inexpressible agony, suffering excruciating pain, and despised and rejected, nevertheless He cried, 'Father, forgive them.'[6]

Why? Because Jesus knew the way of revenge, the way of *lex talionis*, (eye for eye and tooth for tooth) to be catastrophic. Our Natal and Reef townships are eloquent proof of that. King noted further:

> In spite of the fact that the law of revenge solves no social problems, men continue to follow its disastrous leading. History is cluttered with the wreckage of nations and individuals that pursued this self-defeating path.
>
> Jesus eloquently affirmed from the Cross a higher law. He knew that the old eye-for-an-eye philosophy would leave

everyone blind. He did not seek to overcome evil with evil. He overcame evil with good. Although crucified by hate, He responded with aggressive love.[7]

Call of the Cross

Calvary's Cross speaks to both blacks and whites.

To whites the Cross says we must repent (personally and politically), ask for forgiveness, end the system of exclusive power and privilege, and face the challenges of redress and restitution. This not only means restoring detained leaders as is happening now, but land reform, commitment as far as possible to equalising standards of living and education of blacks, and their full involvement in the decision-making in this country. It will also mean finding our place in a politically subservient, or at least secondary, role.

I recognise this is the bitterest of pills for our white conservative right wing to swallow. It means giving away the white political power base in exchange for a non-racial democracy. This is for many whites an unspeakable thought and out of the question.

But the question is not whether whites retain their former power base, but whether they will in God's strength do what is right and leave the consequences to God. We must surrender the lesser to embrace the greater. It is surely better to seek a new non-racial South African identity and, pray God, have peace, than cling to an exclusive white identity and power base and live permanently in a low-intensity civil war.

For blacks the Cross also has a very demanding implication, for it means *forgiveness* of whites, no matter how hard and costly. One black leader said recently: 'The call for "one settler one bullet" was a call for retribution against whites for crimes committed against blacks.' Said the spokesman: 'If you whites think we are going to absolve you of the crimes you have perpetrated against the black people of this country you are mistaken.' Outside the due processes of law, this unforgiving line of an eye for an eye will leave the whole nation blind. For there will also be conservative whites in good supply to take up their own version of the *lex talionis* should a war of retribution and counter-retribution begin. The emotion is understandable indeed, but perilous to the processes of long-term peace.

With the high moral demand from blacks to forgive must also go repentance. Blacks need to repent of any spirit of vengeance, hatred, power lust and retaliatory violence towards whites. Maybe as whites must repudiate the Verwoerdian way, so also some Zulus, and maybe other blacks in other groupings, should repudiate the violent Shaka way which is another dead end. The spirit of forgiveness among blacks will also require rising black politicians to refrain from an endless castigating of whites for their past sins. This can become counter-productive and finally quench the spirit of repentance. To push someone's nose in their sin for too long could end up making them revert in reactionary mode to that very sin.

We will need to follow Jomo Kenyatta's words on Kenyan independence: 'Unless we build our nation on forgiveness, we will lose the day.'

Thabo Mbeki has said that the prize all should be seeking is an end to apartheid. And 'if you proceed from the position of the pure, and the price you might have to pay is to forgive and forget, then the matter ought not to be so difficult.'

At which he amazingly adds of certain imprisoned whites who have inflicted horrendous things on blacks: 'And let those people who acted in whatever nasty ways be affected by such an amnesty.'[8] That is the right spirit.

IV LAW FOUR: LOVE HEARS AND SEES THE OTHER SIDE

This law relates in measure to the second law of loving the enemy. St Augustine put it simply. *Audi alteram partem* (Hear the other side).

Once we have started the process we are always astonished at our folly in not having done it before. For example, after the first major meeting between the South African Government and the ANC, one Nationalist delegate was later quoted as saying, 'I don't understand how we could have been so stupid.

We should have started talking years ago and avoided the mess we got into.'

In Oslo at the 'Anatomy of Hate' Conference, Leon Wessels said, 'I also readily concede that we should have spoken and listened to other political groups much earlier.'

Surely all whites should feel this.

After those first Government-ANC talks in 1990, other Nationalists admitted to being deeply stirred to hear from the mouths of the ANC why they had resorted to the armed struggle.

ANC leaders also indicated how affected they were in listening to the other side. Likewise Communist Jo Slovo was quoted as saying the whole experience was 'carthartic' (*Weekend Argus*, May 19th, 1990).

Of course the tricky thing in South Africa is that there are not just two sides: there are many. And everybody needs to be heard, understood and involved in the negotiating process. More on this in Chapter 15.

But suffice it for the moment to note that any marginalising of major players, for whatever reason, can only produce offence and insult and maybe even violent reaction. It is a short-sighted tactic if ever there was one. It also distorts all the communication processes.

We must avoid at all costs a situation where different sides are thinking: 'I know you believe you understand what you think I said, but I'm not sure you realise that what you heard is not what I meant!'

Communication

Communication and hearing the other side are vital. At the best of times, this is a difficult and complex process. In apartheid South Africa with its legacy of mistrust, pain and oppression, along with the further complications of different cultural backgrounds, the interference in communication is immense, especially between whites and blacks.

Communication only begins when the idea or message, either verbal or non-verbal, from the sender is assigned meaning in the mind of the receiver.

The information we transmit is only the raw material with which our receiver works. The receiver may have heard everything *said*, yet failed to receive the true *content* of the communication. To grasp what is involved in communication and in hearing the other side, we need to see its inner mechanisms. One might express it this way: A desires to communicate with B. A therefore 'encodes' his message, ie he puts it in a formula (eg a sentence, or handshake or embrace) and sends it to B, who on receiving it, decodes it. In other words, he assigns meaning to it. B then encodes his response to what he thinks A has said. This newly-encoded message is now transmitted to A who must decode it and renew the process.

The first thing to underline is that in both the encoding and decoding process, both sender and receiver bring their cultural, educational, social, political and even economic histories to the exercise.

Communication can go Wrong

The whole thing can therefore go hopelessly awry. For example, wrong symbols may be chosen which, through ignorance, are inappropriate and are therefore misunderstood. So A chooses to hug B to show how much he likes him. But in B's culture a man who hugs another man is seen as a homosexual. B's response therefore is negative as a result of misinterpretation of A's friendly symbol.

In the same way prejudice or conditioning can make interaction extremely difficult. A Conservative Afrikaner believing that all ANC people are 'terrorists' or communists will fear any communication with them. Or a member of Inkatha genuinely trying to talk to a member of ANC may well be misunderstood, and vice versa.

Where a symbol of communication is in conflict with a known attitude, confusion results and communication fails. Thus the government leader who wants now to strike a friendly deal with an ANC leader, or any other, finds that previous signals sent, especially in terms of oppression and discrimination, conflict with the new signal which says, 'Let's sit around a table and talk.' Mistrust or suspicion of ulterior motives also blocks meaningful communication.

Understanding these difficulties makes it clear how vital it is that people do sit with each other long enough to appreciate fully what the other person or group is saying. Then communication, negotiation, reconciliation and solution can come.

Former Presidents Sadat of Egypt and Beghin of Israel did sit down together and with the help of former President Jimmy Carter came to some significant understanding. At the historic Camp David Accord each one heard the other side and progress took place.

South Africans face some daunting years and some monumental political challenges. We need, therefore, to commit ourselves to practising love's basic laws. If we can remember that politics is all about people, and if we will deal with our own hearts first; if we will love, humanise and forgive our enemy, and beyond all that hear and see the other side, then, and I suspect only then, will we come through to the new day we all so dearly long for.

10 Love's Ways in the World

Since wars begin in the minds of men, it is in the minds of
men that the defences of peace must be constructed.
Constitution of the United Nations Educational,
Scientific and Cultural Organisation

Our motto must continue to be perseverance. And ultimately I trust the Almighty will crown our efforts with
success.

William Wilberforce

And walk in love.

St Paul (Eph. 5:2 RSV)

Lesley Richardson, the wife of David Richardson, one of my
African Enterprise colleagues, is a good example of a person
who understands love's ways in the world and seeks to do
her bit. Remember Tex Harris's parable of the fellow tossing
the little fish back into the sea? Each positive thing counts.

Recently Lesley said to me; 'I have had to come to terms
with the fact that I just cannot take on my heart the whole
situation in our Maritzburg townships, but I can care for a few
black children in a special way and to that I am going to confine
myself and do my positive best right at that point.'

Her particular belief is along the line of Walt Disney's
dictum that 'The future of a nation lies in the minds of its
children.' In South Africa the future of our children's minds,
she says, is a national crisis.

So Lesley set about pioneering non-racial *preschools* in 1980
in Imbali Township in Pietermaritzburg. There she came face

to face with the stark reality of the disparities between black and white in education. Few of the available preschool programmes were suitable for use in crosscultural and disadvantaged settings. Lesley adapted what she had and researched preschool materials from every available source. She struck gold when she discovered the thirty years of research by Dr David Weikart of the High Scope Foundation. High Scope had studied preschool needs in disadvantaged communities worldwide and had produced an excellent curriculum that really worked in the township, subeconomic and rural preschools Lesley was seeking to serve.

Lesley gave up her much-loved job as principal and teacher of the school she founded, and accepted a bursary to study at the High Scope Foundation in Michigan, USA, with a colleague who was a senior lecturer at a teachers' training college. When they returned to South Africa they set up the first High Scope teacher training programme in 1986. Training teachers who had formerly been childminders and creche mothers provided whole new careers, empowered many women and gave them new acceptance and self-esteem in their own communities.

Now over 100 schools with 120 trained teachers provide quality preschool training for hundreds of disadvantaged (and some highly advantaged) children. Extra staff and field workers have been employed from among the High Scope graduates and currently fifty more teachers are in training. The need is enormous, but the consequences of a quality start for these youngsters who will help build a new South Africa is inestimable.

Lesley returned to High Scope in 1988 and after further training was licensed to train trainers of teachers. Ten women are currently taking this training and will by 1992 be able to offer the High Scope teachers' course to many more women than Lesley can accommodate. She will no longer be alone in this great task.

The point is that whatever others may do which is negative or destructive, positive and concerned individuals must do their bit where they can and while they can. Said Martin Luther King.

When evil men plot, good men must plan. When evil men burn and bomb, good men must build and bind. When evil men shout ugly words of hatred, good men must commit themselves to the glories of love. Where evil men would seek to perpetrate an unjust status quo, good men must seek to bring into being a real order of justice.[1]

We have spoken of love's laws. Their operation is evident in Lesley's story. But so also are love's ways.

There is no fixed line between them but an interplay.

Some of love's ways in the world are:

1 Love looks and thinks ahead.
2 Love wills and chooses well.
3 Love operates according to conscience.
4 Love acts positively and works out its profession.
5 Love lives out biblical social values.
6 Love facilitates reason and reconciliation.
7 Love perseveres courageously.

Let's look at these.

I   Love Looks and Thinks Ahead

Someone once said that a politician thinks of the next election and a statesman of the next generation.

Ted Engstrom, one of the great Christian leaders and administrators in the USA, conducts numerous seminars on Christian leadership and management all over the world. In a seminar I attended, he caught the principle of looking ahead as he wrote in huge letters across the blackboard –

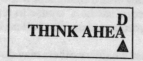

We could see clearly that he'd failed to calculate the space available. At which we got the point! Thinking ahead first involves *looking* ahead and taking the long view. Then comes thinking about how to get there.

What the politics of love require is an investment in Christian political principle which affirms that nothing which is morally right can ever in the long term be politically wrong. And this applies as much to political structures as to anything else. It affirms, moreover, that loving God and our neighbour is a risk we can and must take. The consequences we can by faith leave with God.

As I wrote to a cabinet minister some years ago, the politics of love embrace the principle that it is better to lose in the short term with that which must ultimately win, than to win in the short term with that which must ultimately lose.

The politics of selfishness, though perhaps winning in the short term, must finally lose. The universe, God, life, Scripture and history ultimately side with the right and sanction it and bless it. It is right which finally produces the first prize: wrong does not.

Doing the right thing, as we have already noted, takes courage. But much more fearful is the prospect of letting the politics of national, racial, tribal or party selfishness run their dreadful course towards the abyss.

In taking the long view, the *politics of love* therefore calls us to the adventure of doing right in the political arena and seeing God work it all out. The politics of love pulls us in hope to the future and prises us loose from both the false optimism that we can do wrong and get away with it and from the futile fatalism which says we can't finally do anything to avert a racial slug-out!

The politics of love affirms that, God helping us, we can indeed not only burst free from the clutches of past follies, political logjams, and from the pessimistic mechanisms of historical inevitability, but in doing so we can actually await with positive excitement the surprises of God in history on our behalf. These will arrive as we embrace and demonstrate that the Kingdom of God transcends all earthly identities; the power of Christ and His Gospel transcends all earthly powers; and His way transcends all earthly ways. For it is the more excellent way, and indeed the way to a new society.

Thinking

Then of course there is not only the process of looking ahead, but the thinking process itself.

South Africa in the past has pretty well destroyed itself by wrong thinking or the refusal to think where our wretched political ways were taking us. That thankfully is changing.

The challenge to *think* is especially vital for those on right or left who tend to emotional and racist knee-jerk reactions. These can only lead to conflict. The constitution of the United Nations Educational, Scientific and Cultural Organisation rightly observes that 'Since wars begin in the minds of men, it is in the minds of men that the defences of peace must be constructed.'

The real challenge is to think Christianly and with a Christian mind. To think Christianly, of course, does not mean having a mind which is specifically preoccupied with religious topics, but a mind which can think even about the most secular topics from the perspective of Christian presuppositions. The Christian mind is a mind which has so trained, informed and equipped itself that it will by habit handle secular matters from within a Christian frame of reference.

To think Christianly means to look at everything from the perspective that this world is created, made and owned by the living and biblical God who requires that our choices be made in accordance with His laws and principles. This will be our manner of thought about everything.

An old prayer says it for all of us: 'God be in my head and in my understanding, God be in my mind and my thinking.' It is a prayer much needed by all South Africans.

II   Love Wills and Chooses Well

Related to thinking straight is the privilege of choice. We need to use our wills aright. Origen of Alexandria back in the third century noted that 'the power of choosing good or evil is within the reach of all'. More than that, our choices affect the world, for mankind is not a zero where choices make no difference. Observed Goethe: 'He who has a firm will moulds the world to himself.'

Frederick van Zyl Slabbert has the view that 'The most important factor may yet turn out to be the *will* of the major participants to make a success of it' (ie the process of negotiating a new order and a new day). Realistically he adds, 'There is enough bitterness, hatred and vengeance in our past to sap this will to its limits.'[2]

To know this to be true is to find fresh resolution that it shall not be so. We will not let our wills be sapped. But we should be under no illusion about the fact that we will not see the truly Christian way come forth in this land unless we *choose* it and will it and set our resolve upon it. Hence the subtitle of this book – *Choosing the Christian Way in a Changing South Africa*. We must consciously choose it or we will not get it. In this we will bear in mind the corollary articulated by William James, the great nineteenth-century American philosopher: 'When you have to make a choice and don't make it, that is in itself a choice.'

Clem Sunter, Anglo-American's scenario specialist, speaks often of what he calls the *High Road* leading to a harmonious and economically strong nation. All else is the *Low Road* leading us to national disaster and tragedy. His big point, however, is that the matter of which road we take is basically a matter of choice. We can and must choose to take the High Road or, by default, we will through tragic neglect *choose* the Low Road.

Choices

Willem de Klerk, the President's brother and Professor of Communications at Rand Afrikaans University, to whose insights we will have cause to return in Chapter 11 when we explore further the posture and prospects of the right wing, sees the choices in terms of three directions.

The first is that of a revolutionary take-over of power and the creation of a black majority state within which group rights will not be protected at all: the second, that of a sharing of power in a federal dispensation within which minority rights will enjoy some protection: and the third, that of a division of power by means of partition, in terms of which South Africa will be divided into sovereign black, coloured and Indian states as well as a state for whites.

This last, the partition option, is the one being advocated by the Conservative Party. But it will in Dr de Klerk's view run us 'over a precipice' and plunge us 'down into an abyss'. It will amount, he says, 'to nothing less than pulling down the pillars in an act of self-destruction'.

He has the view that, given enough things going wrong, especially in black politics, many in white South Africa could still *choose* this path and commit a 'historic act of idiocy'.[3]

To opt for a true non-racialism and to choose by the dictates of Calvary love the right way of a free and just society is thus crucial. More than that, if we are ready to choose aright, we will see to it that our choices are in accordance with those principles which will work for the greatest long-term good of all. And those choices will also be guided by *conscience*.

III   Love Operates according to Conscience

Perhaps we need to elaborate on this as both blacks and whites (and especially those whose politics are a matter of gut re-actions) need so much to be guided by this mysterious and yet critically important moral monitor which resides in each of us. For this is the place where God has 'put eternity into man's mind' (Eccles. 3:11 RSV).

The word *conscience* is derived from two Latin words meaning to 'know with'. Conscience is not just a knowing, but 'a knowing together with' something or someone. Among all human beings there is this 'knowing together' with a will that is over or above our own – a supernatural, supramundane and super-powerful will which makes demands on our own will and which has a right to do so. This will, Christians believe, is the will of God, an inner moral law which dictates how we should love and whether we are behaving according to moral law.

Conscience then is a 'knowing with' God how, when and where we are at one or at odds with His will and mind. Conscience can, however, according to the New Testament, be 'seared' by lying influences or through the spirits of deceit

(1 Tim. 4:2). Beyond that conscience can be 'corrupted', says St Paul, through impurity, unbelief, and the mental influences of corrupt people (Titus 1:15).

It is important therefore that we are alert first to ensure that our conscience is operating according to truth, purity, godly principle and an uncorrupted mind. Second if it is thus operating we must *obey* it. In fact as the Apostle Paul put it, and as I would describe the purpose of this book, 'The goal of this command is *love*, which comes from a pure heart and a good conscience and a sincere faith' (1 Tim. 1:5).

The person with this aim will manifest a *love which wills and chooses well according to conscience*. And that love, let South Africans note, will deliberately choose even to work with the former enemy if that is in the best interests of the country and for the greatest good of all.

Lincoln

Abraham Lincoln demonstrated this capacity dramatically with a man called Stanton, a one-time rival and arch-enemy in the race for the presidency. History tells us that Stanton hated Lincoln and did everything to denigrate and degrade him in the eyes of the public. Cruel unkindnesses even about Lincoln's physical appearance were part of Stanton's endlessly bitter diatribes against his opponent.

Lincoln, of course, was elected President and then had to choose his cabinet to prosecute his programmes for the nation. When the time came to fill the very important post of Secretary of War, Lincoln, to everyone's astonishment, and indeed to the accompaniment of an uproar in his own inner circle, announced that his choice for the job was Stanton. Everybody round the President reminded him of the ugly and cruel things Stanton had said about him and that this man was his 'enemy'.

'Yes, yes, I know Mr Stanton,' said Lincoln impatiently, 'and I am aware of all the terrible things he has said about me. But after looking over the nation, I find that he is the best man for the job.'

And so Stanton became Secretary of War, a capacity in which he served with distinction. After Lincoln's assassination, when many great things were said about him, Stanton's plaudit was one of the most moving and significant. He said: 'Lincoln was one of the greatest men that ever lived and he now belongs to the ages.'

Not only did Lincoln transform an enemy into a friend, but he made him a partner and colleague.

Here was love which willed and chose well according to conscience. Such willing and such choosing is very necessary in South Africa at this time.

And the reason it is much needed is because its own inner arguments and pronouncements can inform each of us *deep down* what is the right thing to do. The black man who says 'no negotiation with whites – no place for whites – no response to them except giving them their just desserts', will find his *conscience*, if he truly listens to it, protesting and saying 'No! That is not the way. Choose the path of forgiveness and true togetherness.' Likewise, the white who says, 'I'm never going to be ruled or dominated by any black so-and-so', will, if he listens to *conscience*, hear a voice within saying, 'That attitude is wrong. Humble yourself. Repent. And face honestly the rights of the majority group and where that must lead politically, even if at first blush that majority might put my own minority group at risk.' The thing is to hear what conscience says and do it.

IV Love Acts Positively and Works out its Profession

I remember in 1986 meeting a wonderful black pastor in the Eastern Cape at the height of the crisis that precipitated the introduction of the state of emergency. When I asked him how he was, despite the fact that everything in his world was in a shambles, he replied, 'Positive!' – and beamed at me. I found that amazing and instructive, because South Africa is a place where it has been, and often still is, very hard to stay positive. As Alan Paton once said, 'This is a country where you hope on Monday and despair on Tuesday!'

And even now in the Mandela–De Klerk era this is still happening. The struggle for all to stay positive and hopeful is a real one, for disappointment knocks daily at our doors.

However, we dare not capitulate to the negative. For, is not the Cross a minus sign crossed out and made into God's great positive plus sign over the world? In fact He took the single most negative thing which had ever happened in the world, namely the judicial murder of His own Son, Jesus Christ, on a criminal's gallows, and made it into the most positive thing in our planet's history, namely the means by which sinful, negative human beings might come to eternal salvation.

The trouble with South Africa is that it is a nation whose whole foundation is negative. It is a nation built on a series of negatives: that humans of different sorts *cannot* get along together, *cannot* live harmoniously side by side, are *not* equal and are *not* reconcilable. For decades the many who tried to counteract that with positive labours were met with denunciation, opposition, social pressure, or even banning or imprisonment. We had a true national odyssey into the negative. And it will take much work to free ourselves from the habits and consequences of that negativism.

Calvary love keeps calling us back to the positive, both in the micro and in the macro.

Micro

One of the sadnesses of South Africa is that the problems of negativism and defeatism are so great that many people feel paralysed. There is a sort of silent majority, but there are also the exceptions, thankfully in increasing numbers.

We have seen that Lesley Richardson is one of them.

My brother-in-law, Tony Bester, is another. Tony used to run a small Boys' Town Process School for about forty-two black street children, eleven of whom have no traceable families. These are for the most part flotsam and jetsam street children whose lives would have hit worse than rock bottom but for the intervention of people like Tony. Each life represented in these children has been an essay in negativism until now. But even now there are endless battles against negativism.

On one occasion Tony's boys had a dreadful clash of fisticuffs with white boys from a nearby orphanage.

In the days following this clash, Tony and a master from the orphanage, each in their respective institutions, began to work to build positive, forgiving and understanding attitudes into their youngsters towards the other group. A week or so later, they got the youngsters together and an amazing, healing and moving reconciliation took place. Attitudes have changed, understanding has dawned, new possibilities fill the horizons of each youngster. Norman Vincent Peale would call it the 'Power of Positive Thinking'. Nay more, the power of positive acting.

Bonginkosi

I also think of the late Daphne Tshabalala. Daphne was headmistress of a school in Edendale. One day during her tea break she threw a crust of her sandwich down on the ground for the dog to consume. But before the dog reached it, a little child rushed forward, avidly seized it and downed it. She discovered that the child had not had either an adequate breakfast that morning or anything the night before.

That little episode led Daphne and Barbara Davies, a former colleague of mine in AE, to launch a school-feeding project called Bonginkosi which is Zulu for 'Praise the Lord'. It is a project whereby the needs of hungry schoolchildren would be linked with the resources of churches which would put up the money to provide a hunk of bread and a bowl of nutritious soup on a daily basis to each child in a given school.

Daphne and Barbara saw a problem, were not paralysed by its macro nature around the country, and simply began in a micro way to do something about it. Today through this project we see some fifteen thousand children fed on a daily basis and the project is expanding.

Other Examples

Other marvellous examples are found in Caesar Molebatsi's work among the youth of Soweto, in Vorn van de Linde's agricultural self-help project called ACAT (Agricultural Co-operative Action Trust), Dennis Bailey's Sawubona Trust with traumatised township youth around Pietermaritzburg, or

Frank Chikane's Herculean labours for justice through the South African Council of Churches.

But the sort of problems these ministries grapple with need action not only at the micro level but the macro level also.

The ambulance ministries carried out by many fine individuals, both black and white, are not enough in themselves. Structural issues relating to economic systems, constitutions, community infrastructure and so forth all have to be worked on. We will say more on this later.

Macro

Suffice it for the moment to note in regard to the macro side of things that South Africans face a time of unprecedented possibility to rise and bless the world, not to mention ourselves. We have the opportunity to demonstrate by positive labours that a nation can at the macro level right itself, repent, turn, change and manifest the truth our planet is waiting on tip-toe to embrace – namely that different peoples in a heterogeneous society can by God's power and principles live together in forgiving love, mutual interdependence, humility and partnership. We must cling to this vision.

I am convinced that positive hope and vision will free those who have built racial or tribal fortresses for themselves which have become their prisons and which will become their graves unless the negative is surrendered and the positive embraced.

So God says, 'Away with thoughts of *irreconcilability*, for with me all things are possible – even a new, just and harmonious South Africa.'

Work out our Profession

As mentioned before, the call to us all in this hour is positively and excitedly to work out what we profess as a Christian nation, something we have so far failed abysmally to do.

We need to grasp, while South Africa is in this transitional phase, that the new thing could be unimaginably dreadful or unbelievably wonderful. The choice is ours. We can choose the cesspool of strife and tragedy, or we can choose the demanding but splendid destiny of becoming a truly Christian nation working out what we profess. One of the keys to which path we take rests very specially, I believe, with the Afrikaner, and most especially the conservative Afrikaner. But it's no easy way for him, for it is the Calvary way. Yet he, maybe more than most, is equipped with his deep Christian convictions to set out on it.

The ease with which this happens will depend on whether the Afrikaner people will forgo the old identity (*identiteit*) of yesterday to find the new identity of tomorrow, and on whether they can 'let go and let God'. In political terms it means surrendering this hugely cherished notion of 'group rights'. For to think 'group' is still to think racially, even tribally, rather than nationally. To think nation is to surrender 'group'. Even better, to think Christianly is to think 'true liberty, equality and fraternity'.

But if we choose to stay sectional, clinging to racial or group thinking, and if as Jesus said we love only those who love us or are part of our own in-group or our own sub-culture, then why bother to hold on to our profession as a Christian country? For how then are we different from other pagan or communist countries? And if we aren't different from them, why not cut our Christian profession and officially declare ourselves a secular, pagan state? Then what we do will be consistent with what we profess, but we will reap the negative rewards of such paganism.

If alternatively we can rise to the glorious and epic challenge of acting positively by God's power and by Christ's principles to work out what we profess, then I believe we will know God's protective care and blessing on the land.

V Love Lives out Biblical Social Values

In 1987, a remarkable little thirty-page volume was released by Professor Bernard Lategan and three other theological colleagues at the University of Stellenbosch. It was called *The Option for Inclusive Democracy*.

With the very high percentage of people in South Africa's Christian sector they felt there was a great possibility for 'consensus regarding social values'. Apartheid they see as having arisen out of a disregard of these values. But if the values could 'command the loyalty of all' there would be a harmonious way into the future. 'What they plead for now is "real democracy" in which predetermined classification of groups on the grounds of race, ethnicity or tribe shall not be a feature of the social order.'[4]

First they adduce a number of theological truths out of which are extrapolated a series of biblical social values.

Here is their theological list. It is a list to which the *Politics of Love* should cling.

1 *Human equality*
  All people are equal in their dignity which is given and guaranteed by God.
2 *Human unity and interdependence*
  In interdependence men and women come to full humanity only with and through other people. And if they form themselves into groups, these must serve the interests of all people, including those outside the group.
3 *Human freedom*
  Human beings are accountable for their deeds because they have been given freedom of decision making.
4 *Social responsibility and human rights*
  Social justice is a condition for peace in society.
5 *Human government*
  The function and standard of government is service and the upholding of good for the benefit of all.
  All human actions, including those of governments are subject to moral criteria and laws. Ideology, of course, may cause a demonic debasing of these criteria.
6 *The reality of sin*
  Human sinfulness and frailty is a reality all social and political thinkers have to keep in mind. Otherwise we fall prey to starry-eyed utopianism.

In my family I seek to hold up certain moral, spiritual and social values to my children. And although at the ripe old age of six one of my daughters once said to me, 'Don't talk rubbish. Daddy', nevertheless I have pressed on undaunted! I don't mean talking rubbish, but elevating principle! Why?

Because I love my children and know their greatest long-term
happiness lies in embracing and obeying those principles.

Likewise if we love the world with God's love, we will as
Professor Lategan and his colleagues urge, hold these principles constantly before society and say, 'Keep these in mind
and things will work best for the greatest long-term happiness
of all.'

VI   Love Facilitates Reason and Reconciliation

One of the loveliest Scriptures in the New Testament is Paul's
word that God 'gave us the ministry of reconciliation' (2 Cor.
5:18). Not only does this mean bringing people to God but to
each other.

The father in the Prodigal Son story (Luke 15) had to
facilitate and pray for three journeys to take place in the life of
the wayward boy – first a journey to himself, then a journey to
the father, and then, equally important, and I believe implicit
in the story, a journey to the brother. I have little doubt the
father's heart, prayers and labours played a part in all three,
especially bringing the two alienated family members
together.

In alienated situations, such as South Africa's, love will seek
to bring the alienated parties together. It will not wilfully
contribute to keeping them apart. It will not widen chasms,
nor deepen bitterness. It will work to keep 'reason' alive and
reconciliation the goal.

My own conviction is that at a thousand levels in the years
ahead there is going to be the need for people of loving
goodwill and integrity to facilitate the process of bringing
alienated people together at both macro and micro levels.

We will have cause to expand on this when we think about
negotiation.

VII   Love Perseveres Courageously

Without the spirit of perseverance, many otherwise bold
spirits will falter and turn back.

In South Africa this would land us, in Matthew Arnold's words, 'wandering between two worlds, one dead, and the other powerless to be born'.

In contrast stands the spirit of Livingstone who once said, 'Anywhere – provided it be Forwards.' On another occasion he said he was committed to Christ and to His way 'with no reservations – no regret – and no retreat'.

This also means a courageous spirit. As Plutarch, the great Roman writer of the first century put it, 'Courage consists not in hazarding without fear, but being resolutely minded in a just cause.'

This spirit of courageous love is much needed by all in South Africa, especially when prospects of moving to a new day seem threatened by the dark thunderclouds of ongoing strife, suspicion and power struggle. Blacks will need this courageous love as obstacles and obstructionism from whites keep rearing their ugly heads.

Whites also greatly need this as they begin to see on the one hand some of the darker side of black politics, and on the other the full implications of where repenting from the ways of apartheid must take us.

The problem is that facing the unknown future with all of its uncertainties unnerves us and makes us want to turn back to our old familiar ways of oppression and control.

While the old apartheid game was wrong and even dangerous, nevertheless we whites knew how to play it. But now all is uncertain. So our nerve falters. And the way of love and principle seems not to be worth it. Let's therefore try another.

But love says, 'No! Persevere! Soldier through! It will come right if enough people work at it!'

A marvellous illustration of such courageous loving was the great William Wilberforce whose forty-five years' work to abolish the slave trade is mentioned earlier in this book.

In 1831 he sent a message to the Anti-Slavery Society, in which he said 'Our motto must continue to be *perseverance*. And ultimately I trust the Almighty will crown our efforts with success.' He did.

Yes, love perseveres. And in South Africa also love will prevail if we persevere.

VIII   Conclusion

To look and think ahead, to will and choose well, to operate
according to conscience, to act positively and work out what
we profess, to live out biblical social values, to facilitate reason
and reconciliation and to persevere courageously – these are
some of love's ways in the world. And they remain equally
valid, whether in the dark times or the bright.

It's a matter of putting our hands, personally and nationally
into the hand of God. For it is He who knows the Way.

Part Four

LOVE'S CHALLENGES

The light shines in the darkness, and the darkness has not overcome it.

John 1:5 RSV

11 Reaching the Right

De Klerk has sold us down the river.

White shop assistant

The Whites are not a nervous little huddle of people ready to capitulate if the pressure gets just a little worse.

Die Volksblad

We shall not be intimidated. We shall defend our rights with every means at our disposal . . . You cannot share power; it is a political lie. The moment you try to share power; you lose it.

Dr Andries Treurnicht

I sat among them.

Ezekiel 3:15

In South Africa the Politics of Love face a multitude of challenges. One of the greatest is that of reaching the political right wing where fear, religious zeal and a fierce white nationalism have combined in precarious chemistry to lay hold upon the hearts and minds of nearly a million people.

Can't Be The Way

'Hek, No!' said Hendrik Pieterse on his Northern Transvaal farm. 'This can't be the way. I'm involved in the army. So I know what's going on. I'm also a Christian. It's true I'm politically conservative, but many of us are getting a bit tired of being blamed for everything and never getting any credit whatsoever for the way we and the police have to work in very dangerous and difficult circumstances. I want to tell you that the ANC, backed by the Communist Party, have an extremely efficient and thorough organisation and up here they have terrorised and organised all the youth to defy all authority, to refuse to go to school, even to destroy schools, plus some of the factories. This leaves many adults without jobs. They are intimidating anyone who wants to work and co-operate with normal society or who does not agree with them. In these last weeks I have also seen them attacking and destroying the property and homes of certain black businessmen.'

Pieterse paused and looked towards his horizon. 'No, these black young people are totally unaware of the fact that they are destroying their own means of education for the future and their own future capabilities of earning a living in the factories. I see these young people doing countless millions of rands worth of damage and destroying thousands of jobs. The aim seems to be revolution and total chaos so they can ultimately take over the country. These people don't want to go to the negotiating table to negotiate, but to demand. They have the Nationalist Government over a barrel and I am thoroughly depressed about the whole thing.'

In the nearby town, Hennie De la Rey, who owns a vegetable shop, was equally concerned. 'I am convinced,' he affirmed, 'that there is much greater social harmony where there is a social division and where people who are the same can live together.'

At this point he illustrates some recent research which shows that only 29 per cent of all Afrikaners fully accept complete mixing in church and school. De la Rey goes on, 'The only solution here is residential and political segregation. And it is not too late to achieve this. Surely the Afrikaner deserves somewhere that he can call his own.'

Such people believe that God gave them their land and they feel strongly that if they were to be finally denied their own place, the temptation to turn to violence would be great. All the more so when in their view there could be a thinly veiled communist takeover of the country using ANC surrogates.

They see it as their God-given duty to resist an atheistic, communist government by every means at their disposal.

The Rev Fritz Simon, a friend of mine, recently began pastoring in a country town in the Orange Free State. One day soon after arriving in the town, he passed the local gunshop. 'I was horrified,' he said, 'to see the place packed out with conservative whites buying guns and ammunition. But now I am pretty shock-proof. Every day it is the same. A huge, mighty and roaring trade is going on.'

Small wonder when the rhetoric from certain leaders on the far right says, 'Give us a million guns.'

Fritz one day met the local traffic cop in his town, who professes to be a Christian. 'But,' said the cop, 'the only way in South Africa is to shoot all these black so-and-so's. Otherwise there is no answer for us.'

'And the man says he is a Christian,' lamented Fritz with a shrug of despair.

Of course the traffic cop's political despair has fed his violent posture. Despair and insecurity sadly can do such things.

Durban City Hall

Though Andries Treurnicht comes from the Waterberg, that homeland of arch-conservatism, he knows he has significant support in many places. After all, in the 1989 election his Conservative Party (CP) won 45 per cent of the Afrikaner vote, as against 46 per cent for the Government and 9 per cent for the Democratic Party. And that, he knew, was part of an upward trend over the last three elections. For in 1983 his party won 18 per cent of the total white vote, then 26 per cent in 1987 and finally 31 per cent in 1989. A healthy slice.

And a nice trend for him, he would have known, as he walked on the evening of March 9th, 1990, into Durban's City Hall in the heartland of English Natal, the so-called 'last outpost of the British Empire'!

The place was packed with fifteen hundred wildly enthusiastic supporters. His line was simple. The National Party would be responsible for a revolution in the country if it dismantled apartheid. Besides which, President F W, Future

Worries, de Klerk (the country's new alternative to P W, Past Worries, Botha) had no mandate from white South Africa to 'negotiate the surrender of his people's political rights'.

The government, he went on to say, 'is actually refusing to enforce some of its own laws. They are unbanning terrorist movements and communist movements which can stir up the masses and spread violence, chaos and looting in South Africa and the homelands. These things are happening. There is not a single place in South Africa which is not being threatened by violence.'

Treurnicht took brief breath, then galloped on: 'Look at what happened in Durban at the African National Congress rally. Instead of the South African police maintaining law and order, three thousand marshals controlled the crowds.

'That is telling the government: "If you can't maintain law and order, we'll do it for you."'

'But,' mused one sugar farmer in the crowd, 'it *could* just show that the ANC can be good at disciplining and controlling their followers. I just hope they can keep doing so as we move into the future.' He turned his attention back to Treurnicht.

Treurnicht went on to note how the National Party played a trump card with the whites about

the threats of sanctions, disinvestment, economic isolation, an increasing armed struggle and an ultimate bloodbath if they did not get all political parties in South Africa to the negotiating table.

'But,' he thundered, 'we shall not be intimidated. We shall defend our rights with every means at our disposal . . .

'You cannot share power; it is a political lie. The moment you try to share power, you lose it.'[1]

That's heady stuff, I thought to myself when I read the report next day in the paper, and the sort of thing which appeals in elemental terms to embattled whites. Of course, some aspiring black politicians, in reaction to having been silenced for so long, are using similar rhetoric to whip up black emotion, especially among the young, in a welter of condemnation of all that is being done at this time by a self-reforming National Party. 'Lord, however will we win through,' I prayed, 'if this all or nothing line and no power-sharing takes hold too widely?'

Then in May 1990 Treurnicht gathered not fifteen hundred in a city hall, but sixty thousand ardent, passionate followers, at the Voortrekker Monument, sacred symbol of Afrikaner nationalism and historical grit. And, let it not be forgotten, thousands of these are members of the police, army, school systems and civil service. Their view of things is simple and uncomplicated.

'We shall never, ever surrender,' said one bearded farmer leaning, rifle in hand, against his horse.

Interview

Paul Bell is Deputy Editor of South Africa's distinguished *Leadership Magazine* which under Hugh Murray's guidance has done a sophisticated job in bringing the diverse views of South Africa's varied leaders to the attention of the public.

But I think he must have wondered what he was in for when he went to interview Koos van der Merwe, a Conservative Party MP and one of its leading spokesmen. He found a man, a lawyer by training, who had obvious intellectual agility and who made his public utterances 'like battering rams'. Bell found van der Merwe's view that the CP Afrikaner would not be 'pushed or sold out without a fight', to be 'chilling' – even if that resolution turns out 'to be a scarecrow'.

'He says,' noted Bell, 'that black leaders cannot restrain their followers from violence' (a view seemingly supported for all conservatives by the widespread outbreaks of violence which have buffeted the country) 'and he expresses, in a manner which seems faintly to suggest the opposite, the hope that the CP can restrain their own.'

Bell kicked off by asking him how South Africa's 'ten days that shook the world' affected the CP and its strategy.

The so-called new 'hard man of the right' replied:

The events have accelerated our movement in the logical direction we are headed. We think people will eventually realise, as they are realising in Eastern Europe, that you can't juxtapose different peoples together. At Yalta the great powers decided to force numerous different nationalities together in the strong hug of the communist bear. Now, less than fifty years later, it has failed because it cannot work. You cannot suppress nationalisms.

De Klerk is trying to juxtapose different nationalisms, Afrikaner nationalism, Zulu nationalism and all the others, and he will cause the ANC to hug them together. He's making exactly the same mistake as they made in Eastern Europe. The CP knows that won't work and wants the country to accelerate to that realisation. That, to us, is the most positive aspect of those events. We want to skip the experimental phase, which failed in Eastern Europe, and move to the solution phase . . .

The modern trend is that a people, a 'volk', doesn't want to be dominated. If I use this language, I am completely in line with modern thinking, Eastern European thinking, African thinking.

Radio Botswana asked me what we would do if we won an election. I said we want exactly the same as Botswana, namely a geographic part of Southern Africa under our own rule.

We demand only self-determination in our own state for the Afrikaner people, meaning the Afrikaner and other whites who associate themselves with Afrikaner ideals, thereby constituting a white nation. If the other peoples want to enter into what is now commonly referred to as a non-racial democracy, who am I to tell them not to? On that basis we say there are two sides to the coin: we can't force our will on you; neither can you do it to us. Hence we will devote our energy and our organisation to establishing an Afrikaner state. We are entitled to do so.[2]

Land and Boundaries

As the interview progressed, van der Merwe, to Bell's manifest exasperation, hedged vigorously on what the boundaries of this so-called 'Boerestaat' (Boer State) would be.

In the end he affirmed: 'Eventually, we are prepared to negotiate the boundaries of our land. We are not prepared to

negotiate the fact that we want part of South Africa in which
we want to govern ourselves – we are not even talking
about that – but we are going to negotiate the size of it, the
boundaries.'

Would that mean that the CP et al. would be at de Klerk's
negotiating table? Van der Merwe continued:

> We have insurmountable difficulties with President de
> Klerk. First, he no longer represents the majority of white
> people; we do. Second, he has arrived at a critical junction
> and, despite the international acclaim, he can't get out of it.
> Probably the two most important actors in this drama, the
> ANC and the CP, are both apprehensive and cautious and
> not at all enthusiastic. Here is de Klerk's dilemma: the two
> main actors each have a non-negotiable claim which stands
> in direct opposition to that of the other. The CP says: 'We
> want a part of South Africa, which is ours and which we
> govern.' The ANC says: 'No, we want the whole of South
> Africa which we know we will dominate because of
> numbers.'
>
> And why doesn't de Klerk want to answer our questions?
> Because he knows that if he opens that curtain just one inch,
> either the CP or the ANC will shy away immediately, like a
> jet taking off. And it will ruin everything. If today de Klerk
> says one man, one vote, there will be a complete uproar
> among white people, there will be ugly scenes and the CP
> will be so strong it will be unbelievable. If he says there is not
> going to be one man, one vote, then there go Mandela,
> Sisulu, Mbeki and the rest of them. He can't solve the
> problem.

Violence

Bell now teased out of the big Afrikaner what his thoughts
were on violence. Could this all end in a white-black slug-out?

To Bell's relief, van der Merwe answered: 'We reject violence. However, Government has created a certain mood, and
in that mood you may find violence from left and right and
from black and white. We sincerely hope we will be able to
contain our people.'

Then came the bit which sent chills up and down Bell's spine:

> But let me point out the potential for violence among whites. The ANC has scored a victory against de Klerk with what I believe is ten thousand soldiers.
> But hundreds of thousands of whites, among the million CP supporters, are trained soldiers. We've been trained for the last twenty or thirty years in all forms of warfare. If you add that to the fact that our forefathers paid dearly for a part of South Africa, that we fought the British because they wanted to rob us of our right of self-determination, that we lost twenty-six thousand women and children, that we lost Japie Fourie and all the others, do you think we will simply surrender to Mandela? It is out of the question.
> When Mandela becomes leader, the cabinet will quickly become mostly black, then the mayors of towns. Our towns and schools will be invaded. They will nationalise our property, they will take all we have toiled for. There is no compromise: this is what they want. Mandela, having raised unrealistic expectations among blacks, will not find it easy to contain all his followers. Treurnicht, however hard he may try, may perhaps not appease every individual conservative.
> What it boils down to is: the ANC wants to enforce upon South Africa the one-man, one-vote system. The CP says no, we want our own state. I recognise this as a deadlock position with a definite potential for violence. I know what violence and war entail and I would certainly rather find a peaceful solution.[3]

Hanging in the Balance

How delicately all things here hang in the balance. For editor, Ken Owen, 'malign influences' on right and left are spreading. As evidence he cites right-wing white leaders of the Afrikaner Resistance Movement saying from public platforms that the unarmed white man is dead, while black youths in some townships strut around with T-shirt slogans saying 'One settler, one bullet'.

He also observes that right-wing English voters are ominously 'leaping in small but significant numbers clear across the Nats to the CP.'

More ominously yet, he notes that for black people a nightmare expressed some years ago by a coloured writer is becoming a reality. 'The white man sits silently polishing his rifle in the sun.'[4]

Analysis

As well placed a person to understand this and analyse it is Willem de Klerk, the President's brother and, of course, a true-blue Afrikaner.

In a nutshell he sees the CP line as curving away from Clem Sunter's *High Road*, 'then running over a precipice and plunging down into the abyss'.[5]

While some analysts write off CP chances, De Klerk is more cautious, however, and notes several arguments working in their favour. Further ups and downs in the South African economy with a consequent lowering of living standards may result in strongly increased resistance to the government.

Another factor is that as political trauma continues, the effect on many whites could be that their hopes for a power-sharing solution are destroyed. Disillusionment sets in and the National Party is blamed by the CP constituency for the chaos. Its own alternative of partition is thus presented as the only way towards solution.

Then there is the argument that the CP's approach of 'ethnic mobilisation', by which a strong play is made on Afrikaner nationalism and identity, has the potential to be as effective today in the 1990s as it was in the 1940s during the run up to the Nationalist take-over of power from the old United Party.

The idea of ethnic mobilisation is that process by which the CP attempts to build an extended infrastructure on all different levels of Afrikaner community. The CP thus makes itself the agent for rebuilding Afrikaner nationalism with powerful new symbols and myths, plus, of course, playing on fears of the 'swart gevaar' (black danger). This kind of thing can have magnetic appeal to many insecure and anxious whites.

This takes us into a final argument favouring a CP build-up, namely its capacity to exploit these gut emotional forces of fear and hope, in contrast to the National Party's weaker emotional appeals which are now currently based on reasonableness, doing the right thing, and vague expectations for an uncertain and evolutionary future.

Four Roots

Willem de Klerk identifies four roots in the basic philosophy and ideology of the Conservative right. The first is 'the quasi-religious doctrine' that Afrikaners are a chosen people whose destiny is to maintain a separate existence.

The second relates to a doctrine of racial exclusiveness whose strength lies in an insistence on maintaining one's identity rather than mixing with any other races or groups. This sort of mixing is seen as a 'transgression of the order of nature'. While the initial boundary for this identity was in the past the Afrikaner volk or nation, it might now be extended to other whites, most notably the English, but only to whites.

The third route identified by Willem de Klerk is what he calls 'The utopian point of departure that a permanent solution is to be found in separateness and that a separation of power will finally settle all conflict.'

He sees the fourth root as the moral justification that the right of self-preservation is one of life's highest values. Of course, in its reversed dimensions, it includes the right to discriminate. This kind of nationalism 'demands exclusion, seclusion, the drawing of boundaries and the concentration of power. By these tokens, self-determination becomes a norm and power-sharing with people of other races is seen to conflict with the proper ordering, even divine ordering of nations.'[6]

All this, of course, takes us back to the very early theological, philosophical and political wellsprings of apartheid. The story of that birthing I elucidate in detail in *The Passing Summer*, pp. 108–50. I would encourage the reader to look over that material.

In this sense the Conservative Party and the political right wing are replaying the record of yesterday which gave birth to apartheid. The CP thus takes up the old Verwoerdian mantle and makes itself a highly ideologised and rigid movement which is completely uncompromising in nature.

Clearly the capacity of this element in South African life to produce upheaval, to inspire white intransigence and to escalate black anger is not inconsiderable.

In commenting on this, Willem de Klerk writes,

> This scenario spells full-scale war, with millions of victims. It will rage on our northern and eastern borders and in the interior. Control exercised by the security forces of the white state may be hampered by foreign military intervention, mobilised in terms of a consensus between East and West that the rights of blacks have to be protected against such a racist régime.
>
> Otherwise, it may lead to a permanent Lebanon-type situation – only on a larger scale. And that is the most hopeful scenario![7]

De Klerk goes on:

> The other scenarios then follow of their own accord. With everything spiralling out of control and a total lack of stability, the economy has to collapse, with economic activity, markets, foreign trade and other economic relations and resources short-circuiting one after the other.
>
> This leads to the spectre of a domino scenario in which collapse on one front triggers off the next.
>
> The scenarios may be multiplied from a number of perspectives. As far as the outside world is concerned, the mildest scenario is that of South Africa being written off in a few dramatic steps or over a period of time. A harsher scenario is that of total isolation and internal chaos. The harshest scenario is that of intervention from outside on the grounds that the régime is totally illegitimate.
>
> What we are dealing with is a scenario of either hurtling headlong into the abyss, or sliding into it.[8]

For Willem de Klerk and for countless other South Africans, a take-over of the nation by the right wing is an appalling prospect which would amount to a pulling-down of the pillars in an act of national self-destruction. 'But still . . . there are those who say South Africa is capable of committing this historic act of idiocy.'⁹

Counter

To counter such an act I believe there is no power adequate other than the politics of love. This way will first of all require us to understand the pain and the insecurity of a long embattled people. Ezekiel said of those in Babylonian exile, 'I sat where they sat.' Loving someone is the first prerequisite in changing them, especially when they neither want to be changed nor see any reason for such a necessity. To surrender, or *feel* you are surrendering all you've fought and laboured for for centuries, as the conservative Afrikaner feels, is no easy thing. If no attempt is made to understand those feelings, they will as surely as night follows day become tragically entrenched.

The appeal at this point will also have to be to those basically Christian roots which are there in the South African right wing. The word must be, 'Be and work out who and what you profess to be as Christian people.' To appeal to anything else will be to appeal in vain.

Perhaps the South African right wing needs to pause afresh and reflect on the mistakes made by conservative German Christians in the 1930s when they pressed their 'Germanness' ahead of their 'Christianness'.

Such an embracing of 'Christianness' over 'Afrikanerness' *must* come from the South African Conservative Party and right wing, otherwise the German experience could tragically repeat itself in these parts.

If even the Way of Love which seeks to dispel fear, sectionalism and insecurity is not accepted, then the possibility of some form of 'Boerestaat' will have to be put on the negotiating table in preference to civil war. It will be a counsel and course of despair. But at the end of the day the idea may finally thrust itself tragically into serious purview.

But, as Thomas Hardy once noted, 'I have plumbed the depths of despair and have found them not bottomless.' For even there can God be found to lead us out to higher and better things.

shocked mourners. Bishop Matthew Makhaye, speaking from
the poignant place of the black Christian, made this statement:
'As ministers in and of the Church of God, we by word and life
preach the Gospel of Christ crucified, risen, ascended and
glorified. The essence of that Gospel is love, peace, and joy.
This Gospel we proclaim to all of God's people irrespective of
their political affiliations, and we preach it in all places without
consideration of their political inclinations.

'This we do,' Makhaye affirmed, 'because we believe Christ
died for all and our God's sovereignty is over all His creation.
In the name of Christ we condemn evil in all political institutions and parties and we praise good. We deplore and grieve
deeply at the violence and mindless killing of so many people,
gripping the greater part of the Pietermaritzburg area and
other parts of the country.

'We request, therefore, all our people wherever they may be
and whatever political party they belong to, to receive our
ministrations without giving such ministrations party political
identity. We pledge ourselves to continue faithfully, in obedience to God and our calling . . . to preach and minister
to all.'

Bishop of Natal, Michael Nuttall, said, 'With the psalmist
we cry out "How long, O Lord, how long?" We pray that the
death of Victor Africander may help to reveal the bitter truth
of what is happening and that somehow by God's grace it may
be used for healing in a broken community.'

Not long after this, a hate-crazed assailant came into the
Cathedral office and stabbed the receptionist and shouted:
'That is a message for the Bishop,' as he fled back to his world
of irrationality and hatred.

The reality of violence in South African life, a problem
going into deep recesses of the South African national psyche,
is one of the supreme challenges to the Politics of Love.

As long as violence continues in South Africa, we are set to
spiral into what Nelson Mandela calls 'a full-scale civil war'.
He sees the prospect of such a thing as 'real and terrifying'. My
experiences living in Natal have likewise convinced me of this
danger, not to mention things I have personally witnessed in
places like Uganda and Southern Sudan.

Natal is certainly enough of a crucible to persuade one of the grave perils ahead if the sort of spirit and approaches tried here to resolve political struggles become entrenched on the national stage.

Frederick van Zyl Slabbert, former leader of the opposition in Parliament, punches straight from the shoulder when he says in an IDASA publication:

Nothing exposes the bankruptcy of politicians more brutally than violence; nothing betrays the fragility of the social order easier than its consequences; nothing challenges the quality of a country's leadership as unrelentingly as its continuation. Violence makes nonsense of civility, of 'talks about talks', of negotiating democracy. There can be no democracy without a democratic culture. And any culture that depends on, or draws its inspiration from violence and brutality negates culture and democracy.

The hallmark of democratic negotiation is tolerance for difference and respect for diversity. Violence is its unholy antithesis.

Given the violent nature of much in South African life, and the extensive nature of this plague, it becomes instructive to see something of its tragic face and its inescapable laws.

I THE FACE AND TRAGEDY OF VIOLENCE

At 5 p.m. on Sunday evening Mandla Bhengu came running to his house in Edendale with five boys chasing him. His sister identified the five boys. She knew them. They were armed with knives.

Once Mandla was inside the boys shouted for him to come out. When he refused, they bashed the door and broke all the front windows. Then Mduduzi Chamu, the Bhengu family neighbour, a fourteen-year-old youth, ran from the road to help the Bhengu family. The boys grabbed him and stabbed him all over his back. They thought he was dead. They picked up a brick and hit him on his temple. They said that if anyone came forward as a witness, they would 'get them and fix them'. Then they left. The Bhengus called Mduduzi's mother, who phoned the ambulance, and he was taken to Edendale hospital.

The family was afraid as they made statements to the lawyer later on in the day. Mandla was placed in a safe home for the time being.

Please, they asked, would someone from the Imbali Support Group stay with them overnight?

The Imbali Support Group was started by Graeme Swan, a Canadian intern with African Enterprise, and by Mbulelo Hina, also a colleague, plus people like the great-hearted and intrepid Monika Wittenberg of PACSA (The Pietermaritz-burg Association for Christian Social Awareness), a group which works significantly in our area with victims of the trouble. It is mainly a group of whites and Indians who will stay in the homes of black people in the Imbali township who feel they might be attacked or shot. It is a ministry of astonishing faith and Christian courage. Graeme Swan's bullet-ridden car, later gutted by a petrol bomb, testified vividly to the courage of all those involved in this work.

So now – would someone from the Imbali Support Group stay with the Bhengus? Of course. Beshara Karam went. The politics of love at work.

Not So Lucky

Mandla Bhengu did not die. Alex Nzaca was not so lucky. His home was burned down. He was shot and died next day. His house is opposite the 'Welcome to Beirut' sign which graced the entry to his township. Around 3 a.m. on this fateful day a petrol bomb was thrown through a rear window of the house. The husband went to investigate and was shot through the window in the left buttock and in the stomach. His wife said some eight shots were fired. Other witnesses heard three. His wife and two children escaped through the front window unharmed. The ambulance took Alex to Edendale hospital.

Anthony Nobbs, my AE colleague and another member of the Imbali Support Group, received the call about 3 a.m., and rushed to the Nzaca's house. Distraught, he ministered as best he could. At 10 a.m. next morning he checked out Alex's condition at the hospital. He had just died on the operating table.

'What did you find at the house when you got there?' Anthony was asked.

'Well,' he said, 'there was a riot investigation unit there and the police were helpful. In fact, two of the Indian officers had entered the burning house when they thought a child remained inside. The house was basically burned out. The only firefighting being done was with a neighbour's garden hose. The family will not be moving back. At 3.45 a.m. another house was petrol-bombed, but was only slightly damaged.'

Fact-finding Tour

Many of the people seeking a solution to the causes of this violence have asked the government for a judicial enquiry. At the time of writing this has not yet happened. But some of the causes were brought home to a group of us taken on a fact-finding and briefing tour round the 'civil-war' zone of Edendale Valley on the edge of Pietermaritzburg at the height of the troubles. The exercise is the sort of thing, among scores of others, which IDASA, a real beacon of light in South Africa, has done in the past four years in furthering their declared goal of *building a democratic culture* into South Africa's fundamentally counter-democratic culture!

Apartheid Chickens

'It is not helpful or possible,' said John Aitcheson, our briefer and a Natal University academic who monitors the violence with professional precision, 'to say who fired the first shot. But of course in some ways we are seeing some of the apartheid chickens come home to roost.'

Aitcheson went on to note that the Edendale Valley was originally a series of farms owned by Methodist missionaries. Later it was taken over for extensive black settlement. Since 1948, however, there had been no real land tenure nor proper political representation. The whole thing had been a classic saga of the impoverishments of apartheid. The place had finally been put under the homeland administration of Kwa-Zulu. The task for KwaZulu was very difficult and frustrations on all sides took root. Inkatha, observed Aitcheson, had been established initially as an organisation to give Zulu people a cultural identity. Membership was actively encouraged and many joined. In the 1980s the UDF (United Democratic Front), a legal front for the then banned ANC, was established nationwide. As a political movement, later also banned, its membership increased rapidly. In Natal, members of the UDF, called 'comrades' among the disaffected youth, started to clash with members of Inkatha. Alienation eventually flared into violence, first sporadic and then endemic. The dimensions of the problem made it difficult for the relatively small police force to cope, particularly as they were often perceived as siding with Inkatha. The vendetta spirit set in. Chronic unemployment aggravated the whole situation. Criminal elements further exploited the alienations and capitalised on the developing chaos. 'Now,' said John, 'you see the fruit of it all.'

As our minibuses of church leaders, businessmen and MPs wound through the area, stopping here and there to meet and speak to people, Archbishop Dennis Hurley, the Roman Catholic archbishop of Natal, next to whom I was seated, shook his head and murmured, 'It is tragic, tragic, tragic!'

Our first stop was on a hillside at the edge of Ashdown township which is a UDF area bordering an Inkatha area. All along the periphery of the township were burned-out and gutted houses. A stricken old man said, 'One of my children has been killed. I have lost everything. My house has been burned down. No one told me why.'

The in-between people, I thought. Like the one who said to me, 'We mothers are just watching and waiting. We can't do anything. We can't fight. We can't find solutions. We don't know what is happening. We don't know the roots of the conflict. But the Lord says, and we know it, that we are just visitors and just passing through. We are with Jesus Christ. And we keep praying.'

From there via a church hall, packed with displaced and dejected women and children, out to an encounter with Chief David Ntombela, labelled by many locals as an 'Inkatha warlord', at a large tent in an open space in an area called Taylor's Halt. The tent was intended to be used for a proposed reconciliation rally to be addressed by Chief Buthelezi and Dr Nelson Mandela the following week. This in fact never materialised.

Ntombela looked like something out of a storybook. A great swashbuckling character sporting a belt of bullets and an enormous holstered revolver. His three guards were armed with sophisticated pump-shotguns.

We were politely introduced by Dr Khoza Mgojo, a senior Methodist leader. Ntombela put his and Inkatha's side of the story. They were only responding to provocative attacks upon their buses by young comrades, who stoned their vehicles as they went through Edendale, he said. 'Finally, enough was enough. We had to retaliate. We can't have our buses stopped. This is very bad because if it happens people will starve. What do you think they will do if they cannot get through Edendale to work?'

'And what about the proposed meeting here next week with Chief Buthelezi and Dr Mandela?' asked one of our group. 'It is important,' said Ntombela, 'because these leaders must come together and sit and talk. It is no use them talking to people outside. They must talk to each other. Children must go to school and no one must be recruited by the other side by force. But everyone knows there was no trouble in this area until the UDF came. That is when it started. But now we must all listen to the leaders. Now is the time for everybody to think about God and Jesus. We cannot go on killing and assaulting. We have had enough.'

I noticed sceptical looks in our group. Yet there was recognition that this man was putting his viewpoint. Right or wrong, that's how he saw it. Somehow the group was seeking to hear all viewpoints and take them seriously. As with an estranged couple, you do have to hear both sides, listen hard and be committed not so much to either side as to both sides and the relationship which both need to reach if healing and reconciliation are to come.

'Khoza,' I said as we came to the end of our time, 'don't you think we could have a prayer together here?'

'Indeed,' said the big man. 'Go ahead.' So I did, regardless of one or two awkward looks in our group. 'But, hek,' I said to myself, 'there will never be any way out of this unless we can get the Lord in on the act to anoint the best and most necessary endeavours of all human peacemakers.'

I noticed as the prayer ended that there was a visible relaxing in the countenance of the old chief and his three guards, even amidst their awful anxiety, belligerence and who knows what of guilt or innocence.

Imbali

Our group had mixed looks of mystification, scepticism and a sense of helplessness as we trundled back down the hill from Taylor's Halt into the cauldron of Edendale Valley. On our way back, as we passed pathetic little clusters of people who had evacuated their homes and were carrying beds or belongings on their heads down to the Valley, one of our group said, 'How can he talk about Jesus, prayer and all that, given all he and his cronies are said to have done?'

Yet the fact that he could, as mysterious an aspect of the anatomy of this country as you could find, tells me that there *is* something down there in him and in most South Africans that is spiritual, even if in some it is distorted. On this we have to build and from that platform move to new answers and a new day.

As we got back to the Methodist church in Edendale I was told a gang had just gone through Imbali. 'Mr Tshale is dead,' lamented Mrs Nyembezi, a prominent member of the community. 'They shot him.'

'I would like to go there,' I said to the driver of our minibus. 'Could you take me to the Tshale's house?' Archbishop Hurley plus others in the group and in our particular minibus were likewise anxious to go. Seeing, of course, is believing. And feeling. And understanding.

A pitiful scene awaited us at the Tshale's house in Unit 13 of Imbali. A cluster of shocked and shattered women sat in the front room, including the daughter of Mr Tshale, who had saved herself by hiding under a bed. In the bedroom, prostrate

on a mattress on the floor was Mrs Tshale, with a nurse and
several other ministering women.

'Two youngsters came in,' said one. 'And then bang! bang!
with their guns. Mr Tshale fell right there.'

The nurse pulled back a little rug to reveal wet blood
beneath, and newspaper to soak it up.

'They've taken Mr Tshale to the mortuary.'

Words at such times are cheap. And even prayer can feel
that way. Yet I felt constrained to pray and did, commending
the stricken woman to the Lord's comfort and mercy.

In the next room was the daughter. Archbishop Hurley
prayed for her. A prayer of anguish. And a cry for the madness
to end.

Then we went next door where the humble house had been
partially torched. Two older men this time had gone into the
house, the only occupants being two terrified children of
eleven and six who had escaped out the back door. Round the
corner five more houses had been burned. Wailing women
pointed down into the little valley a couple of hundred yards
away: 'They are down there,' they said, heads shaking,
tongues clicking, eyes streaming with tears.

No one says who 'they' are. But if it is a UDF area it means
Inkatha. If it is an Inkatha area, it means UDF.

My mind went back to February 1990. Mandela had said
that as a result of government policy 'violence by the African
people had become inevitable.' Perhaps. Yet I also wondered
what part the rhetoric on various sides about 'armed struggle'
had played subsequently in furthering this violence. Such talk
was understandable, but it could not be the Christian way for
our nation's highest good. Certainly we cannot condemn one
group's violence and approve another's.

President de Klerk's words on February 2, 1990 still therefore address this issue and point the way:

'It is time to break out of the cycle of violence and break
through to peace and reconciliation.'

II VIOLENCE AND ITS LAWS

1 Types of Violence

Of course there are different kinds of violence. For example, *psychological violence* happens when injury is done to a person's integrity and self-respect.

Then there is *structural violence* where extreme force is exerted on people by the effects of a given social or political structure (eg the Indian caste system or SA apartheid). The structure curbs freedoms or discriminates in such a way as to 'do violence' to people's humanity, dignity and equality.

Then there is of course *physical violence* when people wound, maim, torture, damage or kill each other.

In *The Passing Summer* (pp. 375–6), we noted Professor Klaus Nurnberger's understanding of how the chain of violence has often worked, especially in South African society. Nurnberger thus speaks of *institutional violence*, which is found in the system when people's human rights are removed and their significance violated. On top of this come specific strong-arm tactics, as South Africa has seen over the years, to enforce objectionable legislation, such as the Group Areas Act, Unequal Resource Allocation, Job Reservation, Race Classification, Land Acts, Separate Education, and no vote in the Central Parliament.

This, Nurnberger says, gives rise to *reactive violence* from the grass roots, when people start to protest at the oppressiveness of the system, the ANC's strategically planned violence in the black townships in 1985, for instance.

Then comes *repressive violence*, which is the state's response to reactive violence. More police or military force is used to screw the lid down. Not only is the huge South African police force deployed everywhere, but the military gets brought in as well. Even more sinister in South Africa was the secret police unit called the CCB (Civil Co-operation Bureau) which was employed to perform a host of sinister tasks.

All these sorts of repressive violence finally produce *destructive violence*, when people in fury and frustration turn their destructive energies against almost anything in sight. It may be

against each other (eg Pietermaritzburg townships in 1987 and
1988) or against a library or a school or a clinic or a municipal
bus, or even, as happened in Port Elizabeth a good many years
ago, against a nun who had worked among black people in that
township for many years. Likewise in the late 1980s in people's
courts in the townships, incensed youths acted as both judge
and jury and passed brutal sentences, sometimes even death,
on their own parents.

The institutional violence of apartheid is probably most to
blame for leading us to become a violent society, but knowing
the origin of the violent impulses in our society does not
thereby legitimise our giving way to them. A man who finds his
wife abed with another man may know why he has a murderous impulse upon him, but that does not legitimise the
murderous act. The woman who loses two children in an
accident may know the cause of her suicidal emotions, but her
self-destruction is not thereby validated. South Africans may
know why they want to fight each other and thereby commit
national suicide, but that gives no moral grounds to do so.

Yet that is just what the way of violence and armed struggle
will finally do. It will produce our national suicide or something akin to it in that, like the US Civil War, it could take us a
hundred years or more to work out the consequences. So we'd
better know the laws which govern the way of violence.

No one has probably put them better than Jacques Ellul, the
great French theologian and sociologist.

2   Laws of Violence

(i) *The Law of Continuity*:   Says Ellul, 'The first law of
violence is continuity. Once you start using violence, you
cannot get away from it. Once a man has begun to use violence
he will never stop using it, for it is so much easier and more
practical than any other method.'

In some of South Africa's townships today, this principle of
violence, being difficult to curtail once it is in the system, is
vividly illustrated. The original causes of violence have been
almost forgotten, and there has been a spiral of attack and

counter-attack. How this is to be stopped is a source of perplexity to white and black leaders alike.

Certainly addressing some of the identified wrongs would help. An impartial judicial enquiry into the cause of the violence would help. The operation of love's laws of forgiveness and understanding from both sides is essential. Radicalised youth should be given an official forum to air their grievances. Thereafter much emotional healing will be needed and the repatching of broken lives. Thankfully this violence is not on the larger scale of a full-blown racial or tribal confrontation, though recent spreading of it to other areas of the country is worrying.

And, of course, if any of this 'spread of violence' is the work of 'Third Force' *agents provocateurs*, as Nelson Mandela and others suspect, then such Third Force stirrers of something so dangerous and explosive should be apprehended forthwith and have the heaviest possible sentences imposed on them. For stirring violence is like putting lighted matches in a dry, winter forest. Catastrophic conflagration has to be the consequence. Let us be warned.

(ii) *The Law of Reciprocity*: This is the second law, as Ellul says:

> It is stated in Jesus's famous word, '*all* who draw the sword will die by the sword' (Matt. 26:52). Let me stress two points in connection with this passage. There is the insistence on 'all'. There is no distinction here between a good and a bad use of the sword. The sheer fact of using the sword entails this result. The law of the sword is a total law. Then, Jesus is in no sense making a moral valuation or announcing a divine intervention or a coming judgement; he simply describes the reality of what is happening. He states one of the laws of violence. Violence creates violence, begets and procreates violence. The violence of the colonialists creates the violence of the anticolonialists, which in turn exceeds that of the colonialists. Nor does victory bring any kind of freedom. Always, the victorious side splits up into clans which perpetuate violence . . .

The man who, in whatever way, uses violence should

realise that he is entering into a reciprocal kind of relation capable of being renewed indefinitely.[1]

(iii) *The third law is the Law of Sameness*:   Ellul says,

> It is impossible . . . to distinguish between justified and unjustified violence, between violence that liberates and violence that enslaves. Every violence is identical with every other violence. I maintain that all kinds of violence are the same.
>
>   There is another aspect of this sameness that characterises violence: once we consent to use violence ourselves, we have to consent to our adversary's using it, too. We cannot demand to receive treatment different from that we mete out.[2]

(iv) *Law Four is the Nothing Else Law*:   Violence begets violence and nothing else. Violence is *par excellence* the method of falsehood. In Ellul's words,

> We have in view admirable ends and objectives. Unfortunately, to attain them we have to use a bit of violence . . . If we revolutionaries are only allowed to use a little violence (you can't make an omelette without breaking eggs), you'll see the reign of justice, liberty, and 'equality'. That kind of thing is repeated again and again, and it sounds logical enough. But it is a lie.
>
>   The end does not justify the means. On the contrary, evil means corrupt good ends . . . Let the man who wants to use violence, do so; let the man who thinks there is no other way, use it; but let him know what he is doing. That is all the Christian can ask of this man – that he be aware that violence will never establish a just society. Yes, he will get his revenge; yes, he will subdue his 'enemy'; yes, he will consummate his hatred. But let him not confuse hate with justice.[3]

(v) *Law Five is the Law of Justification*:   Every user of violence will try to justify both it and himself. Violence is so unappealing, says Ellul, that every user of it has produced lengthy apologies to demonstrate to the people that it is just and morally warranted. Hitler, Stalin, Mao, Castro, Nasser, the guerrillas, the French 'paras' of the Algerian war – all tried to vindicate themselves. The plain fact is that violence is never 'pure'. Always violence and hatred go together.[4]

To these five laws of Ellul's, I would add three others, making our total eight.

(vi) *Law Six – Violence is basically uncontrollable and will degenerate from the purposeful to the mindless*: It is as unrealistic to moralise about violence as it is to legislate against tornadoes. After the awful violence on the Reef in September 1990, when random slaughter even took place on trains, Lloyd Vogelman, a violence monitor at the Witwatersrand University, said, 'The whole nature of violence here has changed. We have never seen such indiscriminate violence in South Africa' (*Natal Witness*, September 15th, 1990). Law Six above affirms just that. The violence will move uncontrollably from the 'purposeful' (that for which people feel able to give some tenuous rationale, whether moral or political) to the mindless and indiscriminate.

(vii) *Law Seven – Violence silences the voice of love*: Che Guevara once said that 'a people without hatred cannot win over a brutal enemy'. To which Martin Luther King replied, 'Through violence you may murder the hater, but you do not murder the hate.' When Victor Africander dies, some of the world's love dies too. And hate is allowed to scamper insanely and unfettered across the landscape. There are no winners, except the devil and his minions.

(viii) *Law Eight – Violence treats people as things*: Violence dehumanises its victims before it demolishes them. It also dehumanises its agent. Again we balance a quotation of Che Guevara against one from Martin Luther King. Guevara said: 'Hatred transforms a man into an effective, violent, selective and cold mechanism of death.' But King observed:

Violence as a way of achieving racial justice is both impractical and immoral. It is impractical because it is a descending spiral ending in destruction for all. The old law of an eye for an eye leaves everybody blind. It is immoral because it seeks to humiliate the opponent rather than win his understanding; it seeks to annihilate rather than to convert; violence is immoral because it thrives on hatred rather than love. It destroys communities and makes brotherhood impossible. It leaves society in monologue rather than dialogue. Violence ends up by defeating itself. It creates bitterness in the survivors and brutality in the destroyers.[5]

And this applies as much to when violence is used to achieve so-called racial justice as when it is used in power struggles for one group to gain ascendency over another. In the end only bitterness and brutality result.

Sum of the Matter

Many in South Africa are much tempted to the ways of violence. But that way will be catastrophic. Every law of violence listed above says so. Beyond that, as Ellul observes, let those who choose that way refrain from appealing to great principles – a declaration of rights, democracy, justice – in the hope of escaping the reaction of the other side or group or persons they have attacked. Above all, let us recognise, and clearly, that violence begets violence. And if any ask 'Who started it?' let them know that finally that is a false question, for since the days of Cain, there has been no beginning of violence, only a continuous process of retaliation.

Whatever the solution to the problems of violence, Christian love has an approach to it found most especially in the example of Jesus.

Jesus's Example

The first thing to insist from Jesus's example at Calvary is that we cannot put together any reason to hate anyone. I may get angry with someone, even hate something they have done, but

Calvary robs me of any brief to hate anyone. Jesus said, 'Love
your enemies and pray for those who persecute you' (Matt.
5:44).

In front of Pilate's cynicism, Jesus said nothing. 'When he
was reviled, he did not revile in return; when he suffered, he
did not threaten' (1 Pet. 2:23 RSV). Instead of resisting arrest
and calling down the powers of Heaven, He went to the Cross.
Faced with the brutality of Roman political might and Jewish
religious ruthlessness, He prayed, 'Father, forgive them, they
know not what they do.'

Calvary also reveals a vital distinction between force and
power. Paul says, 'For the message of the Cross is foolishness
to those who are perishing, but to us who are being saved it is
the power of God' (1 Cor. 1:18). The Cross is the power of
God. Nothing in history has been more full of power and less
full of force, than the Cross of Jesus Christ. Saul of Tarsus set
off for Damascus to demolish the Christians with force. On the
way, he was met by power – the power of a persecuted,
crucified and loving Christ. And power won. Force had proved
futile. Indeed, the man who takes up his fist, his gun or his
knife, is not a man of power. For real power works without all
that despairing machinery. The point is that force is 'power-in-
despair' and in decline. Force is the mark of weakness, and
insecurity, not strength and power.

Challenge

Hear then the ringing words of Bishop Matthew Makhaye,
who speaks again with godly power as he challenges fellow
Christian ministers in South Africa today.

> The situation of your ministry is very unpredictable. You
> are called to speak out and up, loudly and clearly, as you
> appraise the good and condemn the evil; you are to face men
> of power and authority with the challenging word of God;
> you are to allay fears and doubts; oil and heal the open sore
> of mankind. You are to pronounce forgiveness; you are to
> give a word of hope, comfort and encouragement to the
> weak and forlorn; you are to minister meaningfully and
> adequately to the father who sees his house burn down, to

the mother seeing her son burning to death and the daughter who sees the charred body of father and mother in a heap of burning tyres. You are to feed, clothe, shelter and teach the orphans. You are to address boldly and in unequivocal terms the powers that be and the perpetrators of evil, irrespective of status, with the word of God – you must say 'thus saith the Lord'.

And in this context you are now required to recommit yourself in the full awareness of what it takes and costs – remembering that God has not given you the spirit of fear but of courage and power. Stir up then the gifts of His grace within you as He continues to sustain each one of you in your ministries.

In that sort of Calvary spirit, which embodies the politics of love, we can at last break out of the cycle of violence and move creatively towards the goal of a reconciled and peaceful society.

13　Facing the Giants

Beyond the dismantling of apartheid, the real problems
loom.

Breyten Breytenbach

The shape of South African society in future, after the
revolution, will depend critically on the foundations that
are laid now.

Mamphela Ramphele and Francis Wilson

If a free society cannot help the many who are poor, it
cannot save the few who are rich.

John F Kennedy

Little children, let us not love in word or speech but in
deed and in truth.

1 John 3:18 RSV

The stories of people like Ben Nsimbi and Lesley Richardson
express an interesting truth about South Africa, and one much
needed if we are not to become defeatist or depressed: for
every grim Goliath which stalks the land there is a determined
David in place – sometimes many, both men and women – to
challenge his destructive impudence. That said, it would be
self-deluding not to register the full magnitude of several great
giants which face us, and which inhibit a person's ability to
make love's choices.

Poet Breyten Breytenbach puts it this way: 'Beyond the
dismantling of apartheid, the real problems loom.' The problems he lists include destitution, famine, poverty, economic

restructuring, urbanisation, land redistribution, 'a brutalised and ill-educated society holding all laws in contempt', a virulent and armed right, corruption and incompetence.[1]

Victims of these find that their ability to think clearly, to understand, to listen to conscience, to be positive and to think outside their own wretched condition is difficult indeed. And the number of victims is immense.

Time and space forbid extensive consideration of all of these giants but some attention must be given to several lest those who are not victims miss the full dimensions of what love must tackle. Not forgetting our fragile environment, the battleground on which these giants stalk.

In considering these problems it needs to be remembered that statistics can be misleading. Even so, they give us a picture of what is happening, hence our use of them here. They give Goliath's dimensions and, when carefully considered, can both facilitate and stimulate our creative and positive response. The statistics must challenge us and not slay us!

And so to that very greatest of Goliaths: poverty.

I   POVERTY

Mrs Witbooi of Philipstown in the Karoo knows about poverty from experience: 'Poverty is wondering where your next meal is to come from and never knowing when the council is going to put your furniture out and always praying that your husband must not lose his job. To me that is poverty.'

Francis Wilson and Mamphela Ramphele, ('Davids' if ever there were any) open their epic study on *Uprooting Poverty: The South African Challenge* with Mrs Witbooi.[2] The book tells saga upon saga. I quote the experience of a black lady in Cape Town.

Desperation

My husband lost his job about five months ago. It was a big shock but we thought we could cope. I was earning a reasonably good wage. We had to cut a few corners, though.

We had to eat less meat. We had to save on all kinds of things. I had now to catch the train to work, 'cause it was cheaper than the bus even though it took a lot longer. I also took in other people's washing. There are a few people here who pay you a little bit to wash their clothes. I used to wash clothes every Sunday. Then two months ago I lost my job. We were desperate. There was no money coming in now. We had to spend everything we had in the time my husband was without a job. Now they've cut off the electricity and we're two months in arrears with rent. They're going to evict us I'm sure. But we just can't pay. My husband decided to go to Jo'burg. He went a month ago. He said he would get a job there. He sent some money the first week. But I haven't had any money since. I don't know where he is. I haven't been able to get hold of him. I would like to go to Jo'burg to look for him but what can I do with the children? Before he left we used to take turns to look for work because the children can't go to creche because there's no money. Sometimes they lie awake at night crying. I know they are crying because they are hungry. I feel like feeding them Rattex. When your children cry hunger-crying, your heart wants to break. It will be better if they were dead. When I think things like that I feel worse. It's terrible when a mother wants to kill her own children. But what can I do, I'm not a mother worth having.[3]

Shocking

Poverty, of course, is a world problem. In the world at large one in five is poor. That means that people 'cannot satisfy their basic needs in food, clothing, housing, education and health care'.[4] In Africa 50 per cent of the population live in abject poverty. In South Africa, in the 1980s, research shows that 50 per cent of the population lived below the Minimum Living Level (MLL). In many black areas the figures were over 60 per cent while in the 'homelands' (which includes the 'independent states'), the figure sometimes rose to 81 per cent of the people.[5]

In most poor households in South Africa 30 or 40 per cent of their money is being spent on food alone. They have very few facilities in the home. In fact 20 per cent of all black households have no facilities, a black household being defined as a unit where a person or people live. Only some 10 per cent have a bathroom.

Energy

Take also the simple matter of energy. Research done at Valhalla Park near Cape Town indicates that for black houses connected to the Escom Power system, (the country's main and national supply system), the average family was spending R29 per month on its fuel, lighting and heating needs. Those families without electricity were spending R67 per month on paraffin, candles and the like. *Now that's expensive.* Moreover, 80 per cent of black people in South Africa are as yet not connected to an electrical supply system (39 per cent in metropolitan areas are without electricity and a huge 98 per cent in rural areas).

For those who do have an electrical supply there are excessive cost problems. Says *Star* reporter, John Qwelane (*Sunday Star*, September 23rd, 1990): 'One of South Africa's largest electricity plants, Orlando Power Station, is in the heart of Soweto but does not supply the teeming black metropolis. It in fact serves 'White Johannesburg' leaving Sowetans to pay high charges for electricity brought in from Escom, hence the perennial grievances and rent boycotts.'[6]

So the poorer people pay more.

Research Findings

Research shows too that 30 per cent of black households do not have a single book in them. Only 5 per cent of black children of schoolgoing age have a desk or a table to work on. Over a million black households (about a quarter of the total) earn under R200 a month in cash income.

Another startling fact is that 50 per cent of black households, compared with 3 per cent of white households, have incomes under R400 per month, while some 55 per cent of white households and only 1 per cent of black households have incomes of over R3,000 per month.[7]

Inequalities

Poverty itself is shocking enough. But the even more shocking feature of poverty in South Africa lies in these huge inequalities imposed by apartheid's laws: there is a gaping chasm between those who are grindingly poor and those who are massively rich. In South Africa 5 per cent of the population own 88 per cent of the real wealth. Not surprisingly, therefore, 'The bottom line,' says researcher Teddy Langschmidt, 'is that the vast majority of the poor are getting poorer.'

No wonder the ANC and other black ideologues call for 'nationalisation'. The hope is that by this radical expedient the inequalities will be slowly eliminated. Whether this will come about by *this* process is highly debatable (and more on that later), but the cry for something radical is understandable when viewing the facts.

Unequal distribution of income plays an obvious part in aggravating poverty. But the Goliath which marches alongside this and seeks to conquer the most optimistic of Davids is that of population growth.

II POPULATION EXPLOSION

This is of course both the world's problem and Africa's. The world's population is increasing by three people per second, or a hundred million each year! But 76 per cent of the world's population lives in the less-developed countries and a vast 40 per cent of this population is *fifteen years old or younger*.

Africa has the highest population growth in the world (2.8 per cent per annum). The population of the African continent is thus set to rise from its present 560 million to 730 million by the turn of the century, now less than ten years away.[8]

South Africa

In South Africa, our present population of around 36 million is set at least to double every twenty years. By the time we are not too far into the twenty-first century, when today's young adults will be in their middle years, we will have a hundred million people, which is some twenty million more than the upper limit of what the country's natural resources can sustain. While white population growth during this time will decline significantly, (from 15 per cent of the total in 1985 to 10 per cent in 2010), the black population (African) will grow from 73 per cent of the total in 1985 to 81 per cent in 2010. Beyond that, the overall number of children *under five* already equals the number of adults in the 20–25 age bracket. In South Africa some 3,300 babies are born every day.

Another problem which poverty and population growth between them have worsened is that of urbanisation.

III URBANISATION

Themba Ngomane is forty-five. He sits in the sun on the pavement in the sprawling Durban township of KwaMashu thinking of his tribal home 200km away in KwaMadlala in rural KwaZulu. He remembers with sadness his wife Nomsa and six children waiting for him to return.

If it wasn't for them he wouldn't be in Durban now. With no land left on which to grow food and no grazing for the cattle and goats, Themba has been forced to leave his home to seek work. And since everyone has said there is always work in Durban, this is where he finds himself.

Themba remembers KwaMadlala as it was when he was young, in the days when a family could almost live off the land. That was before the place became crowded with houses, before the land had been ploughed from sky-line to sky-line and before the arrival of the deep and scarring dongas down which the red soil sluiced in ever increasing quantities.

It was also a time when there were still trees, and his mother and sisters did not have to walk too far to gather wood or to collect water. Yes, back in the days before the stream beds became clogged with silt and before the rivers ran dry for all but a few days of the year.

Themba hopes that Nomsa is safe, alone as she is with no one but women and old people to protect her. He remembers that Nomsa was not well when he left home, and he wonders whether she has been able to reach the small rural clinic 10km away from his home. But there is no way of contacting her to find out. Neither he nor she can read or write and there are no telephones. He prays that the letter-writer to whom he paid R5 has put the correct address on the letter; also that the writer wrote down what he asked him to, and finally that the R10 that he put in the envelope reaches his family.

He prays too that he will soon find work so that he can buy materials for a 'lean-to' shelter. For as soon as this has been done he will be able to tell Nomsa to come and join him. Living in a slum in KwaMashu will be better than living without food in KwaMadlala.

Themba's story highlights many of the other problems associated with urbanisation. He is one black South African among thousands moving *en masse* to the cities. South Africa has in fact the highest rate of urbanisation in the world (5.1 per cent per annum), one which doubles every fourteen years. While 43 per cent of blacks, say researchers, were already urbanised by 1980, that percentage had leaped to 53 per cent by 1989. By 2000 it will be close to 60 per cent. This means that 36 million people, our present total population, will be living in our cities in 10 years' time.

Durban

Durban in Natal is one of the fastest-growing cities in the world, second only to Mexico City. Researcher Mary Frances George, in her 'Factual Update on the Durban Functional Region (DFR)', published in April 1990, says that the DFR, covering now some 3,000 square kilometers, is populated by some 4,111,018 people. The black 'informal' population alone is estimated to be 2,091,639. It can be stated therefore that 50.87 per cent of the entire population of the DFR live in shack or squatter areas with an average of nine per informal dwelling. This is 69.78 per cent of all blacks in the DFR. And they are there to stay, 86 per cent saying they do not intend to return to the rural areas. The services in these areas, says Ms George, are 'negligible'.

All this reveals that housing the increasing population here and in other cities is one of the grave concerns of all who struggle with problems relating to urbanisation.

IV   HOUSING

Here, indeed, is a Goliath if ever there was one. Note too that 28 per cent of black 'households' are single households, (one person living alone in a hostel or compound.) That person might well be a migrant labourer with a family elsewhere. In the remaining 72 per cent of black households, with children, the average size is eight, but it is also estimated that many households in Soweto, for example, are home to some twenty people.

For some seven million South Africans, home is a shack in a squatter camp or in some first cousin-once-removed to a squatter camp. In Natal, one-third of the people are living in squatter conditions. As our researcher describes it:

The squatter dwelling is a one-roomer. What that means is that the family unit only exists in the sleeping state, because it is only after 9 or 10 at night that everybody is in the room. During the day Mum has the little children and is also trying to cook and wash, and the older children are told to play outside. So where is family life? It is almost totally imperilled. In fact, one could say that in any normal sense of the word, there is a breakdown of family life and there is a breakdown of traditional domestic authority. You don't have a true African culture, you just have a slum culture. But, as some have observed, squatter conditions can in fact be upgraded if the authorities are sympathetic.

Clearly the overall problem is gargantuan. For example, the official current shortage of houses stands in the region of one million units, but my guess is that in fact it is very much more.

The calculation now stands that to house all South Africans adequately will require the building of some two hundred thousand units each year for the next ten years. This would mean putting up about 540 houses every day up to the year 2000. Only about 54–56 per cent of the new demand is currently being met so that with the backlog, the shortage each year grows by about eighty thousand units. So over the next *twenty* years four million new homes are required.

Even more complicated is the problem of affordability even if the homes were built. As we have seen, at least half of the black population, which has the highest need for affordable accommodation, earns less than R400 per month. So the problem is set to hit epidemic proportions as South Africa's city populations explode in the twenty-first century.

Work being done presently by the Urban Foundation has become significant in the field of housing. Thankfully there are enterprises such as The South African Housing Trust (SAHT), a private sector initiative, which is grappling credibly and admirably with the challenge of affordable housing. This kind of initiative needs to be multiplied many times over by others. As to the SAHT, they hope to build fifty-two thousand houses in the next few years. Targeted into those who earn between R400 and R1,600 per month, the Trust, led by Wallie Conradie, estimates that the current effective housing demand in its target market is 1,648,896 units, and that, by 1992, this figure will have grown to 2,072,019 units.

Even to begin to handle this challenge would require an economic growth rate in the country of 5 per cent. Operating on 1 or 2 per cent or less is no good. A massive economic challenge stares the country in the face or the grim issue of just housing the population will knock us all for six. That's why for so long I have had deep reservations about whatever weakens South Africa's economy, for what weakens the economy seriously jeopardises the nation's long-term capability of downing both the urbanisation Goliath and the other closely related one of unemployment.

V UNEMPLOYMENT

The total black (African) population of South Africa is estimated to be twenty-eight million. Of those potentially employable, 26 per cent are unable to find work, but in Port Elizabeth's black townships, when our Africa Enterprise team was ministering there three or four years ago, the average unemployment rate was found to be 57 per cent. In one we went into, it was 75 per cent. In another near Grahamstown it was 90 per cent.

If the economy enters more recession, through further sanctions, unrest, strikes, or whatever, that figure must increase. In fact, our economy must be robust enough to provide at least four hundred thousand new jobs per year for the more than sixteen hundred black people a day coming on to the job market.

This leads many to observe that South Africa is sitting on an economic time bomb. Further contributing to the time bomb is not only our very rapidly increasing population, as stated, but the fact that the majority will probably be inadequately educated and trained. Beyond that, even if they were adequately educated and trained, jobs are not in the present convulsions being created sufficiently fast. Result? As many as six million economically active people will not be able to find jobs in ten years time *unless a huge level of resolution descends on the nation* to move along creative, positive, and godly lines and in harmonious togetherness to help fix things.

Certainly, sufficient jobs will never be found without grappling with the towering giant of inadequate education.

VI INADEQUATE EDUCATION

Not surprisingly, latest research statistics reveal a close correlation between employment, income and education. At present 23 per cent (ie three and a half million) of the adult black population have no formal education. And those in this category who do have work earn only about R180 per month.

Significantly 76 per cent of this 'no formal education' category of blacks are unemployed.

Among black people who do have a university degree, however, (the total in South Africa being only twenty-five thousand), the income in 1989 of those working, was over R2,163 per month.[9] Clearly, then, where people *do* have adequate education, they are much more likely to be both employable and employed.

Heartbreak

So what then is adequate education? Let's take two case-studies. First there is Meshack Mphashoe who has just matriculated. He bids his mother goodbye from their neat brick-and-iron home in Bochebela township and sets out to find a job in nearby Bloemfontein. He is sure that he won't have any difficulty. 'After all,' he says to himself, 'I've been told that a matric certificate is the key to success.'

But Meshack is in for a rude surprise. No one has work for him. Even the employment agencies are unable to help. 'Perhaps if your spoken English had been better,' they say, 'you might have had a better chance.' Or, 'If you had taken accountancy or bookkeeping for matric.' They add his name to the long lists of names of work-seekers – each with a matric certificate and hope in their hearts.

So Meshack decides to apply to enter university. 'Perhaps I should study first,' he says. But again no luck because no space, although Meshack has an E symbol which is the lowest symbol acceptable to the university. So once more he finds himself on a waiting list containing hundreds of names.

Finally, Meshack applies to enter the local college of education. Here he is fairly sure of himself. He has a friend who was admitted to the college with an E symbol only last year. But again Meshack will be disappointed. This time he finds that if he had had mathematics or science on his certificate instead of biblical studies and agricultural science, he would have been accepted. Instead he is not, and his name goes on a list of three thousand students applying for a mere hundred first-year positions.

Meshack is typical of over 90 per cent of black school-leavers who *do* matriculate each year. Only 60 per cent of those who write matric pass and only 16 per cent of these have a pass adequate to secure any kind of university entrance. In other words, most have low symbols and most have taken subjects that will be of little help in finding employment, or of assisting them to study further. Meshack lives with heart-break.

Hope

Halfway across South Africa Victor Dlamini sits outside his parents' mud-and-wattle home on a white-owned farm near Pietermaritzburg. He too is clutching his matric certificate, but he is smiling. He has just received a bursary to enter the Mangosuthu Buthelezi Technikon at Umlazi to do a course in Electrical Engineering. His future is assured and he thanks his lucky stars that the teacher at the small farm school where he started his school career advised him to take mathematics and science as matriculation subjects. He need never look back. Victor is a young man of hope.

He is one of the fewer than 1 per cent of black school-leavers who will take up a technical career.

Meshack and Victor represent two sides of the education coin. There is in fact a mismatch between what is taught in the classroom and the employment needs of South Africa because those coming out of black schools – and, in fact, white ones also – are more geared for white collar work, if there is such, rather than for blue collar work, which is probably where some of the greatest economic needs and opportunities lie. Most people want education which is generally formative, liberal and in the classical tradition. But our economy, we are told, is not really calling for that.

Education and Employment Needs

Robin Cox, one of those passionately concerned about South Africa's educational problems recently brought to my attention some of its parameters.

'We have an education system which is unwieldy, controlled by some fourteen departments, and which seems to be lacking direction. Educationalists and business people are of the opinion that the present education system, a white dominated and implemented system, is not meeting the needs of the South African economy, particularly with reference to the need for more pupils to be trained in technical subjects.'

Here are some recent statistics from Cox and other researchers he has drawn on:

About 80 per cent of all white South African pupils follow academically orientated courses at school (liberal education in the classical tradition), while only 20 per cent opt for technically orientated courses. In black schools in 1981 a total of 99 per cent of all black high school pupils took the 'academic' route and not the technical one.

Of all South African manpower, 10 per cent is trained in technical subjects, but 75 per cent is needed.

In 1986, 14 per cent of *white* tertiary students were at technikons and 59 per cent at universities. In West Germany, as well as in the new industrial countries of the East, the distribution is reversed.

For every thousand black children entering primary school, *eight* graduate in science and technological subjects and *eight* graduate in commerce.

Of all South African scholars, 77 per cent are black. Of these, only five to eight hundred per annum *matriculate* with science and maths, and only two hundred pass at a level adequate to study mathematics at a tertiary level.

James Moulder, a professor at the University of Natal, calls this 'education for unemployment'. And lots of people aren't even getting that.

School Attendance

South Africa has nearly a million white pupils between the ages of six and sixteen for whom attendance at school is compulsory. Education is not compulsory for black pupils. Fig. 1 shows that of the 68 per cent, or seven million black pupils who *are* at school, just over half enter at the age of six. The rest enter later so that by ten years of age, most of the 68 per cent are in school. The graph then plummets like a hang glider in crash mode showing the high number of pupils who drop out of school before reaching matric level. By sixteen, only 20 per cent are still at school.

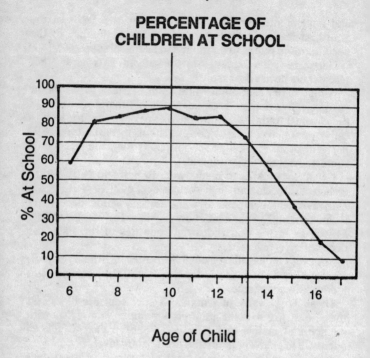

PERCENTAGE OF CHILDREN AT SCHOOL

This is well illustrated by our graph reflecting the 1988 situation and since then, we would guess, not much has improved.

Of the 650,000 black pupils per annum who drop out with inadequate education to become wage earners, (25 per cent of whom only have Grade I education!) less than 5 per cent drop out for ideological and political reasons. The vast majority leave because of poverty. They can't afford the bus fare, uniforms, books, school funds, etc.

Added to these are the estimated three million or more black young people between the ages of six and sixteen who could be at school and are not.

Failure Rate

Clearly poverty is not the only reason for dropping out; another is simply the high failure rate. Of the relatively few who get through to matric, 42 per cent fail that crucial exam. Another 42 per cent receive a certificate inadequate to secure them university entrance. Of the 16 per cent who do pass with a university entrance, the majority do not have mathematics or science and therefore have very limited options open to them. The blame for this lies mostly at apartheid's door and particularly in its past laws of job reservation. This prevented black people from entering most careers. Many became teachers as the only option open to them. Teaching was seen as a stepping stone to a brighter future. But many were and are unmotivated as teachers, they too being victims of poor education and poor training. In fact in 1989, 34 per cent of black teachers (according to the official government figure) were in teaching posts without a matric. In 1983 this figure was 74 per cent, so some progress has been made. But there are many miles to go! Currently strikes, boycotts, inadequate books and facilities and a high teacher-student ratio in classrooms are some of the other factors contributing to the high failure rate in schools.

Complicating things further is the fact that many students believe that if they return year after year, regardless of effort made or innate ability, or subjects taken, everyone must pass! Available facilities in schools are then inadequate to cope with the numbers wanting to repeat, for example, after a failed matric. This creates further problems of discontent, frustration and anger. What a complex vicious circle!

Another shattering and reinforcing statistic produced by Natal University academic, James Moulder, shows that 68 per cent of blacks can't read, write or count, 55 per cent of them adults over fifty.

Moulder suggests that not only are the majority of adult blacks easily exploited, but with percentages such as those given above, it is obvious that South Africa cannot have a strong, modern, driving economy, nor implement true democracy when it has only half the team suitably qualified. As long as this situation is allowed to exist, South Africa will never be a winning nation. Furthermore, if so many parents are illiterate, it is impossible for them to assist their children with homework or any other form of education.

Economic and Other Needs

The magnitude of the problem is evident when we grasp that while South Africa at present spends 6.5 per cent of its Gross National Product on education, it would require nearly 20 per cent of the country's whole GNP to be spent on education before anything like parity could be achieved.

Di Paice, writing in the April 1990 edition of *Leadership*, quotes Elisabeth Dostal of Stellenbosch University's *Future Research Institute*:

> Black education requires R42 billion – more than triple the approximately R13 billion allocated to it by the 1990/91 national budget, and more than half the entire budget of R72 billion – to bring it in line with white education, using per capita parity with whites as the norm . . . In addition, 8,000 new teachers and 345 schools, each catering for 500 pupils, are needed each year to accommodate the children who annually enter the system.[10]

On these facts, it has been calculated that South Africa is almost two hundred thousand teachers short.

Black educationalist, Bozie Mabogoane, makes the additional point:

> No matter how much money is pumped into black education, no matter how many highly qualified teachers are employed in black schools or how sincere and well meaning the minister and his officials may be, *separate is regarded as unequal* and people will continue to speak of inferior, slave education. Although People's Education will take us on to the road to broader and genuine educational success, the first step to be taken is a single education department.[11]

With such a Goliath as inadequate education and its attendant problems waiting to be tackled, a number of Davids have stepped forward from the world of private enterprise. The black-led National Education Crisis Committee is one. Foundations and trusts have also been created, often through the efforts of individuals, with the express purpose of raising money for educational development and improvement. The *Palabora Foundation* and the *Get Ahead Foundation* are but two of these. Working from Phalaborwa and Pretoria respectively these foundations co-operate with disadvantaged communities in different parts of South Africa, working with them to chip away at the apartheid structure through the development of imaginative educational programmes.

With education needing all hands to the pumps, the Church should also make it a major priority to get back once again into education in a big way, and to make the kind of distinguished contribution it was bringing before Bantu Education came along in the 1950s and shut all the mission schools.

Poverty, population growth, urbanisation, unemployment, poor or no education. These indeed are grim Goliaths which stalk the land. Yet these are by no means all. Others, as foreboding, we can but mention.

VII AGRICULTURE

Themba Ngomane's story referred to earlier in connection with urbanisation, touches on some of the environmental issues and alerts us to another Goliath in terms of our agricultural needs.

South Africa has 50,000 white farmers with an average of 1,700ha per farmer. But 700,000 black farmers have an average of 22ha per farmer and 14 million people (42 per cent) live in the homelands which occupy 13 per cent of the land. Agricultural production of the homelands can meet only 16 per cent of the residents' own food needs. Less than 10 per cent of production reaches the market. These are a few of the facts.

Then there are cattle. These are owned for social security reasons and overstocking is consequently widespread. In the Transkei the number of cattle is double what it should be for long-term sustained production. Desertification linked to overgrazing is causing the Karoo to extend northward and eastward and three million hectares of grazing have been spoilt in the Transvaal because of bush encroachment as a result of mismanagement. A further 14 million hectares are at risk. The amount of South African soil lost annually would fill enough trucks to go bumper to bumper seven times around the earth. One third of Africa suffers from famine. South Africa could suffer the same.[12]

VIII   THE WILD-CARD OF AIDS

Many aspects of South Africa's health situation deserve mention, but space forbids. However one aspect of South African health cannot be omitted. This is the wild-card of Aids.

And let us be warned by the Ugandan experience where some 82 per cent of the total population are estimated now to be HIV positive. As to South Africa, a doctor recently said to me: 'This country could be brought to bankruptcy by Aids. It is set to hit us in epidemic proportions. And Aids patients are very expensive indeed to treat and take a long time to die. In fact the Aids bill, if tackled properly, could totally swamp the national budget. I don't know what we can do.'

Some of the facts on the situation are as follows. In March 1990 the SA Blood Transfusion Services found that 2 per cent of their black blood donors were Aids HIV serum positive. They have noticed that over the last couple of years, the incidence has been doubling every eight months. For example, in the Transkei regions, two years ago there were three cases. Last year twelve cases, and in 1990 in the first quarter twelve cases. So a further forty-eight cases were projected for 1990. If those trends continued, by December 1990 the figure would have been 4 per cent, by September 1991 8 per cent, by June 1992 16 per cent, by March 1993 32 per cent and by December 1993 64 per cent.

The projected incidence of Aids HIV serum positive reaching this staggering total is dependent, of course, on ongoing sexual promiscuity and contaminated blood, etc, which may not occur. But if it does, as seems likely, the people with Aids serum positive will reach theoretical maximum by September 1994. Then these people will die within five to twenty years. This is horrific. Let it also be noted, however, this fatality rate will not solve, as many callously suggest, the problem of population explosion, because up to twenty years is a long time during which much more breeding can take place.

By any reckoning this adds up to a massive crisis. Not all South Africans believe this. It is even thought by many that reports of the seriousness of this threat are a propaganda ploy. In another legacy of apartheid, many black people doubt the integrity and trustworthiness of the authorities regarding Aids. This semi-wilful ignorance of the threat compounds it that much more perilously.

IX TOWARDS SOME SOLUTIONS

The giants abound, as we have seen, and we have not done much more than touch their surface to register the various threats, perils and challenges which are before us. At the start I said this sort of overview was necessary 'lest those who are not victims miss the full dimensions of what love must tackle', and tackle it we can and must by God's grace, and in the context of a major, every member, national effort. A Dunkirk-type, 'all hands on deck' movement of national self-help must be embarked upon.

How are we to begin? Here are three first steps towards solutions, three initial stones in our weaponry.

Know the Facts

Research shows most white South Africans are unaware of the real plight of black South Africans. The average white South African says, 'Oh, our tax subsidises blacks, we give them everything, they burn their schools, they are breeding themselves into sub-human poverty, and they don't deserve better.' Most whites are not fully aware of the degree to which black people have been wickedly discriminated against, or of how unscrupulous legislation has prevented them from being adequately educated and prevented them from competing economically.

As many whites are ignorant about black feelings, so many

black people are ignorant about the economic realities. In fact, only 3 per cent of all black adults have ever studied any aspect of economics (eg bookkeeping). Thus surveys have shown that many black South Africans have the perception that because South Africa has most of the world's gold and diamonds then surely we must have most of the world's money. This is an inaccurate perception because the real wealth of a nation is not based on raw materials alone but on the skills, educational levels and productivity of its people.

Thus Japan with its limited mineral resources, but technologically advanced work force, is wealthy while South Africa with its rich mineral resources but poor educational levels is not wealthy. Although the average black South African believes that we are one of the richest countries in the world and redistribution of wealth is a short step away, in fact, if we divided the GNP by the number of South Africans, we would be getting about R5,000 per person per annum. This puts South Africa in the same league as Chile, Venezuela and Bolivia, while Japan's per capita income is about R55,000 per annum! The reality is that we in South Africa do not have huge amounts of money for redistribution. The challenge is adequately to redistribute existing profits so as to create work and generate wealth. More of that in the next chapter.

Clearly the key thing is for us to invest in skills for our people and a wise use of resources. So, for example, we sell a ton of iron ore to Japan for so many rand and then get it back as a Toyota for which we pay a thousand times the sum! Thus does Japan, with its skills, benefit while we, without them, do not! As distorted perceptions influence the choices we make, we all need to seek out the real facts. Each person should be informed and help others to be informed. It is the first step in facing the problems and in positively finding ways to defeat our Goliaths.

Seek Understanding of Each Other

Never was there a greater need than now for South Africa's peoples to seek understanding of each other and discover a genuine togetherness. As leaders seek now to come together and to dismantle apartheid, *each* of us needs to see how we have all been victims of it and how we all need now to help in the process of ending our 'apartness' by a spirit of national 'togetherness' and pulling together.

We are all victims of a terrible prejudice which has come about as a result of this wretched and artificial separation. In consequence we stereotype and caricature. The average black caricatures the average white as being callous and indifferent while whites caricature blacks as lazy and incompetent. Thinking economically, the average black caricatures free enterprise or capitalism as having its own grasping, extortionate and exploitive agenda and as synonymous with apartheid.[13]

Whites, thinking economically and looking at the rest of Africa, see all blacks as inept socialists who will wreck in no time any economy they get their hands on.

All this kind of thing must stop as we seek each other out in order to understand each other, analyse our problems together and seek solutions in positive partnership.

Be responsible

In Chapter 8 we saw that in Wilberforce 'Christian love led naturally into a sense of responsibility to care for the poor, broken and defenceless' and that 'all were responsible to do something about it'. Christian love in Wilberforce and his friends 'gave birth to a moral sentiment that permanently changed England's attitude to distant and defenceless peoples and to her own brutal and degraded masses at home'. We need that Christian love. We need that moral reawakening on a national level to help defeat the giants.

Perhaps here it is instructive to think back to Tex Harris, the United States consul in Durban and his comment also quoted in Chapter 8: 'It is frightening to me as an American and as a Christian . . . that so many people in South Africa are afraid to make a commitment to work for a new day. Everyone sees this as someone else's work.'

Fortunately we have been able to look at some who see nation-saving and nation-building as their work. But every one of us needs to see it as our own responsibility, as something each of us can and must do. For example, if someone has education or a special skill, then he or she should offer their services creatively at some point of need, even if only for an hour a week. Whatever anyone can do, they should do.

Some of the sorts of options people could consider are listed in Appendix A. Please look at it. But in considering these, the value of planning together with those in need must be kept in mind.

When I spoke with Langschmidt in Johannesburg, he stressed this point, saying,

We cannot plan *for* people, we have to plan *with* them. And a process of planning with them might be slow and painful because the fact is that many South Africans are poorly educated and don't understand many of the realities that educated people take for granted. Trust may therefore be tentative, and instead of taking minutes of discussion to develop, it might take years. But take the years we must, if we need to, because we cannot any more just do things patronisingly for people in need.[14]

Tex Harris brings us back also to the faith component: 'Through people's faith in Jesus Christ they can act on the basis of a set of principles which at the basic bottom line are nation-building in nature. It is in the hearts of individual people that the real answer lies. Not in some distant political achievement worked out at the top.'

South Africa has all the resources – political, material, intellectual and spiritual – to save itself. Now it must harness these and do so.

My firm conviction stands that we can indeed dent, if not defeat, our Goliaths as we obey the words of St John in Scripture: 'Let us not love in word or speech but in deed and in truth' (1 John 3:18 RSV).

God grant that we may be enabled to do so. Likewise God be thanked who has matched us with this hour.

14   Structural Sharing

The simple point is that if a Constitution does not reflect an already existing consensus on the nature of political society, then no Constitution can fabricate this.

Frederick van Zyl Slabbert

South Africa can make history. We have all the ingredients to turn expectations upside down and to show that we can achieve things contrary to all national and international expectations.

Chief Mangosuthu Buthelezi

I have news for you – Nationalisation is not the only word in the economic vocabulary of the ANC.

Dr Nelson Mandela

Wealth cannot be redistributed for social services, or any other for that matter, unless it is first created.

Harry Schwarz

Each of you should look not only to your own interests, but also to the interests of others.

Philippians 2:4

With those giants and their awesome magnitude still very much in our minds, we are inevitably constrained to think about some of the structural, economic and political needs of our land.

Reporting on the Oslo Conference on 'The Anatomy of Hate', in September 1990, Lance Morrow in an essay in *Time Magazine* (September 17th, 1990) noted that there were two kinds of people there – the *subjectivists* (poets and moralists) who looked for the seeds of hatred within the human heart, and the *objectivists* (economists, historians, lawyers) who 'dismissed such vaporings and located the causes of hatred in the conditions of people's lives'.

There is no need to set the two in antithesis, for both are true. Even so, moralising alone is inadequate and perhaps there was validity, after listening to extensive moralising, in the impatient outburst at the conference from Elena Bonner, Andrei Sakharov's widow: 'Moral concepts are lovely, but the key is governing these things by law.'

She was right. To whatever extent we have moralised about the love ethic in politics, we get nowhere unless finally such concerns and principles become enshrined in law and in structures of justice, democracy and economic fair play.

Arrow

South African blacks know this to be true. South African whites somewhat anxiously fear it to be so. That is why when Nelson Mandela on the day of his release spoke about 'nationalising' the commanding heights of the South African economy, his message went like an arrow through both black and white hearts.

'That's right, that must be done, that will fix things,' said Ntsu Ramahadi, a student in Soweto.

'Oh, No! I don't believe it,' moaned Herby Brentford, a white businessman in the Free State. 'That will wreck everything.'

The idea that the gold mines, banks and other major business enterprises might be nationalised and that land might be redistributed sent as many chills through the white business sector as it sent cheers through the black consumer sector.

Sitting in his London lounge, and watching the speech on TV, investor Harry Singleton leaped from his chair. 'This is madness. How can Dr Mandela possibly talk like this after everything socialist in Eastern Europe has collapsed! And look at those disastrous African socialist countries! This scares the pants off me.'

In one sentence Nelson Mandela catapulted the economic debate to new levels of intensity.

As we have seen, the issue at heart is the imbalances of wealth between black and white and most especially the chronic poverty of so many blacks. We have to ask ourselves which economic system will change this.

Root Causes

This requires, initially, a journey back to some of the root causes creating the economic imbalance.

Clearly it is our long and sad political history which has brought us to this place. Most notable in the twentieth century were the Land Acts. The one in 1913 allowed blacks to occupy but not own 7 per cent of the land, while the 1936 Act, in a fit of political generosity, nearly doubled the figure to 13 per cent. This assured poverty for the blacks and wealth for the whites who owned the other 87 per cent.

The Pass Laws and Migratory Labour, which have fuelled economic growth since the days when diamonds and gold were first discovered, inevitably enabled white South Africans to prosper hugely while black South Africans sank. Black people were allowed to sell their labour in the towns and cities, but were not allowed to settle there with their families. Since they were regarded as temporary residents, there was no reason to provide them with adequate schools, shops, roads, housing or other basic infrastructures. They were allowed to fill only the lowest-paid occupations and in many cases were prevented from bettering themselves or owning businesses.

Then, from 1948, came the formal apartheid system which imposed terrible restrictions on black South Africans, preventing free movement in the country. Where jobs were not available in places of residence, black people were not allowed to go in search of work in other areas.

Business and industry were often attracted to areas where there was a plentiful supply of labour: poorly-paid labour. There was very little incentive to pay a living wage. Hence the rampant prevalence of poverty.

Worse still, once poverty was in place, it trapped people into

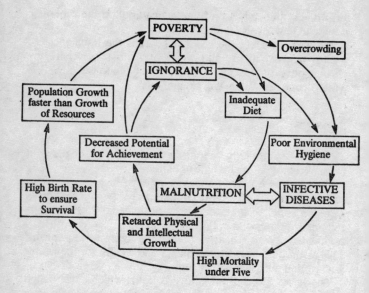

a downward spiral. One calamitous consequence followed another.

In *The Passing Summer*, I catalogue and explain this spiral. The reader may like to check pages 194–5. Pictorially you see it in the diagram above.

And so it is that political injustice, economic exploitation and chronic poverty combine to put economic reform and a total political overhaul at the top of every black person's agenda for the coming years.

Beyond that, poverty generates the desperation and mindlessness of endemic violence. Says noted South African columnist Gerald Shaw: 'Much of the current violence is rooted . . . in poverty and everything that goes with poverty.'[1]

On reading Shaw's column, I was reminded of the day we went round the Edendale Valley amid all that violence. Again and again, briefers and interviewers said, 'And of course so many of these people are *unemployed*. That is a big part of the problem.'

Fundamental Changes

Poverty in South Africa clearly has to be tackled and up-rooted. Our white society needs to recognise that basic and fundamental changes are necessary, although we can't be so naïve as to think there are any quick fixes. Dr Ramphele maintains that as a minimum basis there must be no discrimination on the basis of race or sex, and there must be the implementation of an egalitarian society.

Wilson and Ramphele make this observation:

> Undoubtedly one of the most important shifts in the balance of power between black and white in South Africa since the National Party came to power in 1948 is the rise of the independent trade union movement since 1972. Indeed, it is the most important shift in power since the Act of Union in 1909 entrenched white control in a structure that provided blacks with no peaceful political path to government.
>
> The fundamental importance of trade union movements, whether in Charles Dickens's England or in Lech Walesa's Poland, is that workers, backed by real power, are able to challenge the economic and political establishment. Trade unions have proved to be the workers' most effective weapon against dehumanisation and exploitation at the work place. The independent trade union movement in South Africa is no exception.[2]

That is so. But the challenge is to involve all society, not just the trade unions, in working creatively and sacrificially on solutions, not only to dismantle all discrimination and inequality in our society, but to start to live and behave as a new society as quickly as we can.

Everyone should look to their own structures, be they in business, commerce, industry, education, the Church, or the home, and get things right there. Everyone has to be committed to being part of the solution rather than part of the problem. This practice must start now. And not just with aid programmes, à la Ethiopia. While these may be necessary at times as a first step, and an ambulance exercise, the real uprooting of poverty begins with the enrichment and re-building of communities and societies.

And if it does not, John Kennedy's celebrated dictum will hold true: 'If a free society cannot help the many who are poor, it cannot save the few who are rich.'

Don't Kill the Goose

It remains true that in the process of seeking to fix the problem, we must not kill the goose which lays the golden egg.

Trade unions are effective weapons for challenging injustice, but they need to be used responsibly. The warning should not go unheeded that sometimes, in asking for unrealistically high wages, 'trade unions risk pricing themselves out of the market and companies will turn to less labour intensive production methods'.[3] Even now many are automating.

It is very crucial that our economy stays strong, so that not only may our expanding population be satisfactorily fed, housed, clothed and educated, but also so that political change and its complex processes may be adequately financed.

'The resolution of most of the burning issues facing South Africa,' says economist Lawrence McCrystal, 'such as unemployment, urbanisation and housing, excessive population growth, haves and have-nots, and upgrading the quality of the urban environment, depends on *the capacity of the economy to deliver the means to resolve them.*'[4]

Therefore, to let the economy of this land be shattered, to allow foreign investment to flee, to diminish employment prospects for the sixteen hundred or so people a day coming into the job market and to tear ourselves to pieces by violence, political convulsion and economic slow down, and then finally to imagine that a socio-economic and political phoenix will rise magically from the ashes to bless the new South Africa – all that is just political and economic pipe-dreaming.

No, the economy must keep developing. But what we *can't* have is a situation here where the rich keep getting richer and the poor keep getting poorer.

Principles

So then, what Scriptural principles can serve as guidelines for an economic order relevant to this context, especially when we bear in mind that the basic purpose of economic life is to 'liberate us from being dominated by scarcity and to provide us with the conditions necessary to a fully human existence'?[5]

Here are several, most of which were referred to in *The Passing Summer* (pp. 456ff).

1 *Does the system take material adequacy and absence of scarcity seriously as a basic ingredient in human well-being?*
Does it labour for financial adequacy and the elimination of poverty?

2 *Does the economic system fit God's intentions for the good of humankind?*
God is always concerned for the good of *all*. Does the economic system remember, as the Bible endlessly exhorts, the poor and the economically weak? And will it in the South African context take cognisance of the statistic stated earlier that in South Africa some 60.5 per cent of our black population live in poverty? And in some areas the figure is much higher.

3 *Is the system committed to the basic unity of the human family?*
Does the system for example work against divisive tendencies between people or groups of people? And does it also support and strengthen the basic unit of the family? Obviously in the past things like migratory labour have devastated black family life.

4 *Does the system include belief in the value of each individual human being?*
Is it committed to individual freedom and opportunity for individual creative development and expression?

5 *Does it consider human beings to be equal?*
At the very least this means management seeing workers not just as impersonal cogs in a *money-orientated* exploitation process but as valued participants in a *people-orientated* production process.

6 *Does it take seriously the universality of human sinfulness and make provision for the effects of self-centredness?*

This is not to eliminate economic incentive but to curtail greed.

7 *Does the system also recognise the individual's right to sell his or her labour and be worthily remunerated?*

These criteria should apply not only to a new economic order but to our private lives and our daily dealings with people.

Two major challenges that face South African economic thinkers are how to share the cake more fairly, and how to expand it. Failure on either score imperils the overall society. Henry Ford II put it this way: 'If business concentrates on *social goals* at the sacrifice of short-term profit, it may find itself destroyed by its neglect of its long-term future. On the other hand, if it emphasises *profit* to the exclusion of social goals, it may find itself abandoned and destroyed by the people it has ignored.'

Sharing the Cake

In this we need to bear in mind the fact mentioned in the last chapter that if the GNP were divided by the total number of all potential wage-earning South Africans, each would receive about R5,600 per annum. (For Canada the figure is about R50,000). Our nationwide per capita income would therefore not be very much; the figure highlights the necessity of both sharing wealth and expanding it. However our challenge in this section relates primarily to bringing about a fairer distribution of wealth, land, resources and the means of production.

The early Christians shared their lives both spiritually and economically (see Acts 2:42–7), though this was very difficult to maintain. The accumulation of huge wealth among some while others languished in abject poverty was very much contrary to the generous principles they sought to follow. Paul spells out some of these principles in 2 Corinthians 8 – his famous chapter on financial giving. The Apostle is not concerned here to see everyone equal in poverty, but rather everyone equal in financial adequacy.

Economic reform must therefore go hand in glove with political reform. So must land reform. No longer may 84 per cent of the people *occupy* only 13 per cent of the land while 16 per cent *own* 87 per cent! This shattering land apportionment explains why blacks will not accept the view that all we need to do is open the system and encourage blacks to enter it on a basis of 'equal opportunity'. 'The morality of this view,' notes educator Franklin Sonn, 'must be questioned against the larger issue of whether a late start is indeed an equal start.' He adds: 'If the business sector does not give real attention to the question of historic disadvantagement and backlogs, the very basis of the current economic system will remain seriously at peril.'[6]

Because of these things, massive land reform and redistribution, such as took place in Japan after the war, will be necessary in South Africa before final solutions are reached.

Incidentally, the Japanese programme, which was accompanied by great projects of agricultural education, resulted in the transfer of ownership of 35 per cent of the total cultivated area of Japan. It involved the purchase of over thirty million different pieces of land from two million families and their resale to over five million families. It can be done.

So equal education, equal job opportunities, equal access to the labour market, equal pay for equal work, equal access to land and resource acquisition – all this should be provided for in an economic system reflecting the politics of love.

Expanding the Cake

To avoid a sharing of abject poverty and misery, as is found in many African countries where so-called 'African Socialism' is the economic way, it is necessary for economic thinkers to grapple as much with the processes of wealth creation as with those of wealth distribution – though this must not involve raping the earth or denuding it of its God-given resources.

Commenting on this, a Durban economist wrote to me:

The South African economy has in fact been in a downward spiral for years with pitifully low and negative growth rates due to high inflation, and poor productivity. This has been caused by the inefficiency and magnitude of our State bureaucratic systems, and the lack of a truly free-market economy through over-concentration of centralised power structures, high defence costs, heavy emigration of skilled professionals, and all exacerbated by the international economic sanctions campaign. However, I am convinced that we have the human skills and are blessed by natural resources in South Africa so that we can in fact massively increase our economic growth rate, if allowed to operate in a free and open society and in a deregulated environment. South Africans have proved their resourcefulness and skills over and over again when let loose in international competition. That resourcefulness and those skills must come to our economic rescue now, as never before.

In this regard we underline again that economic planners need to do some fresh thinking about South Africa's problem of selling most of its raw materials at low cost to other countries instead of using them here to create finished items that would sell at much higher prices. For example research shows that Italy makes more money from South African gold than South Africa does. They buy our gold and turn it into jewellery, with the original gold being worth only 13 per cent of the finished item! Instead we should be training people in South Africa to design and make jewellery to gain full benefit from our gold resources. The same is true of our sand which people in other countries make into silicone chips. Likewise with our coal. And on and on.[7]

Clearly here the educational needs highlighted in Chapter 13 have huge spin-offs if properly addressed. Said Mahatma Gandhi, 'Look after the people, and the population will look after themselves.'

The point, as mentioned, is that wealth is generated not simply from countries rich in natural or mineral resources but from countries which invest in equipping their people with abilities and skills.

But let it be noted that this educational push needs to be in a democratic and economically free environment. Argentina with its rich resources complicated its educational and economic efforts with an undemocratic military dictatorship and ended up with a failing economy.

Russia pushed on education, but cluttered its economy with

heavy socialist controls which likewise produced, as they have everywhere, a failing economy.

Socialism's Failure

In an amazing article, Nic Borain, son of Alex Borain of IDASA, wrote as an initially enthusiastic young socialist of his visit with other young men to the USSR. He told how the editor of the Moscow Communist Youth Organisation daily newspaper, though a political appointee,

> harangued us for over an hour about the evils and absolute unworkability of socialism . . . The sentiments behind these ragings were expressed by everyone we met – more cautiously by only the most senior members of the Communist Party.
>
> The economy has clearly failed to meet the requirements of the population and the list of reasons they give reads like a tirade from the New Right!
>
> Almost without exception the people we spoke to blamed socialism for their ills. When those of us with deep philosophical and political roots in the South African socialist movement protested that it wasn't socialism per se that was the problem, but rather the errors committed in the building of the society and economy of the Soviet Union specifically, we were laughed out of court.
>
> 'It is the ideas themselves; 1917 was a disaster for us; we need a market economy.' was a refrain we heard time and time again.[8]

Ken Owen, Editor of Johannesburg's *Business Day* wrote, after being in the USSR, of 'Life in a Failed Society'. The signs of disintegration were everywhere, he said, and the socialist 'system is finally grinding to a halt. For the average Soviet citizen, life is reduced to an endless, arduous struggle for simple shelter, food and clothing.'[9]

Another friend of mine just back from the Soviet Union said simply: 'It is a Third World country.'

Such a failed system will not do for South Africa.

Wealth Creation

With the challenge before us both to generate wealth and
distribute it, to expand the cake and share it, one has to ask
which economic system best accomplishes both these goals.

Beyond Ideology

In thinking about these questions we have registered the
abject failure of most socialist economies. Yet under South
African style capitalism, most blacks feel they have been
exploited, impoverished and often dehumanised. Wealth has
been generated, to be sure, but it has all gone to whites.
Miserable though the failures of socialism are, are they not
preferable to life under capitalism?

These realities and sentiments being what they are, South
African leaders are required by the exigencies of history and
the different types of failure in each economic system, to begin
to struggle with the mechanisms of getting beyond economic
ideology to a system tailor-made for our unique context.

The point to hold on to is the Christian one, that *the ultimate
purpose of an economic framework is to provide everyone with
material adequacy necessary for a fully human existence*.
Beyond that, the system needs to enhance the higher ends of
social harmony, human brotherhood and our God-given
creativity.

To achieve this we need to hold all ideologies, political or
economic, loosely. We need to give flexible space for compromise and for human ingenuity in this unique South African
context to work out something original and ingenious.

That's why the endless touting around of comparisons
between 'Socialism' and 'Capitalism' (both swear-words to
different groups of people) may have now lost its usefulness.

Professor James Moulder, of Natal University, is totally
forthright on this and says:

When capitalists and socialists argue with each other, they
have two options: either they compare their theories or they
can compare facts about capitalist and socialist societies.

More often than not, they don't do either of these things. What they do instead is compare their THEORIES with FACTS about the societies their opponents admire. In other words, instead of comparing theories (apples with apples) or comparing facts (oranges with oranges), they compare their theories (apples) with their opponent's facts (oranges). Not surprisingly, when they do this they confuse each other as well as everyone else.

This is certainly true in South Africa. They end up, in Moulder's view, arguing that 'the unattainable society which they can imagine is superior to the unattainable society which their opponents can imagine'.

The point he makes is that 'in both societies, some people get sacrificed. In capitalist societies some poeple end up in slums, all in the sacred name of competition and freedom, in socialist societies some people end up in labour camps, all in the sacred name of compassion and equality.'[10]

Moulder declares the debate between capitalism and socialism sterile. This seems to me hugely relevant for South Africa. The debate has become sterile because, while many blacks are using socialist language, whites can point to the collapse of socialism throughout Eastern Europe and much of the Soviet Union, and to the disaster areas of virtually all socialist countries in Africa. And while whites sing the praises of free enterprise, blacks can point to their exploitation under that system. The fact is that neither the capitalism which blacks have experienced in South Africa nor the socialism which many blacks have experienced in the rest of Africa would seem to suit our needs.

Moving Goalposts

'What we need to do,' Moulder says, 'is to move the goalposts. We need to create a debate in which nobody can blur the difference between what we would like to have and what we can have.' Moulder notes that there are certainly two things we cannot have. And this strikes me as fundamental.

'We cannot have a free enterprise system that doesn't

generate inequality and poverty. We cannot have an egalitarian system that isn't restrictive and frustrating.'

Moulder's means of moving the goalposts involves adopting three rules.

The first says that it is always legitimate to ask how we can increase the productivity and wealth of an organisation or society.

Rule two says it is always legitimate to ask how we can distribute the profits and wealth of an organisation or society more fairly.

The third rule says it is never legitimate to ask the first question (the one about productivity and wealth) without asking the second question (the one about distribution and fairness). And the other way round.

For Moulder, it is rule three which is the really crucial one, and which moves the goalposts and changes the name of the game. 'Just as anyone who wants to increase wealth must tell us how to distribute it more fairly, so anyone who wants to distribute wealth more fairly must tell us how to generate it more effectively and efficiently.'[11]

If in the negotiating process of the years ahead and in the accompanying economic debate this kind of line could be meaningfully pursued, then we have a chance, and a good one, of breaking away from the mistakes of the past. We might manage to avert our eyes from the manifest weaknesses of both systems, and move from the realm of economic swearwords into that of Christian principle. The result will surely be a creative form of mixed economy geared uniquely to our special needs.

Love

At which point, I believe, we can and should unashamedly reintroduce the idea of Christian love. I know it is a mistake to imagine that any human institution, constitution or economic system can perfectly represent Christian principle, since human frailty and sin will inevitably infect the whole human enterprise. But it is equally mistaken to imagine that human institutions cannot approximate in greater or lesser degree to that love principle which takes the other person or group seriously.

So it is that creative social and economic systems should represent both a positive expression of love and a serious effort to guard against the effects of human sinfulness.

Constitutional Structures

All of which brings us to the imperative of building love into our constitutional structures as well as our economic ones.

In this we are aiming for justice, both political and economic. Reinhold Niebuhr once noted that 'It is man's capacity for justice which makes democracy possible, but man's inclination to injustice which makes democracy necessary.'

That means fighting against what the Psalmists called 'mischief by statute' (Ps. 94:20 RSV).

'Can wicked rulers,' he prayed to God, 'be allied with thee, who frame mischief by statute?'

To the Psalmist the idea seemed incongruous indeed. Yet mischief by statute is exactly what South Africa's racist constitutions from 1910 onwards have produced. Pray God we don't repeat the errors as we seek in these years ahead to frame a new constitution for the new day.

All of which brings us once more to the matter of principle. And thankfully this is something many others hold to as well. I have had the privilege over a good many years now of getting to know the ANC's Thabo Mbeki, and the thing which has always struck me was the sense of principled reasonableness which seemed to control him.

In an interview (February 1990) he made the point that in drawing up a new constitution 'the first step has to be an agreement among everybody about *the fundamental principles* that must underline that new constitution'.[12]

It is so. And in my view a Christian consensus here should be possible. For what is justice other than power implementing love? And how is justice to be secured on the widest basis for the greatest number other than by entrenching it within the structural framework of a constitution which controls and governs a nation's life?

In the first instance, a constitution is nothing more than a piece of paper with some ideas on it about how a society should be structured and run.

Obviously the strength of a constitution lies in the commitment to those words written on that piece of paper. Clearly the American constitution is strong because the American nation as a whole is committed to what is written on that piece of paper. Previous South African constitutions, by contrast, have been very weak because the majority of the nation has not been committed to them or willing to live under their ideas.

A Common Framework

South Africa needs a common framework of principles through which it will come not only to a constitutional settlement but to social peace and harmony. These principles will have to bridge the various divides of current party politics and yet be specific and definite enough to provide a clear basis for a new dispensation.

It is here that the Christian community can make a real contribution in being consensus builders, bearing public witness to the fact that there is such a set of principles and such a framework available in Scripture. These principles transcend the various racial and ideological barriers in our present society and they can therefore be a real meeting point for our diverse peoples. I myself believe that it is important for there to be a general acceptance in the South African public mind about the kind of thing we can and should be aiming for. And we all need to be working to achieve it, however modestly, in our own individual spheres of influence.

Christian peacemakers can also set and hold these biblical principles before the major political players in the situation.

Some of the principles Christians would want recognised in the constitution-making process are these:

1 *Human Equality under God*
Nothing in a constitution should undermine or deny this principle and everything should affirm it.
2 *Human Freedom under God*
A godly constitution will balance each person's freedom in relation to the freedom and dignity of others.

3 *Social Justice under God*
In enshrining social justice, the constitution South Africa
needs must also provide mechanisms whereby a more just
distribution of material resources between rich and poor can
take place.
4 *Government under God*
A godly constitution will recognise that the state is God's
servant. Its power and task are derived from God so it may
serve the good of all its citizens equally. Its legitimacy will be
judged by the people in terms of how truly it does this.
5 *Human Sinfulness under God*
God has judged us sinners. And so we are. Therefore constitution designers should be aware of this and guard most
especially against the human lust for excessive power and
control. This would argue for some measure of dispersing
power away from an excessively powerful centre.

Human Rights

Not surprisingly all the above have implications for human
rights. These, says Bernard Lategan, 'are based on God's
claim on people to treat their fellow human beings in the same
way as He does . . . For this reason it is essential that a society
should spell out basic rights to which everyone can appeal.'[13]

   In thinking from a Christian perspective, some of the rights
we are required to secure would be these.
(i)   The sanctity of life.
(ii)   The right not to be permanently deprived of land.
(iii) Equality of opportunity both in the political system and
in education and work.
(iv) The right to rest from work one day in seven.
(v)   The right of a servant of God not to be the slave of
anyone else.
(vi) The right to be protected from the arbitrary exercise of
power.
(vii) Equality before the law.
(viii) The right to an environment which enables quality of life
and is a result of responsible stewardship of the earth's
resources.
(ix) The right of the individual to sell his or her labour.

At heart, all human rights revolve around the right to be fully human, for the origin of human rights lies in creation. We never acquired these rights or had them conferred on us by a government. We have had them from the beginning, having received them with the gift of life from the hand of our Creator. They are inherent in our creation.

God's Personhood

In *The Passing Summer* (pp. 453–4), I noted that one could also think of certain constitutional principles which flow simply from the nature of God Himself as we see this in the Bible.

Pride of place would go to where the Bible starts with *God as Creator*. Having created human beings in His image, all are equally valuable, and their value should be reflected in the way a constitution is set up. There will be no structural abuse of human dignity and value. Nor will individuals or groups of individuals be treated preferentially in a way which offends or violates the equality or value of others. A godly constitution will therefore avoid all discrimination.

The Scriptures also depict *God as fatherly and loving*, which means that the spirit of mercy, care and protection for His children is integral to His make-up. In constitutional terms, this clearly implies the merciful protection and care of those least able to protect and care for themselves. It also implies an insured care and protection of our shared environment.

The Scriptures also present us with a *God of justice*. This is clear in both the Old Testament and in the New. This would speak constitutionally of equality of protection for all before the law. Such concerns involve protecting the rule of law, namely the right to stand innocent until proven guilty; the right to confront one's accuser; the right of all to representation in courts; and the possibility of winning one's case even if it is against the state.

The Bible as a whole, and the politics of love as a concept, call for us to protect the rights of the individual and to set him above the state in importance and value. Winston Churchill once wrote:

No one can think clearly or sensibly about the vast and burning topic of the value of a constitution without in the first instance making up his mind upon the fundamental issue. Does he value the State above the citizen or the citizen above the State? Does the Government exist for the individual, or do the individuals exist for the Government?[14]

Laurie Ackermann, Professor of Human Rights Law at the University of Stellenbosch, has stressed that the rights of people to enjoy their own culture or use their own language should be protected as *individual* rights. Group rights, he says, should simply be the aggregate of a particular group's individual rights. In this sense, and only in this sense, does the idea of group rights have a validity not open to abuse. Professor Ackermann comments:

If, however, the protection of group rights means the entrenchment of existing privileges and restrictions such as, for example, superior residential areas, superior government schools, superior hospitals and so forth, such a concept would be wholly at variance with universal, international, human rights norms.[15]

Of course, in South Africa we are polarised by group rights and this looks in the negotiating phase of the de Klerk–ANC era to be looming as a significant obstacle. To surrender this is understandably the Becher's Brook hurdle for Afrikaners. Yet in a new heterogeneous society, individuals can and will associate themselves freely in groupings to protect their individual rights on a collective basis. But the focus must be kept more on the individual than the group, thereby minimising the racial mindset of group confrontation and group conflict.

All of this is of course very general. Much more specific and politically worked out constitutional thinking from a Christian perspective has been done by a Christian group based in Johannesburg called CREID (Christian Research, Education and Information for Democracy). The group periodically releases specially-focused research papers, some popular, some academic, on a wide variety of issues, 'constitution' being one of them. Readers wanting to get into this question

more fully should write to CREID at 8 Inverness Road,
Westdene, Johannesburg, 2029.

Majority Rule

That noted, we need to ask a final question. Will all our
national thinking on constitutions, etc lead to so-called majority rule? The answer must be yes. Apart from anything else,
sheer arithmetic and demographics affirm this to be so. By
2020 for example, less than thirty years from now, South
Africa could have ninety to a hundred million people, only
nine or ten million of whom will be white. There is no way
whites can remain the dominant political force.

But this is not so terrifying a prospect if we stop thinking
racially (which is what group rights is still doing) and start to
think of a *different sort* of majority rule – ie rule by a non-racial
majority of blacks and whites who all share the kind of values
we have sought to set forth in these pages.

To go any other way, for example clinging to the group
thing, and insisting on structural protection for whites so they
can never be dominated by a black majority, is only to prolong
the agony or precipitate a catastrophic racial civil war at worst.
So we should not proceed from the position that the group
concept is fundamental, otherwise we will jeopardise successful negotiations.

If whites will only capitulate on *racial and ethnic thinking*,
and engage more vigorously in the process of 'thinking nation'
and contending for certain biblical social values to control that
nation, then both a non-racial constitution, supported by a
majority of all South Africans, and a harmonious non-racial
society will emerge at this exciting end of Africa. And not only
we, but the world will be blessed and inspired.

We need to get away from race altogether so that we achieve
a 'common South Africanness'. Barbara Masebela, head of
the cultural department of the ANC, speaks from a black
perspective saying, 'We have to teach white South Africans
that they are not Europeans: they are Africans.'[16]

More than that they are human individuals. And from the
biblical point of view it is the human individual whose sacro-
sanctity is paramount. However, Sir Fred Catherwood of the

European Parliament says this does not excuse us of *concern* about people who rightly or wrongly see themselves as some form of minority group.[17]

Peace

As we seek to find peace and a new day, perhaps the words of the great St Paul can have relevance: 'If it is possible, as far as it depends on you, live at peace with everyone' (Rom. 12:18). The search for peace *must* finally find consummation in the working out of a righteous economic system and a constitution which will enshrine and protect the peace we all long for.

Both the processes and the final result are fragile in the extreme and can be jeopardised by power-hungry or selfish people, even by people who are not obviously any of these but who stick rigidly to their own thinking as the only way forward.

We might seem to have more than adequate grounds for profound discouragement, given the huge polarisations and anguished history of South Africa. But let us take heart from the fact that even George Washington, when he went to the Constitutional Convention of 1787, lamented as he did so: 'I almost despair of seeing a favourable issue to the proceedings of the Convention.'[18] But they won through. In South Africa we can do the same. And we must enshrine it in a consti-tutional framework for which generations of future non-racial South Africans will rise to bless us.

That will mean some mighty labours in negotiating the new day. And so to that we turn.

15   Negotiating the New Day

'Henceforth, everybody's political points of view will be tested against their realism, their workability and their fairness. The time for negotiation has arrived.'

President F W de Klerk

'I have cherished the ideal of a democratic and free society in which all persons live together in harmony and with equal opportunities.'

Dr Nelson Mandela

'Negotiating can be compared to a game of tennis. If one wants the game to continue to the end, one should never play in such a manner that the other person wants to leave the court.'

Wynand Malan

'Come now, let us reason together,' says the Lord.

Isaiah: 1:18

Each of you should look not only to your own interests, but also to the interests of others.

Philippians 2:4

Stephen Mulholland, a prominent South African editor has said the interesting thing about South Africa is that the answer to every question about what will happen is 'Yes'.

For example,   Could there be a military coup? Yes.
                Could there be a bloodbath? Yes.

Could there be a rightwing takeover? Yes.
Could there be a black Marxist takeover? Yes.
Could there be peaceful evolution? Yes.
Could there be more of the same, repression
    and reform? Yes.
What about a Federal System? Yes.
What about Rhodesia style hot-house econ-
    omic growth? Yes.
Could there be economic collapse? Yes.
Do you want to stay here? Yes!
Do you want to emigrate? Yes!!!

CHOICES

The man speaks well, for it is so. But what of course he means
is that the future in South Africa is still open. No historical
inevitabilities doom us to catastrophe, assure us of success or
predestine us to one option or another. We can in fact still
determine our future by choices and most especially by the
mechanisms of negotiation.

The time for this may well be short, however, in terms of
determining our future. Beyond that there is a real danger of
South Africa's future being decided by unthinking and unin-
formed emotional reaction instead. This is because of the
many people, especially among the traumatised youth, whose
ability to make informed decisions and wise choices has been
eroded by the structures of apartheid, by poverty and little
education, by ill health, by violence and much more. All of
which presses us to make our choices rightly under God and
with all speed.

Right Spirit

If we are to succeed we will need the right spirit and the power
of a key Pauline principle.

It is found in Paul's letter to the Philippians and is a simple
sentence of political and spiritual dynamite: 'Each of you

should look not only to your own interests, but also to the
interests of others' (2:4).

It is preceded by an almost equally compelling first-cousin
utterance: 'Do nothing out of selfish ambition or vain conceit,
but in humility consider others better than yourselves' (v. 3).

Our principle is climaxed by Paul's elucidation of the example of Jesus himself who being in the very nature of God,
did not consider equality with God something to be grasped,
but made *himself* nothing, taking the very nature of a
servant . . . 'And being found in appearance as a man, he
humbled himself and became obedient to death – even death
on a cross!' (vv. 6–8).

In September 1985, the day after the ending of the National
Initiative for Reconciliation Conference in Pietermaritzburg,
we convened at the African Enterprise centre an extraordinary gathering that had this passage as its charter and guiding
principle for the day.

The range of people extended from Archbishop Desmond
Tutu (then Bishop of Johannesburg) to Chief Mangosuthu
Buthelezi; from Dr Frederick van Zyl Slabbert (then leader of
the opposition) to National Party MPs Leon Wessels, now
Deputy Minister of Foreign Affairs, and Wynand Malan, later
a co-leader of the Democratic Party. Dr Johan Heyns, Mod-
erator of the Dutch Reformed Church, was sitting down with
Alan Paton and with Archbishop Philip Russell, then
Archbishop of Cape Town and head of the Anglican Church.
P W Botha's chaplain was there, so too Dr Khoza Mgojo of
Federal Seminary, Dr Stanley Mogoba and Caesar Molebatsi
among others.

The full range of people was truly remarkable. So was the
diversity of backgrounds and history. Yet, in spite of that, we
had an astonishing encounter with that scripture of 'looking to
the interests of others' truly controlling us.

Archbishop Tutu opened his comments by saying: 'I am
amazed that we are sitting together like this – me with a
Krugersdorp Nationalist MP! [Leon Wessels] It is incredible.'

Asked van Zyl Slabbert: 'How on earth did such a group get
together?'

All of us felt that sense of incredulity. Most particularly
when we related meaningfully. Now, of course, in the

Mandela–de Klerk era, with the government doing the unthinkable and sitting with the ANC, all we were into that day in 1985 seems tame. Yet it did not seem so then.

No Scapegoating

If thinking of the interests of others is one of the first preconditions for negotiating a new future for South Africa, another has to be a repentance all round from our delicious but perilous delights in endless scapegoating.

Scapegoating is the process of laying *all* the blame at the door of one's adversary, but always exonerating oneself. The trouble with it is that it is dangerously self-deceiving and enslaving. For it absolves us from facing our own political and social sins and their consequences.

This mechanism of shifting blame on to others is one which we all use. Husbands do it with wives, and bosses with staff. An angry child kicks the dog. South African whites blame all problems on the ANC or on sanctions or the communists. Blacks blame 'the system'. If you drop the ball at some point you can blame whites, capitalists, the system, the West or neo-colonialists.

None of this is to say that the scapegoat we choose, whether communist, capitalist or nationalist (white or black), may not in fact be responsible for some or most of what we accuse him, but this does not move us forward. Beyond that, when indulged in during a negotiating exercise, especially a delicate one, it becomes a wrecker. Hence Wynand Malan's point: 'Negotiating can be compared to a game of tennis. If one wants the game to continue to the end, one should never play in such a manner that the other person wants to leave the court.'

If we want to know whether we are scapegoating, there is a clue that may help: if we are fixated on unpleasant actions or strategies in others, without humbly and repentantly acknowledging blame in ourselves, then we are scapegoating. Many of us in South Africa have developed this into an art form.

Blame and Forgiveness

To avoid it two things are necessary. The first is humility to acknowledge blame. Not like the woman telling her friend,

'I've a wonderful husband, you know. Whenever we argue and he's in the wrong he always apologises.'

'What about when you're in the wrong?' queried her friend.

'Oh, that's never happened,' came the cheerful reply!

The second quality necessary to lift us out of the scapegoating syndrome is the spirit of forgiveness, already alluded to earlier in this volume.

Clearly this is crucial in our South African logjam if negotiations are finally to succeed at both macro and micro levels. For example, unless blacks can forgive the CP its attitudes or actions, and the CP some of the black acts of violence, final negotiations will bog down. Likewise unless ANC leaders can forgive wrongs imagined or real in the political life, for example, of Inkatha leaders and vice versa, then a dangerous logjam will indefinitely threaten the whole peace process. Forgiveness, of course, does not condone wrong things done, but faces them, judges them and then lets them go.

Prisoners of History

Sometimes our rising to this kind of demand is facilitated by grasping the degree to which other people, especially one's adversaries, are prisoners of their personal or group history. Inevitably we all have our histories and these *do* tend to imprison us, sometimes in spite of ourselves. Just think of Peter, after three years with Jesus, seeing Him risen, having six weeks of post-resurrection teaching, finally going through the tumultuous phenomenon of Pentecost, *yet* when Jesus tells him to go to Cornelius, the Gentile, Peter is captive to his Jewish history and conditioning and says No! (Acts 10:14). Finally he does go and is freed from his prison of prejudice by Cornelius, the Gentile, who is freed from his prejudice too by the visit to his home of Peter, the Jew. Thus do adversaries or strangers each have the keys to each other's prisons.

Imagine if each group in South Africa understood the principle of history's imprisonments and applied it mercifully and in the spirit of understanding to their particular antagonists, not just at top level negotiations, but on every level of interaction.

Everybody There

This becomes particularly important when one thinks in the macro exercise not just of *some*, but of *all* the major players who will need to be party to a lasting solution for South Africa.

The tricky thing, of course, is that there are not just two sides, there are many, and everybody needs to be both heard and involved in the negotiating process. Asked in an interview who 'everybody' was, Thabo Mbeki of the ANC replied: 'Everybody is everybody.'[1]

And if this is truly to happen, *every* individual in the country has a part to play in promoting, encouraging and enabling the process to take place. Wherever there is interaction, each of us needs to make room for people from different groups and of differing opinions, seeking opportunities to hear them and interact with them.

The *Johannesburg Sunday Star* (March 25th, 1990) carried an article entitled 'You're in Their Power'. Surrounding the article were no less than twenty-three photographs of key players in the national situation. The article's subtitle read: 'And the good news is they're all committed to negotiation'. Sadly missing were the faces of hardliners such as Andries Treurnicht of the Conservative Party and Eugene Terreblanche of the AWB (Afrikaner Weerstandbeweging = Afrikaner Resistance Movement). Regardless of that, Afrikaner conservatives will have to be accommodated in a final solution. Otherwise there is trouble ahead.

But the range of other people listed in the article reveals the magnitude of the negotiation Everest which straddles the South African horizon in these coming years.

The article spoke of at least twelve or thirteen groupings and concluded: 'After a lot of history and a bit of luck, South Africa's political leaders who really count are heading for the negotiating table after shooting at each other for about thirty years. They could broker peace – or another thirty year war.'

This is true. And if it is not to be a thirty year war, something more than a bit of luck is needed – namely a supernatural effort under God to work those laws we have talked about and need constantly to remind ourselves of: firstly seeing politics as all about people; secondly dealing with one's own heart; thirdly humanising and forgiving the enemy; fourthly hearing and seeing the other side.

Such laws do not, of course, allow any group to sideline or marginalise another group with a significant power base. On this we need to be very clear.

The Perils of Marginalising

Dr Oscar Dhlomo, a political thinker of clarity and perception, has written of the perilous consequences when Frelimo in Mozambique marginalised Renamo, when Angola's MPLA tried to marginalise UNITA, when Zimbabwe's ZANU did the same with Nkomo's ZAPU, and when P W Botha did it in his era with the ANC and PAC, etc. He also cautions about the consequences here in terms of past or possibly future ANC or PAC postures towards Chief Mangosuthu Buthelezi and Inkatha.

> What are the lessons we should learn from all this? If you want to bring out the worst instincts of any political party, you do that by trying to marginalise it and pretend that it does not exist or that it does not count in the political game. The more the party is ignored the more it embarks on exploits that will draw attention to it and convince those who are attempting to isolate it that it is still a force to reckon with. The 'we have nothing to lose' syndrome takes over and the party exempts itself from acting within the bounds of decency in its 'struggle for survival' and to draw attention to itself.

Dhlomo concludes with both a warning and a challenge:

> There is no doubt that if our major political parties continue to play the game of political isolation, marginalisation, vilification and name calling, then we have a very good chance of going through the Mozambican, Angolan and Zimbabwean experience. It is our political leaders who have the power to save us from this impending catastrophe, and they can do so by talking to each other and encouraging their parties and followers to practise mutual respect, mutual

tolerance and freedom of association. This is what multi-party democracy is all about.[2]

THE PROCESS ITSELF

And so to the negotiating process itself, so crucial as our pathway into the future at dozens of levels. The fact is that whatever happens at top level in the forthcoming months or years, South Africa is probably set for at least a decade of negotiations at every level. So we are going to have to give more and more attention to the process and its mechanisms if we are to come through satisfactorily.

Negotiation can be defined as a coming together of two or more parties in a voluntary problem-solving exercise by which they seek to resolve their differences through joint analysis of the problem before them, leading into an accord which will positively control their future relationship in facing a given situation or task. If this negotiating process is successfully carried out, it will leave the various parties in harmony, satisfaction and even mutual cooperation in terms of their shared futures. The negotiating process should also create a positive springboard and a sure foundation for future problem-solving and ongoing relationships.

Real negotiations will not involve an uneasy and precarious truce where no one feels satisfied, all feel cheated and everyone sees himself as a loser thanks to the tactics of the other side. Rather all will feel winners because the bigger cause of a united and harmonious nation will have been served as each group has made space for the other and their heritage in each contribution to the overall solution of the common problem.

Models

While the big debate goes on at the macro level, negotiation will also need to go on at the micro level, between, for example, workers and managers, household employers and employees over adequate wages, pension schemes, housing conditions etc. Youngsters will bargain with their teachers over school conditions and company workers over mechanisms of advancement and promotion. And at a thousand other levels every day, people will be working out their human and personal relationships across every conceivable kind of divide.

Those who can't or won't enter the negotiating process or the spirit of it, as it goes on around them, will be crushed, broken or overtaken by the traumas of clinging rigidly to the patterns, policies and perceptions of the past.

Eyes on the Prize

Key to this whole process is seeing what we want and 'keeping our eyes on the prize', to cull a line from an American Civil Rights song.

The point is that both leaders and led in South Africa must get a clear vision of what we want and then be part of the process of going for it. We want peace and harmony and not civil war in our nation. We also want justice in our structures, not a travesty of it as we have had in the past. We want a nation where people are treated equally and fairly and are not discriminated against on the basis of colour. We want a way of life and an economy from which all benefit fairly, and in which everyone is pulling together in the same direction rather than pulling in opposite directions with the consequences of fragmentation, paralysis and alienation. We want government to work smoothly and according to a mutually agreed constitution and not via coups, convulsions and political cataclysms. We want the young to inherit a land which is happy and whole and not a lamentable landscape of ashes and tragedy.

If that is going to happen we are all going to have to negotiate it in the spirit of our Jehovah God who still says: 'Come now, let us reason together' (Isaiah 1:18).

Forsaking the Old Ways

This will mean that on every level of interaction we will also have to forsake some of our old ways of thinking about how negotiation gets done. This will start with abandoning the old assumption which says, 'When I am weak, *how* can I compromise? And when I am strong, *why* should I compromise?'

The rude shocks from Soweto 1976 onwards should have disabused all whites of such ideas, but seemingly they did not. At least not until the late 1980s when almost all the wheels of our society appeared to be coming off amidst the rage, frustration and overwhelming indignation of a black majority which had finally run out of patience.

As far as the negotiating process goes, we will also have to forsake our old ways of seeing it simply as a means of lifting the battlefield on to the bargaining table. It will not do for us to see negotiation as two opponents who have exhausted each other in civil conflict, achieving a dubious and unstable peace through a process of desperate, often hostile demands. Out of that kind of mechanism can come only an uneasy and precarious truce, and this must have the seeds of its own destruction within it.

Likewise, as underlined, we will have to move away from all negotiating postures which see only the other person or the other side as the cause of all problems, feeling that everything would come right if only the other people saw it and did it our way. This will mean that we stop fishing for answers through various kinds of uneasy compromise when each side has surrendered some little slice of its winner-take-all position.

As Ron Kraybill, of the Centre for Intergroup Studies in Cape Town, has noted, that sort of agreement, if reached, is grudging and trust remains low. Its enforcement is difficult and there is the daunting task for those who strike such a deal of convincing their supporters to back an agreement for which the baseline rationale is, 'It's the best we could get, given the circumstances'.

If this is the kind of negotiation South Africans have in mind when they anticipate their future – and indications are that many important players do envision something similar – then the process promises to be long and arduous indeed.

Given the depths of the South African conflict, only a partnership rather than an adversarial approach will finally work, or we will all be the losers. So will our children and grandchildren. The crux is for all sides to grasp that the desire of people to be free, to achieve their fullest potential, to have their human dignity, and be respected and esteemed and to secure this as a legacy for their children is so fundamental that

no long-term answers will come for our land while any constituency or group feels these treasured values denied them.

A Better Way

In fact, the partnership alternative in negotiation is still open
to us and achievable. A body of research and theoretical
interpretation has emerged over the last decade that, if recognised by key players in South Africa, could profoundly enhance the possibilities for successful resolution of the issues
facing this country.[3]

Kraybill has noted the now established fact that so-called
'*deep rooted conflicts*' are not resolved by negotiated settlements which are some form of uneasy and precarious truce,
with neither side really satisfied. Research seems to have
shown that deep rooted conflicts are not based, in fact, on
relatively transitory interests, such as land, money and natural
resources, but rather revolved around 'basic human needs',
these being needs that in fact go deeper than the material side
of things.

They include, for example, security, identity, recognition
and human development, all of which are universal needs and
which 'cannot be compromised, cannot be made subject to
some legal judgement, and cannot be bargained'.

Because they are so basic it is manifestly clear that they have
to be truly resolved rather than superficially resolved by 'the
mere restraint of the opponent'.

Kraybill makes the further key observation that due to the
irrepressible nature of the basic human needs, each party to a
dispute has to recognise that its own long-term interests are
best served 'by recognising, honouring and collaborating to
meet the basic needs of an opponent with whom one is locked
in such conflict'.

The point for each side to grasp is that in deep rooted
conflict, the beginning of it all lies in the 'limitless realm of the
human spirit, not in matter'.

This being the case, the evidence now emerging from all
modern research shows that traditional diplomacy and traditional power politics are not in fact able to bring the kind of

solutions in these situations which will become stable and lasting. Old-style adversarial methods, where the other partner remains an enemy or an opponent, will not do.

A far more satisfactory route, say Kraybill and other modern negotiators, is that of starting not from fixed demands and positions, but from a deeply serious attempt in the first instance 'to grasp the dimensions of the problems they are proposing to solve. Agreeing on the problems is often hard, but once this is accomplished, discussion about solutions becomes far more efficient . . . There should be no proposals put forward by any side until the analysis of the situation is complete and a definition of the situation is agreed.'

So joint analysis, what some call mutual education, is where the whole thing has to begin.[4]

This kind of analysis and mutual education then sets the stage for problem solving which becomes a joint activity to resolve the problems which all parties have agreed upon in principle as needing to be addressed.

Useful Tools

Edward de Bono, another expert on conflict resolution, enforces this viewpoint. He writes,

> In conflict situations each side is much concerned with its own point of view. The opposing point of view is only examined as a commander might examine opposing defences: for weaknesses. Yet an understanding of the other point of view is a most useful step in conflict resolution.'

For this he employs two tools which he calls the EBS and OPV principles.

> EBS stands for *Examine Both Sides*. It is traditional role reversal in which each side has to spell out – honestly and fully – the case for the other side.
>
> OPV stands for *Other People's Views*. This is a more general-purpose tool. 'Thinking-situations' usually involve many more parties than the person doing the thinking. The OPV exercise consists of identifying these other parties and

then looking at the world from the point of view of each of these parties.[5]

Working with Enemies

Even when it initially seems, says de Bono, that it is sworn enemies who are sitting down to negotiate, nevertheless they can come to see the need to sort things out for everyone's good.

Let it also be noted that when the cost of failing to find one another will be so catastrophically high, as is the case with South Africa, then even 'enemies' need to become 'partners' in working out mutually beneficial solutions.

So the basic question returns to us. How can all sides be made to feel that both they and their former adversaries have their inalienable rights secured? To secure this for all is the first and much to be coveted prize. And keeping all eyes on that prize is the starting point of a successfully negotiated future.

The Final Test

Obviously the final test of whether negotiations are successful is whether constituencies, what Kraybill calls 'the folks back home', will buy it. In this he underlines the findings of most modern research – namely that if the *process* in the thing is right and is felt by the respective constituencies to be 'representative, fair and reasonable', the outcome, even where it involves, as it inevitably must, some compromise on original positions, will in fact be accepted. And the 'solution' will stick. This underlines even further why all parties and groups of consequence must be there and why marginalising any major player is so perilous.

Using all Resources

Given what can disrupt the negotiating process – ranging from spiritual strongholds of darkness and evil (2 Cor. 10ff) to division, deliberate disruption, civil war, factional or tribal violence, human intransigence with its consequent deadlocks

and all its dreary scenarios – we need to be resolute and ready
to employ all possible means to ensure its success.

The first is human help – I mean help from other humans,
third-party ones. The second part of the answer lies in help
from the Lord our God. That we'll come to in our final
chapter.

Mediators

But first, third-party help. It may and could come to this,
especially once the negotiating process moves beyond the
Government and the ANC to, for example the Afrikaner
radicals on the right and certain black radicals on the far left.

This third-party help could come from a carefully selected
group of well-chosen church people, or from a friendly government (eg UK, USA or Zimbabwe), or from a concerned
international group (eg UN or OAU) or even what Frederick
van Zyl Slabbert calls 'a Council of Wise Men' – a group of
independent people of good will, whether from inside or
outside South Africa.

And if the country is still locked in violence by the time the
negotiating process is formally underway, and if the South
African army and police force have fully lost credibility with
the masses, then let a UN peace-keeping force be brought in as
in Namibia, to restore order and guard the peace while the
negotiating process gets underway. In Namibia, as Van Zyl
Slabbert has noted, UNTAG said, 'We will provide the stability, you sort out the politics.' If South Africa finally needs
that, let's get it. National pride should not rule out such an
eventuality.

Facilitators

On the other hand, maybe the more effective way might be the
humbler, more hidden means of what some call 'Track Two
Diplomacy'. And certainly here leading Christians and church
leaders can and should play a part.

Track Two Diplomacy is an informal, non-governmental
and unofficial type of networking which can contribute
to conflict resolution. It usually involves private people, or

groups of people within a country or from different countries, and generally they are outside formal governmental power structures.

This is what Clem Sunter is talking about when he says that sometimes one has to start low and aim high. This means starting with informal mediation and 'meeting on an informal basis, without publicity, where you feel out the other side and build up a degree of trust'.[6]

Track One diplomacy, on the other hand, is government-to-government, or party-to-party. This is formal, sometimes even rigid, official interaction between instructed representatives of sovereign states or political groupings.

Some of the qualities needed for Track Two Diplomacy, say some of the experts, are as follows, and not surprisingly these are all related to the Christian understanding of love and its demands.

(i) *Compassion*   This means sympathy, enthusiasm, and the desire to help.

(ii) *Patience*   This means not imposing our sense of time or schedule on the whole process.

(iii) *Humility*   We remember that we don't have all the answers to the world's problems, nor are we infallible Mr fix-its.

(iv) *Integrity*   An essential quality for establishing trust between all the parties involved.

(v) *Absence of Personal Interest*   The facilitator cannot advance his or her interests at the expense of the alienated parties involved.

But for this sort of facilitation to take place it will require most especially humility moving in love and love moving in humility. Otherwise the person or group with reconciling concerns will spoil and impede the whole process.

The Rev Athol Jennings of the Vuleka Trust and Koinonia Centre near Durban has thankfully sought in compassionate concern to do this sort of work in many instances. But he has a caution: 'Facilitators need constantly to question themselves as to their reasons for being in such a position. What are we wanting out of it? What are the gains and losses for us?'[7]

Jennings quotes Robert Theobald in *An Alternative Future*

for America: 'You can try to get the credit for social change, or you can get social change. You cannot have both.'

Jennings also stresses that this kind of concern, so much needed in South Africa at so many levels, is costly stuff.

Professor David Bosch underlined this in 1985 at the launching of the National Initiative for Reconciliation: 'Reconciliation takes place when two opposing forces clash and somebody gets crushed in between.'[8]

Like marriage, therefore, facilitation should not be entered upon lightly, inadvisedly or wantonly! But many, motivated by *agape* love, will have to try and not be overly fearful of failing.

Partnership

What is really needed in South Africa is a spirit of reconciliation leading into true negotiation where there is partnership, team work and mutual respect between people who have hitherto been on different sides of the divide. For this to be reached, all sides need to participate in the mutual education of the other and in a joint analysis of the common problem or conflict facing them.

In South Africa we have a common problem, namely how people of different races, backgrounds and cultures can all live harmoniously and creatively together. The glorious challenge now is for everybody to work together to analyse the components of that problem and then solve it to the mutual benefit of all, so that all feel they have come out winners.

Spiritually Demanding

To reach this sort of place is impossible without God's love at work in us. It is also spiritually demanding because it requires, with the Lord's help and in the spirit of the Calvary Christ, that we first of all deal with our own hearts and become willing to forgive one another, to stop demonising one another, to repent of our insatiable desires to vindicate ourselves and blame the other party, and then on top of all of that to work positively and resolutely towards harmony, and co-operation in the spirit of mutual trust.

Of course it should also be noted, as far as Christians are concerned, that if political choices are made in the negotiating process which involve a manifest denial of God and of Christian principle, then Christians, who cannot deny their God, will face massive dilemmas. Thus a communist government for Christians would be a wrong choice for South Africa because communism is not only a failed and unworkable system worldwide, but more seriously it is both atheistic and philosophically materialistic.

That means, as I noted in *The Passing Summer* (pp. 407–8), that it sees

> nothing in the world except matter in motion. It is not Absolute Spirit that leads us forward in history but *Absolute Matter*. This of course robs a person of spiritual essence and makes him totally material and fully explicable in terms of the natural processes at work in physics and chemistry. It opens the door to the devaluation of human life, along with incredible programmes of human and social engineering, regardless of the cost in human life or suffering . . . This evaluation and treatment of human life is anathema to the Christian.

But let us not, therefore, out of default or lack of will to pursue godly and Christian options, tumble into a politically bankrupt and economically discredited atheistic system. That could only take us from the frying pan into the fire.

Aiming for a noble and constitutional ideal enshrining Christian principles might at first blush seem utopian and out of reach for the kinds of sinners we all are. Yet I remain convinced that if the Lord our God can call us into His presence to 'reason together' about our sins before Him (Isa. 1:18), then, I imagine He has the not unreasonable expectation that we could come together and reason together about our sins and failures before each other. After all He asked us to pray 'Thy Kingdom come, Thy will be done on earth as it is in heaven.' This being the case we should in faith work and pray to that end.

That we need help from on high, no one would deny. That it is available, no one should doubt. No one.

Part Five

LOVE MOVING IN POWER

Power belongs to God.

Psalm 62:11 RSV

16   Power for the Task

Jesus is eternally right. History is replete with the bleached bones of nations that refused to listen to Him.
                                        Martin Luther King

The voice of the people has been said to be the voice of God: and however generally this maxim has been quoted and believed, it is not true in fact.
Alexander Hamilton in USA Constitutional Convention,
                                        1787

Those who choose another god multiply their sorrows . . . [therefore] The Lord is my chosen portion and my cup.
                                        Psalm 16:4–5 RSV

All authority in heaven and on earth has been given to me.
                                        Jesus (Matt. 28:18)

Power is something in which most people are interested, but few know how to achieve it, or what to do with it if they get it.
    Some while ago I was introduced by a master at my son's school to a commentary by Spike Milligan on power as experienced in the British military. Various ranks from general down to sergeant-major were being described in descending order in these terms.

General: Leaps tall buildings with a single bound. More powerful than a steam engine, faster than a speeding bullet. Gives policy to GOD.

Colonel: Leaps short buildings with a single bound. More powerful than a shunting engine. Is just as fast as a speeding bullet. Walks on water (if the sea is calm). Talks with GOD.

Lt Colonel: Leaps short buildings with a running start in favourable winds. Is almost as powerful as a speeding bullet. Walks on water in indoor swimming pools. Talks with GOD if special request is approved.

With the *Major* and the *Captain* things deteriorate further. Then there is . . .

The Lieutenant: He runs into tall buildings. Recognises trains two out of three times. Is not issued with ammunition. Can stay afloat if properly instructed in the use of a life-jacket. Talks to walls.

2nd Lieutenant: Falls over doorsteps while trying to enter buildings. Says, 'Look at Choo Choo.' Is *never* issued with a gun or ammunition. Plays in mud puddles. Mumbles to himself.

Sgt Major: Lifts tall buildings and walks under them. Kicks steam engines off the track. Catches speeding bullets in his teeth and eats them. Freezes water with a single glance . . . HE IS GOD![1]

Well, maybe, maybe not. In fact for sure not unless the typist's error on a congregational service sheet is right. Instead of the popular chorus 'Our God reigns', a mistakenly inserted 's' produced for the Sunday service the announcement of the opening song as 'Our God resigns'!

In thinking of our apparent powerlessness in face of the awesome nature of the South African challenge, we can be thankful indeed that God has not resigned, though on South Africa He must often have been tempted to do so, and that we are not required to have a buck private's view of the universe where omnipotence is vested in the Sgt Major!

So we can embrace afresh and believe with new intensity the Psalmist's word that 'power belongs to God' (Ps. 62:11 RSV). We can also rest our destinies on Jesus's forthright and characteristically personal claim: 'All authority in heaven and on earth has been given to me' (Matt. 28:18). That could hardly be plainer. Beyond that He could affirm, 'apart from me you can do nothing' (John 15:5) – not even get South Africa on the right track!

The fact is, as underlined earlier in the book, that this is His world. '. . . all things were created through him and for him . . . and in him all things hold together' (Col. 1:16–17 RSV). And it is He who upholds 'the universe by his word of power' (Heb. 1:3 RSV).

If His word of power upholds the universe then no doubt our need here in South Africa is to come in real dependence on the living God to show us the way through. After all, as Franky Schaeffer has noted, 'Either God is the Creator of the whole person, the whole universe, and all of reality and existence, or he is the Creator of none of it.'[2]

Elijah expressed it this way, 'How long will you waver between two opinions? If the Lord is God, follow him' (1 Kings 18:21).

And it is only in truly following Him that His power is available to us.

SOURCE OF POWER

When Job, from the depths of his problems and agonies, began to question God, he received back a shattering questionnaire from the God in whom all power resides. Here are a few of the divine questions:

Where were you when I laid the foundation of the earth? (38:4).

Or who shut in the sea with doors . . . and said, 'Thus far shall you come, and no farther, and here shall your proud waves be stayed'? (38:8–11).

Have you commanded the morning since your days began, and caused the dawn to know its place? (38:12).

Have you entered the storehouses of the snow, or have you seen the storehouses of the hail? (38:22).

Is the wild ox willing to serve you? Will he spend the night at your crib? (39:9).

Do you give the horse his might? (39:19).

Is it by your wisdom that the hawk soars, and spreads his wings toward the south? Is it at your command that the eagle mounts up and makes his nest on high? (39:26–7).

Have you an arm like God? (40:9, all verses RSV).

To be sure, not. No wonder Job had to reply: 'Behold, I am of small account; what shall I answer thee?' (40:4 RSV). Then he added 'I know that thou canst do all things, and that no purpose of thine can be thwarted' (42:2 RSV).

Here is the creative power and majesty of God set forth for Job and all to see. Without doubt such a one can guide, enable and control our affairs if we will let Him. And He will give us power for the task at hand if we ask Him for it.

I   THE POWER OF SIGHT

It is one thing to say all that and another to *see* it.

In the Old Testament the servant of the prophet Elisha is terrified of the huge Syrian army because he does not see God's power and thus the assurance of victory. So Elisha prays: 'O Lord, open his eyes so that he may see' (2 Kings 6:17). Elisha by faith could *see* the power of God. So, says the text, 'The Lord opened the servant's eyes, and he looked and *saw* the hills full of horses and chariots of fire all round Elisha' (v. 17).

The problem is that modern human beings trust only what they can *see* in the physical world around us. And so God and the spirit world get left out.

Modern secularists, who see the universe as the accidental result of impersonal energy plus time plus chance, will simply live with total indifference to the idea of a spirit world.

But God and His truth are eternal, the same yesterday, today and for ever. They are not made true by our recognition or failure to see. A table may be in the same room as a blind man whether he sees it or not. He may deny its presence and claim it is not there until he bumps into it!

We should not be among those lamented by the prophet Jeremiah who said, 'You foolish and senseless people, who have eyes but do not see' (Jer. 5:21). We *need* the power of spiritual sight.

In fact our crying need in South Africa now is to move into the future with spectacles on which enable us to see our reality and challenges from the viewpoint of faith in a *God Who is There*.

Seeing the Invisible

As said earlier in Chapter 6 it all begins with the individual finding that transforming experience of 'new birth' (John 3). As Jesus said 'Truly, truly, I say to you, unless one is born anew, he cannot *see* the kingdom of God' (v. 3 RSV). In other words, without the new birth in the Holy Spirit we will not even see, let alone enter the kingdom (v. 5).

Then there is the Apostle Paul who, somewhat in the manner of Elisha, could pray for the blinded Ephesians that 'the eyes of your heart' would be 'enlightened in order that you may know . . . his incomparably great power for us who believe' (Eph. 1:18, 19). The power of God is there, but we must see it.

Professor Calvin Cook, recently retired Professor of Church History at Rhodes, has been living for some years with the threat of failing sight hanging over him.

A little while ago he wrote to me about this.

The whole experience has released a number of things within me, particularly the fear of 'uselessness'. It would be marvellous if my wonderfully acute sight could be restored: I could thunder out the line that has become a favourite recently 'Ye blind, behold your Saviour come . . .' At the same time, all my life I have suffered from the delusion that the Kingdom of God had to wait for my arrival on the scene and not the reverse. What really matters is not whether or not we physically see, but firstly what others may see in us of

his glory and then secondly to live 'as seeing the invisible.'
So in a wonderful way I've been able to wait and hope
expectantly for what the Lord is going to do. Either way is a
miracle: to restore physical sight or to see the invisible.[3]

To see the invisible. That's it. After all, by faith, we see radio
waves, electricity, and the wind, all invisible realities, and we
harness them. Why not with the Lord and His Spirit and His
power?

Helen Keller, though deaf, dumb and blind, could nevertheless see Christ and His power by faith. No wonder she could
observe that 'The only tragedy greater than being blind is to
have eyes and still not see.'

II   THE POWER OF HUMBLING
OURSELVES

Of course if we do *see* the Living God there in all His majesty,
power and holiness, it will lead us to humble ourselves both
before God and before one another. This is how God's power
is released in us.

Thus in the socio-political uncertainties after the death of
Judah's King Uzziah, following a long, successful and stable
reign, it was a mighty thing for the prophet Isaiah in the eighth
century BC to record 'I *saw* the Lord' (Isa. 6:1). As he did so he
saw God sovereign over history, holy beyond measure and
powerful in glory over 'the whole earth' (v. 3).

This drove the prophet into a deep and repentant humbling
of himself under God. 'Woe to me . . . I am ruined! For I am a
man of unclean lips, and I live among a people of unclean lips,
and *my eyes have seen* the King, the Lord Almighty' (v. 5).

If we in South Africa, or others in other nations of the world,
allow ourselves by faith 'to see the King, the Lord of Hosts',
we too will be driven in repentance and shame to acknowledge
our sinfulness and the futility of our independent and human-
istic efforts to pull our nations right by our own efforts.

Church

This applies especially in the church. I mentioned Calvin Cook just now. In that same letter he wrote to me,

> Oddly enough I've been feeling that most of our human schemes, especially some of our socio-political theologies are utterly utopian – a case of healing the wounds of my people lightly – until the church can move the mountains of garbage it used to call sin from the landscape. For until people see their sin and actually then receive and experience forgiveness, they will be unable to love and all our proposals for a new society will be unrealistic because we simply haven't the resources we need. More than that the immense heaps of unshriven sin that pile up like mine-dumps in homes, offices, sport and work places leave the whole community given over to maggots and flies! . . . To blame structures alone, and then to say that we can simply remove them, directs attention in a masterly fashion away from the Lamb of God who *alone* can take away the sins of the world.

Without the Lamb it's all maggots and flies! The phrase is reminiscent of Martin Luther King's that 'history is replete with the bleached bones [ie what's left after maggots and flies] of nations that refused to listen to Him [Jesus]'.

Humbling ourselves and facing our personal and national sins is no easy thing. But there is power available after we do.

Humble Before Each Other

One dimension of the power released in humbling ourselves before God is that of a new capacity to be more humble and flexible before each other. We would find ourselves ready not only to change our minds here and there but to recognise that our infallibility before one another may be less than total. We are delivered from sacrificing the good for want of the perfect.

The sort of humility I speak of, which makes historic breakthroughs possible, was amply demonstrated on September 17th, 1787 when after sixteen weeks of continuous work on the American constitution, Benjamin Franklin stood up holding a piece of paper. His voice, by then being too strained and weak, he asked a colleague to read his humble and thankful sentiments at that historic moment:

> Mr President, I confess that there are several parts of this Constitution which I do not at present approve, but I am not sure I shall ever approve them. For, having lived long, I have experienced many instances of being obliged, by better information or fuller consideration, to change opinions, even on important subjects, which I once thought right, but found to be otherwise. It is therefore that, the older I grow, the more apt I am to doubt my own judgement, and to pay more respect to the judgement of others.
>
> I doubt too whether any other convention we can obtain may be able to make a better constitution. For, when you assemble a number of men to have the advantage of their joint wisdom, you inevitably assemble with those men all their prejudices, their passions, their errors of opinion, their local interests, and their selfish views. From such an assembly can a perfect production be expected? . . . Thus I consent, sir, to this Constitution, because I expect no better, and because I am not sure that it is not the best . . . and . . . I cannot help expressing a wish that every member of the Convention, who may still have objections to it, would with me, on this occasion, doubt a little of his own infallibility, and, to make manifest our unanimity, put his name to this instrument.[4]

The thing to grasp is that when we are humble before God and each other, then God Himself gets in the act. That is His promise. 'If my people, who are called by my name, will humble themselves and pray and seek my face and turn from their wicked ways, *then* will I hear from heaven and will forgive their sin and will heal their land' (2 Chron. 7:14).

Other Powers

Humbling ourselves under God also releases other powers, such as the power of forgiveness of which we have already spoken at length. To be sure, forgiving people is one of the toughest things any of us can ever be called on to do. But we can do it once we ourselves have experienced the *forgiving power of God* as Isaiah did once he had heard God's word: 'your guilt is taken away and your sin atoned for' (Isa. 6:7).

Having seen our sin, having humbled ourselves to confess it before God, having received His forgiveness, how can we do anything other than forgive those who have sinned against us?

Humbling ourselves under God also releases a new *hearing power in us*. Said Isaiah: 'I *heard* the voice of the Lord saying "Whom shall I send and who will go for us?"' Elsewhere in this book I mentioned my experience in Oxford in 1980 of sensing God's Word in my spirit saying, 'I have a way through for South Africa. But it will take a listening people.' Yes, we come to Him to listen and hear, not like the old American black in Tennessee who, when asked if he ever prayed replied, 'Why, sure I prays, even if only in an advisory capacity!' But perhaps we stop advising God and begin to listen and hear only after we've really *seen* Him, seen our sinfulness, cried out, 'Woe is me' and then received His forgiveness.

We have reflected on the power of sight and of humbling ourselves. Now thirdly, the power of strength in weakness.

III THE POWER OF STRENGTH IN WEAKNESS

Certainly it is only in listening to God and His Spirit within us that we can even begin to discover both the power of the Gospel and the mysterious power of weakness which goes with it and which is so often to the worldly mind counted as 'irrelevant'.

For the Apostle Paul there was no question of embarrassment over this humanly weak Gospel of Jesus Christ. Thus he could tell the Roman believers: 'I am not ashamed of the gospel, because it is the power of God for the salvation of everyone who believes, first for the Jew then for the Gentile' (Rom. 1:16).

In fact, to the erratic Corinthians he could specifically affirm that the Cross, though weak and foolish and a stumbling-block to the world, was nevertheless the repository of God's wisdom and power. So for Paul and for all Christians everywhere, 'God chose the foolish things of the world to shame the wise . . . the weak things of the world to shame the strong' (1 Cor. 1:27).

Courage to be Weak

The Christian must therefore be ready to embrace the paradox of finding power by manifesting what missiologist David Bosch calls 'the courage to be weak'.[5]

We must say this lest any still believe that the power of the Gospel and its way in society is a triumphalist, easy one, void of suffering and the Cross. It is not so.

Bosch, Chairman of South Africa's National Initiative for Reconciliation (NIR), can therefore tell us that in the spirituality we need for the South African road or any other we need to know that the true mission of Christians is the 'weakest and least impressive human activity imaginable, the very antithesis of a theology of glory. All this is so, not by accident but by definition. It is a necessary precondition for any authentic mission. In this Paul follows his Master.'[6]

This is not to contradict what we have said earlier in this book about the power of the Gospel to be salt and light in a society and to be a mighty agent of change, but only to note that it all happens, if we will allow it to, in the paradoxes of weakness and the way of the Cross, often with suffering.

Obligation to Love

Martin Luther King held to this paradox as he sensed the doubts of his followers about the Gospel way. He once wrote,

My friends, we have followed the so-called practical way for too long a time now, and it has led inexorably to deeper confusion and chaos. Time is cluttered with the wreckage of communities which surrendered to hatred and violence. For the salvation of our nation and the salvation of mankind, we must follow another way. This does not mean that we abandon our righteous efforts. With every ounce of our energy we must continue to rid this nation of the incubus of segregation. But we shall not in the process relinquish our privilege and our obligation to love. While abhorring segregation, we shall love the segregationist. This is the only way to create the beloved community.[7]

By that way of weakness the Gospel showed its power to bring love where there was no love, justice where there was no justice and hope where there was only despair.

IV THE POWER OF CHOICE

Whether of course we are ever to find the power of the Gospel operative in our lives or in our countries is a matter of choice.

Thus does the Lord's prophetic challenge from Moses still ring across the centuries in our ears. 'I call heaven and earth as witnesses against you that I have set before you life and death, blessings and curses. Now *choose* life, so that you and your children may live' (Deut. 30:19).

Joshua was equally precise: 'Choose for yourselves this day whom you will serve' (Josh. 24:15).

South Africa and South Africans and all people everywhere must make a choice. If we want the peculiar power of our God and His Spirit and Gospel to work in us and in our nations, we must choose it to be so.

Choosing to Give Ourselves

One old saint once put his prayer this way: 'Lord, I am Thine – by purchase, by conquest and by self-surrender.' The thing is that when we hear God's question, 'Whom shall I send?' and when we choose the Lord and His way, we are thereby also choosing to give ourselves to God Himself and His agenda for our lives. 'Here am I. Send me!' Not 'Here am I, send my sister.' Under God, it would be dynamite indeed if multitudes across South Africa would say and mean those five monumental words.

We also put ourselves at the place where we are ready to be divinely commissioned and sent forth for service. God who finally has our humble, attentive and obedient ear can at last express His commissioning power saying, 'Go and tell this people' (Isaiah 6:9).

Thus was the prophet sent. And thus can we be.

National Level

On a national level, this kind of thing can lead to spiritual revival, undoubtedly in my mind the most facilitating context for political breakthrough and social reform.

Charles Finney, the greatest American revivalist ever, was always convinced that the Gospel releases a mighty impulse towards social reform and that the great business of the church is to reform the world and to be a body of reformers.

In fact, from the nineteenth-century revivals which flowed from Finney's preaching came 'an army of young converts who became the troops of the reform movement of his age. In particular, "the anti-slavery forces . . . were drawn largely from the converts of Finney's revivals." '8

So too with the eighteenth-century Wesleyan revival in Britain, the social consequences were deeply significant.

In South Africa's hour of need a similar movement could happen, out of which a successfully-negotiated future could come.

This brings us to the power of prayer, that activity which to the world seems foolish and wasteful but without which God's power cannot be released.

V THE POWER OF PRAYER

A little girl was going to bed one night. As she left the family lounge, where a number of guests were congregated prior to a special dinner, she called out, 'I'm going to say my prayers. Anyone want anything?'

The voice of expectant faith! And why not? For has our Lord not said, 'If you remain in me and my words remain in you, ask whatever you wish, and it will be given you' (John 15:7). Elsewhere Jesus put it even more succinctly, 'Ask and it will be given to you' (Matt. 7:7).

So we can ask and we should, and in South Africa, we must.

Immediately after President F W de Klerk's historic speech on February 2nd, 1990, I faxed him, assuring him of prayer. It was a sound and right instinct. And many evenings my family and I remember him and his wife in prayer, and indeed the Mandelas and Chief Buthelezi and other leaders.

Interestingly enough, after a year of inhuman pressures, the President was asked, 'What enables you to keep going and to cope?'

'The prayers of God's people,' was his immediate, forthright and unashamed reply.

And I believe it to be so.

Prayer and Peril

Not long after the release of Dr Mandela, on February 11th, 1990, I noted in an article both the monumental nature of the moment and the urgent need for prayer.

> For such indeed are the unpredictables of history that moments which are full of promise can by the devil's stroke be transformed into tragedy unless Christian principles control the precarious process. God moves in mysterious ways His wonders to perform. But if the Church of a nation, and especially of this nation right now, does not live out Christian principles and pray them in to protect the process, then danger looms. Christians must now pray with intense and earnest intercession and with weapons which are 'not carnal, but mighty through God to the pulling down of strongholds' (2 Cor. 10:4 KJV) that Jesus, who is the Way, will have His way with us. Without such prayer, great and positive forward movements such as we are caught up in now, can be derailed by demonic Powers of Darkness.

Those were the words of February 1990, and by early in 1991, the language of 'derailment' was in extensive use both in South Africa and overseas. For forces of evil and darkness have indeed been at work. Only prayer and intense intercession from the people of God can bind such powers.

As my February article noted,

> This is not an indulgence in medieval fantasies or fairy tales, but in taking seriously the biblical world view of the reality of forces which are 'not flesh and blood' but part of what Paul in his famous Ephesian passage calls 'principalities' and 'powers', 'the world rulers of this present darkness', the 'spiritual hosts of wickedness in the heavenly places' (Eph. 6:12). There is nothing the evil one would like more than to derail all that is now going on which can bring healing, justice and a new day in our land. Prayer and spiritual warfare can head off and protect the positive, political process. So let prayer from the Church of Jesus Christ in South Africa and worldwide be the first order of the day. We don't want anything to go wrong.'

Four Requests

Prayer should focus on four areas. First, for *godly wisdom* for President de Klerk and his colleagues and for Dr Mandela and his, and for all other leaders from Chief Mangosuthu Buthelezi to Dr Andries Treurnicht and others in the PAC, trade unions etc.

At a dinner in March 1990 when my wife and I had the privilege of sitting with the President and Mrs de Klerk, Carol asked Mrs de Klerk what she felt their major prayer need was.

'Insig' (Afrikaans for 'insight' or 'wisdom') was her un-hesitating response.

Without God's wisdom we will not make it, for so often all we bring to politics is the collective wisdom of our individual ignorance!

The second area into which to focus prayer is *physical, mental and spiritual protection* for all the key players.

Third, we must pray for the *spirit of magnanimity and largeness of heart* to settle upon the nation. We are really talking of the Calvary Spirit.

A fourth area in which to focus our praying is that we may all, from the highest to the lowest, work out and be controlled by *Christian principle* at this time. That's what this book has been all about.

And maybe here we should pray for something else: *to keep perspective* and from time to time to laugh the laugh of faith.

South Africa is so full of doom and gloom that we'll be lost indeed if we can't every now and then chuckle our way into the future. Glenn Clark, the devotional writer, once said, 'When God blessed us with the imagination to see harmonies and congruities and logical relationships in this life, He blessed us also with a sense of humour to see the inharmonies, incongruities and illogical relationships – and smile.'[9]

Thus could I applaud the Afrikaans wag I met in Windhoek at the height of the Namibian troubles who said he'd just worked up a new prayer to keep things in perspective: 'O Lord, please give us all just one last chance – and make the whole world speak Afrikaans!'

National Days of Prayer

When the major negotiating exercises get under way the church of South Africa and worldwide should be in saturating prayer for the whole process. Indeed, that will be the time for national days of prayer and fasting.

There are good precedents, both biblical and historical. For example, as the Jewish exiles prepared to return to Judah, Ezra, one of the key leaders records: 'Then I proclaimed a fast there, at the river Aha'va, that we might humble ourselves before our God, *to seek from him a straight way for ourselves, our children, and all our goods* . . . So we fasted and besought our God for this, and he listened to our entreaty' (Ezra 8:21–3 RSV).

The Old Testament is replete with such precedents. But so is history. In fact modern America is rooted in such national moments of prayer and fasting. Thus in May 1774 George Washington and the Assembly of Virginia involved themselves in a day of prayer and fasting 'devoutly to implore the Divine Interposition for averting the heavy calamity which threatens the destruction of our Civil Rights and the risk of Civil War'.[10] National Days of Prayer and Fasting were also called by President Adams in March 1798, by President Madison in January 1815, and three times by Abraham Lincoln in September 1861, April 1863, August 1864.

South Africa in its hour of both opportunity and peril would also be well advised to pursue such a precedent.

VI THE POWER OF STANDING ON KINGDOM GROUND

To choose Jesus and His Way is to become disciples and be identified with Him before a watching world. Nor will we be secret about this, because either our discipleship destroys our secrecy or our secrecy destroys our discipleship.

At which time we will, I believe, find ourselves in the church standing in the strange place I call 'Kingdom Ground', being 'in the world but not of it' (John 17:14–18).

Martin Luther King, in his inimitable style, caught this posture exactly saying,

> every true Christian is a citizen of two worlds, the world of time and the world of eternity. Living in the colony of time, we are ultimately responsible to the empire of eternity. As Christians we must never surrender our supreme loyalty to any time-bound custom or earth-bound idea, for at the heart of our universe is a higher reality – God and his Kingdom of love – to which we must be conformed.[11]

This means among other things that we will not give *absolute* loyalty to any grouping, though political leaders and followers will obviously have certain party loyalties.

But the Christian believer will never give *absolute* commitments to either the status quo or the revolutionary attempts to overthrow it.

In spite of all the apparent differences between the revolutionary and the conservative there is one basic similarity – both identify the purposes of God with their own political agendas.

This being so, Christians in South Africa will heed the warning coming from Methodist Bishop Ernest Baartman who, though deep in the black struggle, could nevertheless say to me not so long ago: 'As we labour for liberation, we dare not let the Church become uncritically identified with any political movement. We must be the conscience of the nation and stand for God's justice. We dare not become so awe-struck with political leaders, black or white, that we don't challenge them with the Gospel.'

No Co-option

In other words, while we need as believers to be deeply caught up in the processes of working for a new day of freedom, justice and equity for all, we dare not fall prey to the danger of having the Church co-opted uncritically into any political movements, though clearly the Church should be engaged in the cause of justice and supportive where conscience and creed allow of movements for political justice and equity. What we can do without in South Africa – and should actively resist – is a left-wing carbon copy of a political theology which is the flip side of a right-wing apartheid theology and, therefore, as much a political lackey as apartheid theology ever was.

The Kingdom Way not a Middle Way

But we need to note that the Kingdom Way is not a wishy-washy middle position of neutrality. When Jesus called left-wing Simon, the revolutionary zealot, and Matthew, the right-wing government department man, into his apostolic band, he wasn't calling them to middle ground and a Third Way, but to Kingdom Ground and the Only Way, where the Kingdom is the 'shalom' way of 'God-ordered relationships'. Kingdom Ground transcends all earthly allegiances and patterns of relating. It is what led the early believers to be called Christians because they did not fit the Jew/Gentile categories of their day.

Kingdom people will therefore feel free to embrace from left, right or centre whatever social truths are compatible with biblical understandings. At Point A, therefore, the Kingdom will make us radical and at Point B conservative. This will confuse the secular mind. No matter.

Polar Truth

In a sense, with political as with theological truth, our inclinations are to inhabit one or the other of the polar regions of truth when, in fact, a true commitment to truth requires straddling not the middle ground but both poles simultaneously.

Said the great Charles Simeon of Cambridge: 'The truth

is not in the middle and not in one extreme but in both extremes.'

Thus Martin Luther King's Gospel commitments made him struggle in Montgomery in December 1955, with being both 'militant and moderate' at the same time. 'I decided,' he wrote, 'to face the challenge head on and attempt to combine two apparent irreconcilables.' The way through, he said, lay in actions 'balanced with a strong affirmation to the Christian doctrine of love.'

Distinctives

All of which bring us to something vital. While the Church may endorse and embrace truth wherever it is found in the spectrum of political postures, it should also be manifest that our Kingdom posture will call for things which neither the left, right nor centre of secular politics would dream of. We have spoken of the priority of prayer, for example, the place of forgiveness, the way of Calvary weakness and the primacy of love for all.

Such Kingdom commitments, as we said, condemn an uninvolved complacency and involve active engagement which cuts diagonally across left, centre and right. This may result in the Christian getting the worst of all worlds. If so, the Cross – for which both oppressor and oppressed, both rich and poor were responsible – will remind us we face no new thing.

In short, the Kingdom, and those who have been apprehended by its King, have a number of distinctive ways which will seem anathema to the political world. But that is our chosen path. For as Moses said to the Lord, 'For how shall it be known that I have found favour in thy sight, I and thy people? Is it not in thy going with us, so that we are *distinct*, I and thy people, from all other people that are upon the face of the earth?' (Exod. 33:16 RSV).

Kingdom Commitments

Standing on Kingdom Ground commits us then to Jesus as Lord and supreme authority. It commits us to His Word and Way in all actions. It commits us to worship, prayer and fasting. It commits us to evangelism and witness that sinners might receive forgiveness, the gift of the Spirit and eternal life.

It commits us to justice, practical care and *agape* love. It commits us, under Christ's Lordship, to the cause of the poor and oppressed and forbids neutrality at that point. Standing on Kingdom Ground commits us socio-politically to bringing down unjust structures. It commits us to labour in the power of the Spirit (Luke 4:18) that the Kingdom may come and God's will be done on earth as it is in heaven. And it commits us not to fear, for 'There is no fear in love, but perfect love casts out fear' (1 John 4:18 RSV).

Standing on Kingdom Ground also reminds us that mankind's kingdoms, whether white, black or brown, whether CP, NP, DP, ANC, Inkatha, PAC or whatever, will rise, be shaken and fall. But the Word and Kingdom of our God and of His Christ 'cannot be shaken' (Heb. 12:28) and will abide for ever.

Hope

And so in closing we come back to where we began with the events of these days leaving both South Africa and the world gasping. History has landed pulsating in our laps and a curious amalgam of heady hope, high-wire political adventure and uncertainty has settled upon the soul of South Africa. Never in the history of our land has such weighty responsibility devolved upon the shoulders of two such different men of destiny – the white President of Today and the black Prisoner of Yesterday. It is the stuff epics are born of.

As we look to what lies ahead, not all will be plain sailing. We have decades of injustice and political mistakes to unwind and passions are abroad which will not easily come to heel. So there will be set-backs, derailments and Calvaries.

But change is here. Whether that change will be better or worse is up to each one of us. To be sure a great dyke is bursting and if by God's power and to His glory we can control and channel its flooding waters, then, cleansed, we will all be delivered up on to new shores of hope and harmony.

Whether in calm or storm, Jesus is ultimately at the helm. In a great tempest at sea, a young boy stood calmly on a ship's deck.

'Aren't you frightened?' asked a distraught passenger.

'No!' said the lad. 'You see, my Father is the Captain.'

Mine too!

Appendix A

ACTION OPTIONS FOR ADDRESSING SOUTH AFRICA'S GIANTS

by Marylee M. James

Following is an abbreviated outline of some practical ways to get involved in alleviating some of the major problems facing South Africa. The list is by no means complete; but experience reveals that once an individual or group takes the first steps (particularly if they do so with the points outlined under 'personal attitudes' well in mind) then many other avenues of involvement will become clear. Do not be daunted by the enormity of the task; if you are faithful to the concept of helping people to help themselves, your contribution is then multiplied many times over.

Personal Attitudes and Relevant Discipling Activities

1 Examine your own heart and seek understanding until you are fully willing to accept the fact that you are not a problem-solver, but a facilitator. No matter what your level of education or expertise, it is counter-productive to assume a unilateral responsibility in addressing these problems. Become willing humbly to offer your talents in an ongoing dialogue with other facilitators and with the communities involved in any action.

2   Learn to dialogue. 'Dialogue' means to listen to the other side *with understanding*. This involves continued questioning as well as listening intelligently and empathetically to what others wish to communicate. It involves the ability to disinvest your own ego from any enterprise in order to produce an achievement which is shared by, and unique to, all those who are involved in the activity. Dialogical interactions improve working relationships. Dialogue with communities in need motivates them to become actively involved in seeking and implementing the solutions to their problems.

3   Pray for guidance in selecting the areas in which you may be most effective. Should you decide either to support or to work with a specific organisation, spend time with that organisation, learning to discern the difference between the productive method of actively responding to the needs and goals articulated by the people being served, and the counterproductive method of making unilateral decisions for those in need. Talk to the people who are served by the agency, to see if you are able to confirm your opinion as to whether the agency is providing for the people, or working with them.

4   Whether you work with an organisation or have the ability and confirmation from your prayers to work on your own, *do not make the mistake of believing that you and you alone understand the disadvantaged and oppressed*. Nothing is less becoming to the Christian spirit than arrogantly to assume to speak for others. Speak *with* them; work *with* them; learn *from* them. But *do not act or speak for them* (see Point 1 above).

5   Some options for relevant prayer, worship and Bible study on this subject:
   a Plan a public event of united Christian witness or prayer in your local town hall or city hall.
   b Plan a study series on scriptural methods of caring for the disadvantaged and for providing for the stability of communities. End the series with discussions for practical applications in the South African situation, and act on your decisions.
   c Plan an evangelistic outreach to business and professional leadership in your area. Alert them to the necessity for

dialogical intervention and facilitation; discuss methodology in the light of an understanding of the ministry of Christ.

d Organise a prayer group to meet regularly, including members of the needy community. Pray together for understanding, for open hearts, and for mutual sharing of both problems and solutions.

The Giants of Poverty and Unemployment[1]

1 Do not assume that your task is to take over the job of the government, or of management. It is, however, your responsibility to provide those in leadership positions with criticism and guidance based upon a Christian theology of stewardship and justice. Use your own networks, your vote, and your personal power to insist that the structural causes of poverty and unemployment are corrected.

2 Use the values and resources of the Christian faith to recognise and nurture the self-respect and dignity of those who are suffering and in need. Emphasise that each person is created by God, made in His image and beloved of the Creator.

3 Every church should have an employment bureau, gathering information on available jobs and seeing that those in need of jobs are directed to them. Those of us who have jobs and are comfortable could exercise self-restraint, become somewhat less comfortable, in order to use that money to employ more people at a reasonable wage. Create jobs! Everyone with property or a home has work that could be done, a job for an unemployed person.

4 Don't expect your gardener or domestic worker to put in a longer work week than you do. If you need help for more hours, then hire more people. (Domestic workers have families and personal needs also.) This is another way to create jobs. Be careful not to reduce wages when you reduce hours.

5 Church property and buildings can be used as bases for training in marketable skills and for creating employment

situations like sewing groups, baking groups, literacy classes, etc. Do not encourage production for the sake of activity; rather, encourage production of locally needed, marketable products.

6   Share the skills and talents you possess: teach an illiterate person to read; teach someone to sew properly and productively; pass along your carpentry skills. Follow up your sharing by evaluating your success: make certain that your pupils find productive ways to use their new skills.

The Giants of Inadequate Education and Training

1   The church and its members can provide a vast amount of training opportunities (see No 5 under Unemployment). Adult training in literacy and skills is something easily provided by volunteers with a shared concern. Some churches have been able to provide, utilising volunteer teachers, classes that enable students to acquire Standard-level certificates or even matric. Classes that provide the necessary training in handling currency, home finance, and managing a chequebook are also very helpful.

2   There is a tremendous need for preschools and creches where children receive the necessary stimulation and instruction to give them a headstart when they are old enough to attend school. Most churches have the capability of providing this service, which the government cannot afford to do. Each region of the country has at least one training facility for those who would operate preschool facilities, for example, TREE in Natal: contact The Director, at Training and Resources for Early Education, PO Box 35175, Durban, Northway, 4065.

3   Having identified a community in need of classrooms and/or funds to pay teachers (ways to locate such communities include asking a local agency for development or the Department of Education and Training), a church group may work with that community to share the process of raising the funds, doing the actual building, and matching funds with the community to pay teachers.

4   The church has always excelled in providing educational facilities for whatever population it encounters. This experience is available to be drawn from, both in terms of lessons to be learned from previous errors and in terms of the practical steps to follow in establishing and maintaining an educational facility.

5   Bear in mind that close to half the population is under fifteen years of age. As these children approach an age to be looking for jobs in South Africa, a liberal arts education alone is not going to be particularly helpful. A curriculum that includes skills training in fields that are needed to boost the economy of the country (agriculture, engineering, administration, business, etc) must be offered in high concentration. The necessity of providing an equal education for all South Africans still must be stressed. This education should also be responsive to the demands of the population for relevant education. Every adult has the ability to insist on these actions (see No 1 under Unemployment).

The Giant of Urban Migration

1   Support business, industry, and development schemes for decentralisation of the economic sphere. Meet with business leaders to discuss methods of improving the economy of rural areas by providing industrial job opportunities and markets.

2   Encourage agricultural education and practice by asking for laws and procedures which protect farmers. Provide bursaries for students who wish to study agriculture, making this field of education one of high prestige.

3   Arrange to meet with a church that is located in or near an area of informal settlement. Together, meet with community leaders of that settlement to determine how housing needs may begin to be met. One possibility is for the combined churches to provide funds and materials to build one house according to the specifications of the community and with the help of the community. When that house is sold (and loans for

the house may be secured with assistance from church members) then those funds can be utilised to build another, and then another.

4   Encourage entrepreneurship in the informal settlements by sharing your own business expertise with the entrepreneur. For example, marketing skills, methods of production, and sharing of your own network of associations can make all the difference for a struggling new businessman.

The Giant of Health Problems

1   Meet with a local medical or nursing association, or with a health training facility, to discuss ways and means of training community health workers as educators in preventative health care measures. Organise your church or club to provide bursaries for students of the training programme.

2   If you are a medical practitioner, organise some of your colleagues to provide free seminars in health education for the public; utilise the media to provide a greater number of easily understood programmes on Aids, tuberculosis, infant care, etc.

3   Take programmes from Point No 2 into the schools. Make health care part of every curriculum. Organise a group that will be willing to subsidise videos, or even to pay the salary of a health care worker in each school.

4   Educate yourself on health issues. Make a point of reading the available literature on Aids, and on preventative health care; seek medical guidance where the literature is unclear.

The Giant of Environmental Neglect

1   Almost every area of South Africa is close to some community that does not have pure water. Organise a group from your church to meet that community, and together seek the assistance of qualified organisations to discover how streams may be protected, bore holes drilled, and pure water supplied

to that community. Help the community to find appropriate technology, and to obtain funds to build and maintain the water system.

2 Become conservative in your own use of energy. Ask yourself if you really need to use your car, or if you can walk. Arrange your schedule so that maximum use is made of the car by completing many tasks with one trip. Take a number of people with you who have similar requirements (such as school or work). Be conservative in your use of electricity and water. The fact that you can afford it is no excuse for wasting it. Lower that level in the water tank of your toilet. Obtain showerheads that conserve water. Be conscientious in watering your garden sparingly during periods of drought.

3 Spend your Bible Study class period on listing all the ways that you can conserve the environment. Put your observations into action. Study the Bible's view of ecology.

4 Take your family or your club or your class and plant trees on bare hillsides. Seek the advice of a professional concerning soil preparation and maintenance for the young trees. Nurture them until they are established.

5 Make certain that your vehicles and machinery are safeguarded against spewing pollutants into the atmosphere.

6 Use biodegradable materials, don't pollute waterways with fuel or garbage, recycled cans, bottles and paper.

7 Use your organisation or group to mount an environmental awareness campaign in your area. Get radio, TV and newspaper coverage. Write letters to industries and businesses that violate environmental codes, asking them to 'clean up' their act.

8 Thank God daily for the beautiful Earth He has entrusted to our care. Having done that, cultivate a constant awareness of the fact that our stewardship is judged by how serious we are about this task.

Appendix B

In November 1990 in Rustenburg, a National Conference of South African Church leaders met in an historic gathering. They produced there *The Rustenburg Declaration*. The full document can be ordered from African Enterprise, Box 647, PMB 3200 or from the South African Council of Churches, Box 4921, Johannesburg 2000. Herewith, however, is an unofficial summary by Dr Klaus Nurnberger.

1   We, 230 representatives of 97 Christian denominations and organisations have been surprised by the emergence of a broad consensus among ourselves concerning the unequivocal rejection of apartheid as a sin, confession of complicity with the system, mutual forgiveness, the commitment to ongoing fellowship and the necessity of overcoming the ongoing consequences of apartheid by acts of restitution. We praise God for these unexpected gifts of grace.

2   Conscious of the immense suffering among the less privileged due to injustice, poverty and alienation, we hope that South Africa is on the threshold of national reconciliation based on a new and just dispensation.

3   Some of us who belong to the privileged have confessed their guilt of having perpetrated, benefited from, legitimated, silently condoned, or condemned but not resisted the evil system. Some of us who belong to the victims have confessed their guilt of having accepted their own humiliation and deprivation, of having collaborated in the system for temporal gain, of having sought revenge or of having allowed the fires of intolerance and violence to spread. In all these things we have allowed the world rather than Christ to mould us.

4   We ask God and our fellow South Africans for forgiveness. We call members of our churches and the government of our country to join us in this confession. We appeal to all political

leaders urgently to repeal all apartheid laws, to release all
political prisoners and grant indemnity to all political exiles, to
negotiate a new and just order for our society and to embark
on a policy of restitution. We appeal to all church leaders to
end all injustice in the church and to carry this confession into
the life of every congregation.

5   We assert that our highest loyalty belongs to God and that
the state is God's instrument to serve the common good. We
support the separation of church and state and the freedom of
religion, moral conviction and association for all. We call upon
those who negotiate a new constitution under God to exclude
all group interests in the implementation of justice, to en-
trench the rule of law and a bill of rights, to limit the power of
the security establishment to the protection of the population,
to establish an elective process based on the principle of one
person one vote on a common voters' role in a unitary state
and a multi-party democracy. For the transitional period we
call for government and constitutional negotiations by a fully
representative body and the extension of the referendum to all
citizens.

6   We have reflected on the causes of violence and call upon
the churches to respond by collecting evidence, supporting
victims, encouraging all parties to enter into the negotiation
process, convening an ecumenical task force on violence and
calling for a peace conference of leaders to solve the conflicts.

7   We commit ourselves to proclaim the gospel of Christ, to
call for repentance and forgiveness, to bring people together in
worship and fellowship, to pray for the fullness of the gifts of
the Spirit and the spiritual renewal of the land and to call a
national day of prayer, confession, forgiveness and commitment.

8   We recognise the necessity of acts of restitution: the return
of land to relocated communities by the authorities, the
opening of white schools and affirmative action in black
education, the solution of the problem of land redistribution
including the land of the church, giving priority to the needs of

the poor, homeless and unemployed in the economic system, affirming the rights of women and the needs of the youth. We believe that the church should make available its resources for the renewal and reconstruction of society.

Notes

Chapter 1

The direct quotes in this chapter are drawn from *Saturday Star*, Johannesburg, February 3rd, 1990.

Chapter 2

1 *Higher Than Hope*, Professor Fatima Meer (Scotaville Publishers, Johannesburg, 1988). Quotes and information taken from Professor Meer and various newspaper articles.

Chapter 4

1 'Charles Bester: Conscience challenges a Christian State', Michael Cassidy in *Conflict and the Quest for Justice*, eds Klaus Nurnberger, John V Tooke, Bill Domeris (Encounter Publishers, Pietermaritzburg, 1989), pp. 389–90.
2 *ibid*.
3 *ibid*.
4 Letter from Michael Cassidy to State President, F W de Klerk, December 13th, 1989.

Chapter 5

1 Recorded in *Chasing the Wind*, Michael Cassidy (Hodder and Stoughton, London, 1985), p. 96.
2 Quoted in *The Case for Christianity*, Colin Chapman (Lion Publishing House, Tring, 1981), p. 30.
3 *Beyond Liberation*, Carl Ellis (Inter-Varsity Press, Downers Grove, Illinois, 1983), pp. 174–5.

Chapter 6

1 *The Four Loves*, C S Lewis (Collins, London, 1960).
2 *The Relationship Tangle*, Michael Cassidy (Africa Enterprise, Pietermaritzburg, 1974), pp. 103–4.
3 *The Greatest Thing in the World*, Henry Drummond (Collins, London and Glasgow, 1930, 1953), p. 53.
4 *Discipleship*, David Watson (Hodder and Stoughton, London, 1981), pp. 250–1.
5 Drummond, *op cit.*, p. 55.
6 *ibid.*, p. 61.

Chapter 8

1 An article by Frederick van Zyl Slabbert in *Democracy in Action*, monthly newsletter of the Institute for a Democratic Alternative for South Africa, April 1990, p. 2.
2 *Power, Right, Law and Love*, Edgar Brookes (Drake University Press, Durham, North Carolina, 1963), p. 14.
3 *ibid.*, p. 80.
4 *ibid.*, pp. 83–4.
5 *Wilberforce*, John Pollock (Lion Publishing, Tring, 1977), p. 66.
6 This section taken from *The Passing Summer*, pp. 440–1.

Chapter 9

1 *The Passing Summer*, pp. 426–7.
2 'The Risks of the Reconciler – An Anglican Canon reflects on his vocation of reconciliation', in *Sojourners Magazine*, July 1988, p. 25. Interview with Paul Ostreicher.
3 Cassidy, *op cit.*, p. 428.
4 *Weekend Argus*, May 9th, 1990. Article by Alastair Sparks.
5 'The Long Road Back', an interview by Phillip van Niekerk with Albie Sachs, *Leadership Magazine*, Vol. IX, No. 2, March 1990, pp. 32–3.
6 *Strength to Love*, Martin Luther King (Fortress Press, Philadelphia, 1981), p. 37.
7 *ibid.*, p. 39.

8 'Disarming Talk', an interview by Phillip van Niekerk with Thabo Mbeki in *Leadership Magazine*, Vol. IX, No. 2, March 1990, p. 27.

Chapter 10

1 *Words of Martin Luther King*, Coretta Scott King, ed., (Collins Fount, London, 1985), p. 51.
2 *South Africa: Beginning At the End of the Road*, Dr F van Zyl Slabbert (a paper, March 1990), p. 18.
3 'Backwards in Anger' by Willem de Klerk in *The High Road* (a Leadership Publication, April 1988), pp. 16–22.
4 *The Option for Inclusive Democracy*, Bernard Lategan, Johann Kinghorn, Lourens du Plessis, Etienne de Villiers, (Centre for Hermeneutics, Univ of Stellenbosch, 1987), p. 3.

Chapter 11

1 *Daily News*, Durban, Friday March 9th, 1990.
2 'Window on the Right' an interview by Paul Bell with Koos van der Merwe in *Leadership Magazine*, Vol. IX, No. 2, March 1990, pp. 80ff.
3 *ibid.*, p. 84.
4 'Hanging in the Balance', an article by Ken Owen, *Natal Witness*, Pietermaritzburg, March 13th, 1990.
5 'Backwards in Anger' by Willem de Klerk in *The High Road* (a Leadership Publication, April 1988), p. 16.
6 *ibid.*, p. 20.
7 *ibid.*, p. 20.
8 *ibid.*, pp. 21–2.
9 *ibid.*, p. 22.
10 'Disarming Talk' an interview by Phillip van Niekerk with Thabo Mbeki in *Leadership Magazine*, Vol. IX, No. 2, March 1990, p. 27.

Chapter 12

1 *Violence*, (Reflections from a Christian Perspective), Jacques Ellul (Seabury Press, New York, 1969), p. 95–6.

2   *ibid.*, pp. 97–8.
3   *ibid.*, pp. 100–2.
4   *ibid.*, pp. 103–8.
5   *Words of Martin Luther King*, Coretta Scott King, ed., (Collins Fount, London, 1985), p. 73.

Chapter 13

1   'Dreams of Home' by Breyten Breytenbach, *Leadership Magazine*, Vol. IX, No. 2, March 1990, pp. 86–8.
2   *Uprooting Poverty: The South African Challenge*, Francis Wilson and Mamphela Ramphele (David Philip, Cape Town and Johannesberg, 1989), p. 14.
3   *ibid.*, p. 67.
4   *ibid.*, p. 97.
5   *Community Development: An African Rural Approach*, W J O Jeppe, Africa.
6   John Qwelane, *Sunday Star*, September 23rd, 1990.
7   *Third Alternative*, Teddy Langschmidt (Integrated Market Research, 1989).
8   *ibid.*
9   *ibid.*
10 'The Fear Debate', Di Paice in *Leadership Magazine*, Vol. IX, No. 3, April 1990, pp. 28–9.
11 *ibid.*
12 *South African Environment into the 21st Century*, Brian Huntley, Roy Siegried, Clem Sunter (Human and Rousseau, Tafelberg, Cape Town, 1989).
13 *ibid.*
14 Teddy Langschmidt interview.

Chapter 14

1   *Poised on a Knife Edge*, Gerald Shaw, *Natal Witness*, April 23rd, 1990.
2   *Uprooting Poverty: The South African Challenge*, Francis Wilson and Mamphela Ramphele, (David Philip, Cape Town and Johannesburg, 1989), p. 276.
3   *ibid.*, p. 276.

4   'A Christo-economic view on a constitution for a just SA',
    Lawrence McCrystal in *Christian Forum*, Final 1990.
5   *The Great Economic Debate: An Ethical Analysis*, Philip
    Wogaman (Westminster Press, Philadelphia), p. 155.
6   'Sonn's "seven moral questions"', Franklin Sonn in *Christian
    Forum*, Final 1990.
7   Teddy Langschmidt interview.
8   Article by Nic Borain in *Democracy in Action*, monthly
    newsletter of the Institute for a Democratic Alternative for
    South Africa, July/Aug 1990.
9   Article by Ken Owen in *Natal Witness*, September 18th,
    1990.
10 'Comparing Apples with Oranges', by James Moulder in
    Natal Witness, June 29th, 1989.
11 *ibid.*
12 'Disarming Talk', an interview by Phillip van Niekerk with
    Thabo Mbeki in *Leadership Magazine*, Vol. IX, No. 2,
    March 1990.
13 *The Option for Inclusive Democracy*, Bernard Lategan,
    Johann Kinghorn, Lourens du Plessis, Etienne de Villiers
    (Centre for Hermeneutics, University of Stellenbosch,
    1987), p. 3.
14 *If I Had My Life Over Again*, Winston Churchill, comp. and
    ed. Jack Fishman (W H Allen, London, 1974), p. 169.
15 'New Benchmarks', Laurie Ackermann in *Leadership
    Magazine*, Vol. VI, No. 6, 1987, p. 77.
16 'The Fear Debate', Di Paice in *Leadership Magazine*, Vol.
    IX, No. 2, March 1990.
17 *A Better Way (A case for a Christian Social Order)*, Sir
    Frederick Catherwood, (Inter Varsity Press, Leicester, UK,
    1975), p. 81.
18 'The Ark of America', *Time Magazine*, July 6th, 1987, p. 49.

Chapter 15

1   'Disarming Talk', an interview by Phillip van Niekerk with
    Thabo Mbeki in *Leadership Magazine*, Vol. IX, No. 2, March
    1990, p. 26.
2   Oscar Dhlomo in *Natal Witness*, September 27th, 1990.
3   'The Real Rubicon', Ron Kraybill in *Leadership Magazine*,
    Vol. VIII, No. 10, Dec/Jan 1989/90, p. 13.

4 *ibid.*, p. 16.
5 *Conflicts*, Edward de Bono (Penguin Books, London, 1986), p. 34.
6 'The Hottest Gospel', Clem Sunter in *Leadership Magazine*, Vol. VI, No. 3, 1987.
7 'A Healthy Tension', Athol Jennings in *Leadership Magazine*, *The High Road* (April 1988), p. 32.
8 'Reconciliation', in *Leadership Magazine*, Vol. VI, No. 4, 1987.

Chapter 16

1 *Adolf Hitler: My Part in His Downfall*, Spike Milligan (Penguin, London, 1972).
2 Francis A Schaeffer: *A Christian Manifesto* (Crossway, Westchester, 1982), p. 68.
3 Letter to the author May 21st, 1989.
4 *The Living US Constitution*, Saul K. Perdover (Mentor Bookby, New American Library, New York, 1953), pp. 19–21.
5 *Spirituality of the Road*, David Bosch (Herald, Kitchener, Ontario, 1979), p. 76.
6 *ibid.*, p. 78.
7 *Strength to Love*, Martin Luther King (Fount, London, 1969), p. 54.
8 *Issues Facing Christians Today*, John Stott (Marshall, Morgan and Scott, Basingstoke, 1984), p. 5.
9 *Windows of Heaven*, Glenn Clark (Arthur James, Evesham, 1976), p. 138.
10 *Shaping History Through Prayer and Fasting*, Derek Prince (Fleming H Revel Co, Old Tappan, New Jersey, 1973), p. 139.
11 *op cit.*, Martin Luther King, p. 18.

Appendix A

1 Much of the information in this section is borrowed from *The Scourge of Unemployment in South Africa*, Klaus Nurnberger (Pietermaritzburg, Encounter Publications, 1990).

Hodder Christian Paperbacks: a tradition of excellence.

Great names and great books to enrich your life and meet your needs. Choose from such authors as:

Corrie ten Boom	Jackie Pullinger
Charles Colson	David Pytches
Richard Foster	Mary Pytches
Billy Graham	Jennifer Rees Larcombe
Michael Green	Cliff Richard
Michele Guinness	John Stott
Joyce Huggett	Joni Eareckson Tada
Francis MacNutt	Colin Urquhart
Catherine Marshall	David Watson
Jim Packer	David Wilkerson
Adrian Plass	John Wimber

The wide range of books on the Hodder Christian Paperback list include biography, personal testimony, devotional books, evangelistic books, Christian teaching, fiction, drama, poetry, books that give help for times of need — and many others.

Ask at your nearest Christian bookshop or at your church bookstall for the latest titles.